MEAL™
AND A
SPIEL

HOW TO BE A BADASS IN THE KITCHEN

by Elana Horwich

For my cooking students.

Without you, there would be no *Meal and a Spiel*.
This path has brought me so much joy.
Thank you for being my guides.

MEAL AND A SPIEL™

Edited by Seth Grossman | Design by Jessie Glass | Photography by John Shell

Additional Photography by Elana Horwich, Annie Shak, and Keren L. Greenberg

Published by Olive Press | Los Angeles, CA

ISBN 978-0-692-13044-5

Printed and Bound in China by 1010 Printing Limited

10 9 8 7 6 5 4 3 2 1

2020 2019 2018

" *Learning never exhausts the mind.*

– Leonardo da Vinci

Why is this cookbook different from all other cookbooks?

Most popular cookbooks these days are written by celebrity chefs. I'm not a celebrity chef. I'm a teacher. Plus, I'm lazy. I've figured out the way to make the outright best food possible with the absolute least amount of effort. Actually, I didn't really figure it out. I copied it from the Italians who have been hiding these secrets in their homes for centuries.

I'm not here to wow you with brilliant and complicated cooking techniques. This is not fancy French cooking. You won't be asked to whip egg whites to form stiff peaks or to make a creamy *roux*, because you don't need any burdensome techniques to become a badass in the kitchen.

I'm also not here to simply provide you with a list of fabulous recipes that you can prepare to perfection in order to impress everyone you know. I'm here to empower you to *enjoy* cooking. I want you to become a confident cook who can walk into your kitchen, take a look in your (properly stocked) fridge and pantry, and whip up a fabulous meal like a badass because You. Actually. Know. What. You. Are. Doing.

(Of course, a sure-fire by-product of that confidence is that you will inevitably impress everyone you know. The recipes in this book are easy enough for a weeknight meal and elegant enough for your fanciest dinner party.)

I want you to experience the kitchen as a playroom and cooking as a game, where the goal is not to win, but rather to have fun, to express yourself, to be daring and forgiving. I want you to stop keeping score and start getting lost in the whimsy of cooking. Tune your brain down to low and cook from the heart, so your food will taste like love. Most of all, I want you to join me and my cooking students in adding love to the planet, one meal at a time.

EVEN *SCHLEMAZELS* CAN LEARN!

In the days of yore, every *shtetl* had the town *schlemiel* and the town *schlemazel*. *Shtetls* might exist no more, but *schlemiels* and *schlemazels* still do. A *schlemiel* is someone who trips, knocks over a birthday cake, and bends down to pick it up, only to knock over a cauldron of tomato soup in the process. The *schlemazel* is the guy who gets the soup spilled all over him.

Everyone knows that *mazel tov* means "good luck." *Mazel* is the part that means "luck." A schle-"mazel" is without luck. A born loser. But if you're holding this book in your hands, you're clearly not a *schlemazel*. You have luck on your side. Even if you absolutely have no idea what to do in the kitchen, don't worry. I've got you covered.

I've taught the worst of the worst cooks in the world to cook well—people with a self-proclaimed inability to boil water—so I'm not intimidated by your kitchen incompetence. I've tested my methods many, many times. They work.

Schlemiel, schlemazel—I can teach even you to cook! All I ask is that you're willing to learn.

THE BENEFITS AND PLEASURE OF INTUITIVE COOKING

Unlike most cookbooks, which encourage dependence on following specific recipes in order to make a meal, this book is a guide to becoming an *intuitive* cook.

Intuitive cooking is having an innate understanding of how to create flavors and textures in the kitchen and letting that understanding guide you *just enough* so that it informs your choices, but not so much that there isn't room for a little fun.

This is what I call *feminine* cooking, rather than the masculine style of restaurant chefs. This doesn't mean that men and women necessarily cook differently—most men in Italy know how to cook, and they generally learned it from their grandmothers (hot!), and plenty of the best restaurant chefs are women. But most restaurant kitchens are high-stress, competitive, testosterone-fueled places where instructions are followed to a T or prep chefs get chewed out. That's not how I want you to cook. I want you to enjoy the process, to connect to the food, and to allow it to be a little messy.

Intuitive cooking does NOT mean unleashing some sort of wanton, direction-less artistic whim. It does NOT mean passionately throwing different ingredients into a pot without any knowledge of how those ingredients work together. Intuitive cooking is NOT a free for all, like Ecstatic Dance, or some sort of postmodern abstract expressionist art project. Passion without knowledge is a hell of a lot of fun, but it won't put an exceptional meal on the table.

Intuitive cooking means that you're not married to a recipe. It means adding salt and spices with your fingers instead of a collection of annoying little spoons. It means knowing how to improvise wisely when you've run out of an ingredient, and how to confidently experiment with a new ingredient that you recently discovered at your local farmer's market. It means being less attached to numerical precision in cooking—exact measurements and temperatures and times—so you can have more freedom and, dare I say, flamboyance, as you execute a meal. Being an intuitive cook fosters a deep, visceral connection to the food. You will learn to listen to the food and whisper to it at the same time so your creations can reflect a bit more of you. Or even a lot more of you.

How can I bring you to that level of freedom? By teaching you *how and why* recipes work, in simple terms.

As a self-taught chef, I've navigated through thousands of cookbook recipes, both successfully and unsuccessfully. Most cookbooks give you, let's just say, five recipes for soup all seemingly made in five different ways. They deliver a variety, which is commendable, but they don't teach the *principles* of making soup. To the unseasoned cook, each soup recipe seems like a random collection of steps that the author of the book mystically arranged in secret.

But the truth is, there's a simple method to making soup: 99% of soups start out in exactly the same way, with sautéed onion (and often other aromatic herbs and veggies). A *soffritto*. All soups benefit from being cooked on low heat, the longer the better. Furthermore, the goodness of all soups depends on how good the broth is to begin with. It's not rocket science. Properly explaining these principles empowers the millions of cooks out there who lack confidence in the kitchen.

So instead of handing you a bunch of unrelated recipes, I've laid out a simple cooking process, along with a series of recipes that all follow the same process. This way, you're in on the secret. And before you know it, you too will be a kitchen badass.

A SINGULAR, HARMONIOUS PALATE

In my classes, I teach everything from Healthy Mexican Food to Vegan Girls' Night Out. But in this book, I'm not going to teach you how to make every cuisine under the sun. Rather, this book focuses on rustic Italian home cooking, infused with the healthy California ingredients and techniques of my cooking school. I've chosen this flavor profile because it's not complicated, doesn't use a lot of ingredients, and doesn't require precision. Most importantly, it's delicious!

By keeping the recipes all Italian in flavor, the way I originally learned to cook, you'll understand how to build flavors layer by layer. The repetition of certain ingredients and combinations will begin to make intuitive sense to you. I've found that that's the best way to learn the basic principles of cooking. You'll easily be able to transfer this understanding to all types of cuisines, as I have.

A happy byproduct of working within a single flavor palate is that all the recipes work together. This means that even though I give you specific instructions on how to create menus that flow (Page 52), if you were to randomly choose three recipes from three different chapters, they'll most likely pair well together. How easy is that?!

DIETARY CONSCIOUSNESS

The recipes in this book reflect my consciousness of the different eating styles and dietary needs of my cooking students, as well as my own. This isn't a vegan or vegetarian cookbook, a paleo cookbook, a gluten-free cookbook, a dairy-free cookbook, or a low sugar cookbook. But in a way, it's all of these. Even though the recipes include carbs and meat and dairy—and a even a touch or two of refined sugar—there's something for everyone to eat, no matter your dietary path. I imagine many of you are like me: an aspiring gluten-free, sometimes-vegan/plant-forward carnivore, who enjoys dairy and wheat only when it's really worth it. I only share recipes with you that are worth it! I've included chapters on gluten-free appetizers, vegetable-based pastas, and meatless main courses.

MAKING THE WORLD A HAPPIER PLACE
AND THE IMPORTANCE OF BEING A BADASS COOK

I had a doctor (a proper MD) once tell me that she was reluctant to eat in restaurants because she knew how much angst, ego, and stress there typically is in restaurant kitchens. She believes that the energy of the cook goes directly into the food. She doesn't want to ingest all of that stress. For this reason, she prefers to eat at home, as do I, as do Italians.

Cooking and eating are ways for people to make visceral, personal connections, unmediated by technology. If you know what you're doing in the kitchen—and soon, you will—and if you put love in your food, your family and friends will not only taste it, they'll ingest the energy of it.

Cooking is a way to express your deeper self with your hands, and in so doing, you share love. It enables us to access our innate capacity to nurture, so that we can generously open our hearts to our friends and family, and even society at large. If you feed someone a meal made with love, they'll get up from your table carrying that love with them. A good meal makes people happier, nicer, more patient, and more accepting. Eventually, they spread that feeling to the people they encounter, and before you know it, we've infused the whole world with love, one meal at a time. That's my ultimate goal for this book.

My Story

There's definitely something to be said for choosing the life you want to live and working hard to make it happen. There's also something to be said about saying yes to what life offers you, and letting it unfold the way *it* wants to. Somewhere between the two is a happy medium. And sometimes that nexus can cook up magic.

I was born in Beverly Hills, into a family of disciplined high-achievers. My father Jim, a math-nerd and Harvard Business School graduate, founded a successful manufacturing business, and my mother Ada, a Berkeley-educated Peace Corps alum, was a therapist who became an avid political fundraiser. My parents are well-known philanthropists in the Jewish community.

I'm the middle of three daughters—my older sister is a prominent cardiologist, married to a transplant surgeon, and they have two brilliant children. My younger sister is a therapist and parenting teacher, married to an über-mensch who *volunteered* for the Israeli army, and they're raising three bilingual daughters on a gluten-free, dairy-free diet, i.e. the Los Angeles dream.

And then there's me: by seventh grade, I was on a parallel path toward greatness, achievement, and societal and parental approval. That year, I ran for student government, delivering an improvised speech in rhyming couplets that won me a landslide victory as student body president at Hawthorne Elementary School. Then, at Beverly High, I was the only freshman on the varsity soccer team. On my own initiative, I sought out and

My bat mitzvah, with my family.

gained admission to a competitive East Coast boarding school, where I graduated cum laude. During summers, while my peers hung out at the Century City Mall, I volunteered in impoverished Latin American villages, building latrines. My senior year, I earned early acceptance to Brown University. Ivy League, here I come!

And then, in my sophomore year of college, I chose to upend my life completely.

THE EPIPHANY

I'd heard that nobody had a bad first trip, so one day I decided I should try psychedelic mushrooms with my roommate. As the 'shrooms hit me, I fell into a hysterical laughing fit. Like a child, I wanted to go outside and play in the park. It was Spring Weekend, the quad full of students hanging out, goofing off, drinking beer, tossing frisbees. A mis-thrown frisbee flew my way, and I saw it move towards me millimeter by millimeter, as if time had slowed down. Without even pausing my conversation, I calmly and easily reached out and caught the frisbee, *left-handed*. (Until this point, I'd been an awkward, two-handed "pancake-style" frisbee-catcher.) That catch gave me the confidence to believe the epiphany, when it came.

At the time, I was majoring in playwriting, taking Italian classes because my years of Spanish guaranteed me an easy A. As my roommate and I sauntered through the RISD Museum gardens, the epiphany took form. I realized with a sense of absolute clarity that I needed to write about life and love—and the only way to do that was to have experiences away from academia. It was the voice of destiny speaking within, and it felt natural, because somewhere in my most private thoughts, I had known this all along. I had to go abroad. I would take the few thousand dollars I'd saved from a summer job at my father's carpet business, combined with some *bat mitzvah* money, and I would head to Mexico, study the Aztec language Nahuatl, find work under-the-table, fall in love, and have adventures.

The day after I told my plan to my mother, after she recovered from her conniption, she had a completely random encounter with a friend who had just happened to hear about a live-work opportunity for an English-speaking student in Rome, Italy. If memory serves, my mother's exact words were, "You're so fuckin' lucky!" Italy hadn't even been on my radar. But the plan fell so easily into my lap, and I had already taken two years of Italian— so I figured why not and accepted immediately.

You can tell the difference between a true epiphany and a misguided pipe dream, because a pipe dream will hit wall after wall. With a true epiphany, the universe becomes your enabler, conspiring with you to make it all come together.

ITALY

After backpacking around Europe for the summer, I arrived in Rome by train. The moment I put my feet on the platform, despite the filth and squalor of Termini Station in 1995, inside my head I heard myself say, "I am home." Unfortunately, a week later, everything fell apart. My host family had a lot of rules, including a curfew, and that wasn't going to work for a 20-year-old free spirit newly arrived in a city full of cute boys on Vespas. I couldn't stand to stay under their roof, so I moved into a disgusting

Montegonzi
Pernano
SANTA TERESA
casa Panzanellino
Panzanelluccio
CASAFEDE
La Rimbecca

hostel near the train station. Desperate for better digs, I reached out to my high school friend Jen's family, and they set me up for a month in their Tuscan villa, Geggianello. (Good thing I went to boarding school, where people's families just happen to have villas in Tuscany!)

So there I was, all alone in the enormous stone farmhouse. The caretakers, Maria and Roberto, had a separate apartment, but they'd come to check on me periodically, asking if I needed food or firewood. I refused to let them wait on me—I already felt guilty staying there alone, like a princess in a castle. The least I could do was make my own food. Furthermore, the kitchen there was amazing: dark, Italian wood cupboards; a huge, antique wooden table, topped with marble; modern, high-end appliances; and a view of the expansive Chianti vineyards right outside. I couldn't wait to cook.

The only issue was that my cooking repertoire at the time began and ended with toaster-oven tortilla pizzas. My mother had never cooked—she was a strong, independent feminist raising three girls in the height of the Gloria Steinem era, and, in her mind, that precluded domestic duties in the kitchen. So our family ate out and defrosted. A lot. I didn't even really understand where food came from. When my friend Maria Micelli came to school with a sandwich made from her Italian mother's homemade bread, my mind was blown—you can make bread?! I didn't know homemade food until I was 13 years old, when Angie came to work for us as our housekeeper. This Carribean kitchen badass rocked my grandmother's recipe for Shabbat brisket. Despite the Heinz Chili Sauce and Lipton's Onion Soup Mix, it tasted like love and felt like home. Apart from that, for my teenage years, it was dormitory fare and late-night greasy grub. I'd never learned to cook.

But in Geggianello, the ingredients were so fresh and so good that, in all honesty, it was impossible to mess them up. Everything I made was the most amazing thing I'd ever eaten. It was magic. Perfection was inevitable. Each tomato was so sweet and ripe that when I made a sumptuous pasta sauce, I couldn't help but drink half of it before the noodles were even cooked. I made dessert by cutting up a pear, cooking it in a little water and a handful of Chianti grapes I'd picked from the vines outside. I don't have words to describe the taste, but the image of the velvety purple juices bleeding their way down the pears is etched forever in my memory.

I was determined to thoroughly taste and savor every ingredient available to me. By learning to recognize the subtle difference in flavor between fresh and jarred tomato sauce, fresh and aged pecorino, I was not only refining my palate, but I was also learning to eat slowly, mindfully—to eat well.

When Jen's parents Irene and Malcolm finally arrived, everything changed. I was happy to have the company, despite the fact that my access to the kitchen was now curtailed. That's because Maria took over. Let me tell you, if I thought my food was good because the ingredients were so delicious, Maria showed me what you could do if you really understood how to use those ingredients. She grew up with them. She knew their flavors, their textures, their moods. She knew how to make them all sing the same chord. Ribollita, vegetable puddings, nouvelle potatoes with rosemary, spaghetti with a simple tomato sauce, her meat sauce that made every nerve in my body dance,

TOP ROW: Left - Geggianello in the fall. Right - Geggianello's breakfast room. BOTTOM ROW: Left - Jen with our friend Giovanni, polaroid circa 2001. Center & Right - Roberto and Maria near Geggianello

her chicken liver *crostini al vin santo* that made me want to roll on the floor shouting MAMMMMAAA—that became the basis for my definition of good food.

I loved living in Tuscany, taking walks down the cypress-lined dirt roads, breathing in the fresh countryside air, and snacking on the figs off the neighbors' trees. I enjoyed spending my free time drawing in the expansive gardens of the villa. I even got to participate in *la vendemmia* (the harvest), picking Chianti grapes for 100,000 lira a day (50 dollars). Jen's parents encouraged me to stay. But I had to go back to Rome. It held an irresistible draw for me. I was determined to get to know it, to live there, and to discover myself there.

In Rome, I found work in bars. The Dog and Duck was a tiny British-style pub in Trastevere where I'd throw parties, taking home 30 percent of the profits. One day, in walked Federico, a gentle, gray-eyed *romano* who knew everyone in the place. We fell madly in love. We even adopted a street dog together, my beloved Dulcinea.

Italians joke that the number one reason couples break up is that the woman doesn't cook as well as the man's mother—fortunately for me, Federico's mother was a mediocre cook. That gave me an opening. I felt supported, safe to experiment and play around in the kitchen without being judged. I discovered that the kitchen isn't a place for the subservient—my Italian girlfriends showed me that through cooking women can demonstrate their strength and creativity, and command respect. That's sexy.

My favorite part of the day was when I walked to the Campo de' Fiori market to choose my produce. Despite my skimpy budget, I'd never felt richer: I was living in Rome, cooking beautiful meals for a man I loved. I was young and alive and ready for whatever the world threw my way.

Unfortunately, what the world threw my way was heartbreak. Federico and I broke up. I hadn't completed a word of the magnum opus on life and love that I'd come to Italy to write. And I had no plan.

LOST AND FOUND

For the next few years, Dulcinea and I wandered. Returning the US, I finished my bachelors in Providence, then moved back to Los Angeles where I taught in an inner-city school. My classroom was in a church basement, with an unnecessary wall dividing the room, so that I could only see half the students at a time. They were unruly, to say the least. The head of school grew up in a tough Irish family and encouraged me to be severely strict, but spending my days as a disciplinarian just didn't feel like my calling.

I began questioning my purpose in life on a deep, existential level. So, naturally, I became an actor, and by "became an actor" I mean I moved to the East Village in New York to chain smoke cigarettes in a studio apartment. I did fall in love with Chekhov and physical comedy, but I couldn't stand the rejection that's 99% of an actor's life—so I went back to Italy, back to the safe confines of academia.

I earned a master's degree in Florence, then realized that I wasn't meant for academia. So as my parents freaked out, I went to Northern California to study Ancient Thai Massage. Then back to Rome to practice body work, organize historical tours, and lead yoga retreats throughout Italy. I was all over the place. Another Italian heartbreak later, I returned to LA and started teaching again, and on the side I performed stand-

TOP: Left - Federico, doing what Italian men do. Right - me with Dulcinea at 6 weeks old. **BOTTOM:** Dulcinea, my travel buddy.

TOP: Left - Me in Florence, getting my master's. Right - Dulcinea outisde the Hell's Angels Motorcycle Club in NYC.
BOTTOM: Dinner by Maria at a Tuscan yoga retreat.

up comedy. Fast forward, several years later: surprise, surprise, I'm unemployed.

To say that I was depressed about the situation was an understatement. I had tried everything, and I hadn't found anything that fully fed my soul. Sometimes, I'd go out for dinner with my parents, and they'd run into their friends. "Ah, you must be the cardiologist!" the friends would say. I'd shake my head. "The therapist?" they'd ask. Alas, no. I remember my grandmother saying to me, "You're gonna write a book one day. I know it!" And I almost cried because I wanted to believe that she was right, and yet I had absolutely nothing to write. I was the *fashla*, the fuckup, the family disappointment.

Finally, in a fit of despair, I decided to own it. I gave myself permission to *not* have to figure it out, and set out to do the one thing I hadn't yet tried: *nothing.* I wouldn't do anything at all. If I didn't want to answer the phone, I wouldn't answer it. I didn't have to exercise or even leave the house. I took all types of pressure off myself so I could discover what moved me on the deepest level. I sat comfortably in the question itself. And while doing *nothing*, I spent my days reading cookbooks, shopping at the market, and cooking for cooking's sake.

It became clear that I wanted to work with food. It was the first thing I thought about when I woke up in the morning. I didn't have much confidence in my cooking yet, but I figured I was at least qualified to deliver food to friends who needed prepared meals. It was only when my client Jen Stein asked me to cook my recipes without olive oil for fear that it was fattening, that I realized I was an artist, not an employee. You can't cook good food without olive oil, and the Italian in me was not going to pretend otherwise.

So my plan failed. But before I could plummet again into deep despair, the universe delivered an answer. A friend who'd eaten at my house many times surprised me by saying, "I'd love to cook. I just don't know how."

Without even thinking, I replied, "I can teach you."

"Yeah, but I just don't have the *feel*," she said, fearing that focusing on a law career had somehow obliterated any kitchen instinct.

"Oh don't worry," I said. "I can teach you the feel."

And with that, I opened my fridge to find a bunch of dinosaur kale, the larger version of what they call *cavolo nero* in Italy, and we began to sauté garlic in a pan with olive oil and red pepper flakes. Though I had to give her arm a few gentle yanks to prevent her from picking up her cell phone during crucial moments, she stayed present with the process. We cooked my favorite brown rice spaghetti *al dente*, tossed it in the kale, and sprinkled it with Pecorino Romano.

The next day she called me, inspired. She and her mother wanted to pay me to teach them to cook. Was I free the following week?

I most definitely was!

I sent out an email that said "Only Two More Spots in a Cooking Class," a blatant lie. Six people signed up, trusting the overachieving Horwich name.

I called the class "The Quick Six Fix" and taught the aforementioned *Spaghetti al Cavolo Nero, Rosemary-Spiked Cannellini Crostini, 12-Minute Chicken with Herbes de Provence, Roasted Cauliflower with Lemon, and Guilt-Free Blueberry Cobbler*—recipes that are now in print for you here in this book.

After only one class, my students were confidently making food with stellar results.

Everyone begged me to teach another class. I sent out a second "Two Spaces Left" email, and typed out more of my recipes. This time, ten people enrolled.

Teaching a willing adult to make simple food didn't seem remotely challenging to me. I'd spent years struggling to inspire tired, hungry adolescents to find a personal connection to the wonders of ancient world history at 8 o'clock in the morning. Cooking with eager, paying adults in a classroom stocked with wine, cheese, and chocolate—it was a no-brainer. Mostly because I'm not a morning person. I finally had a vision, a goal, and I was willing to work hard to make it happen.

Slowly but surely, word got out. It seemed that everyone who came to class came back for more and brought friends. Students requested different kinds of classes, asking me to teach them to cook dishes that I myself hadn't even mastered. Fortunately, I'd developed a sophisticated palate while living in Italy. So when students asked me for a fish class, for example, I could accept the challenge, even though I had no idea how to cook fish. (That's right, I filled up my first fish class with paying customers before I had any recipes!) And then with my palate, my kitchen instincts, and hundreds of recipes to dissect in both Italian and English, I experimented and figured out exactly which ingredients and processes would create memorable fish dishes that would be easy for my students to replicate at home.

Eventually, East Coasters caught wind of my classes via happy students who posted photos of themselves wearing Meal-and-a-Spiel-branded aprons on Facebook. They wanted the kind of food they saw in the pictures: healthy, vibrant, California-Italian, and they wanted to have fun with me, Meal-and-a-Spiel style. I booked a ticket on miles, packed a suitcase full of aprons, and hit the road from Boston down to Miami, staying with friends along the way.

THE COOKING SCHOOL

Meal and a Spiel is based in Los Angeles, in my parents' large kitchen in Beverly Hills, usually on Monday and Wednesday nights. The classes begin in the early evening, as cars pull up to the house and park beneath a canopy of trees. The door is unlocked, so students can let themselves in. (I always know when a first timer arrives because they ring the doorbell.)

My parents usually make themselves invisible, but our dogs (Dulcinea and AJ (RIP) and now Ezra) stick around to welcome people and put them at ease. I start the evening out with a cheese board and a glass of prosecco to loosen the energy. Everyone takes a seat around the kitchen island, and students go around the room, one by one, stating their first names and their level of comfort in the kitchen. I don't ask what anybody's profession is, so it sometimes take me years to find out that I've taught a celebrity stylist, a famous jewelry designer, or a senior executive at Snapchat. Within the context of the kitchen, it doesn't matter. I don't want any sense of competition. I want mutual support.

By the time our introductions are finished, I've learned everyone's name by heart, which always impresses the group. For me, learning up to 20 new names at once is a crucial part of my job. The best way to teach someone is to love them, and the first step in loving someone is to learn their name. It's how to make someone feel cared for and safe.

(If you choose to join our online community, please introduce yourself!)

When I introduce myself, I tell the story of how my mother never cooked a meal in our lives, which shocks my students because they're sitting in her gorgeous kitchen. I tell them how I learned to cook—the story you've read above—and how I believe everyone can learn to cook. Some of my students are intimidated by the kitchen. Others simply never prioritized cooking as they made their way through law school or launched a real estate business. Still others spent a lifetime cooking tirelessly for their families and are looking for new inspiration.

People come to me through word of mouth. I wouldn't have it any other way. It guarantees a friendliness, warmth, and sense of community in my classes—and that no one steals my mother's crystal. Some students show up every week for months on end and then I see them once a year for tune ups. Some come every few months, while a handful come only once, go home to make every recipe successfully, and decide that's all they need. People have different ways of digesting what they've learned. Some of you will read every recipe in this book, others will find a handful of favorites, and that's enough. So far, I've really only had lovely, wonderful students—no duds in the bunch—and that includes you!

A SENSE OF PURPOSE

I now see that everything that unfolded for me on this journey had purpose. I had to teach history, because I needed to understand how to connect people to the roots, to the tradition of what we're doing. I had to to be a body worker because I had to feel with my own hands how energy moves through people and how emotional energy gets stuck. So much of what I do is dissolving the fear and stress people have around cooking so that they can enjoy it. I had to study acting because I needed to learn how to be open and how to engage a group of people. I had to learn how to be playful, so I could inspire others to play in the kitchen. I had to do stand-up so I could lose all fear, so I would be able to write and deliver honest, vulnerable, and entertaining spiels. I had to learn Italian so I could read every last Italian cookbook. And I had to be a bartender so I could teach my students to make a fucking awesome skinny margarita.

Eight years ago marked the birth of *Meal and a Spiel*. I now dedicate my life to teaching people of different generations all over the country to create healthy, home-cooked meals. Inspired by Maria, who adds love to her food so that it's not just tasted, but felt, I believe that cooking can bring significant healing to our society at large. All food should bring us back home to a quiet place inside of us that is total comfort, unconditional love, relaxation—a sigh of relief after a long day.

Twenty-odd years ago, on the quad of Brown University, I had an epiphany and left for Italy to truly experience life and love. I assumed I would ultimately write about romantic love, with deep insights on the mysteries of life. I didn't realize that the book I was destined to write would be about something as commonplace as food. Yet I believe that in the everyday act of cooking and eating, we can find profound revelations, opportunities to grow the spirit, and the most beautiful connections with our fellow human beings.

I cook with love and I teach others to cook with love, because it's my mission to create joy, playfulness, and connection. By holding this book of life and love in your hands, you're joining our community. I'm so happy to have you here.

Ingredient Number One

In Italy, they say every sauce and every dish comes out differently depending on who's cooking it. Even with the exact same ingredients and measurements, the way someone stirs the sauce changes the flavor. In other words, you can taste the love.

That's why there's nothing that pisses me off more than someone coming into my kitchen and carelessly stirring my sauce. If the wooden spoon is resting on the side of the pan, it's there for a reason! Americans always come in and start vigorously stirring and tasting like it's some sort of spaghetti sauce rodeo. Whoooooa there! Hold your horses, people! Do you walk into an artist's studio and slap paint on his canvas? Do you enter an operating room and poke your finger in a patient's liver? Do you walk into the Oval Office, go over to the President's phone, and send a grammatically incorrect tweet? No. Make your own damn sauce!

And when you do make that sauce, remember, it's your baby. You don't abandon it or ignore it. You care for it with all the love in your heart. If you don't have the bandwidth to love your sauce, then don't complain when no one appreciates your food. It won't matter what recipe you follow or how much time you spend. Cooking is about love.

Now, I accept that we can't always be free to cook with absolute commitment. When your work or your children need you, that's not the time to cook. You need to carve out a peaceful time to be with the food. It'll relax and invigorate you more than you thought. Your children will unconsciously appreciate the loving energy in the home and will consciously appreciate it when they're grown. Similarly, you might find that the meditative quality of cooking with love will naturally inspire your creative efforts at work. It's no accident that Francis Ford Coppola gathers his new cast together before he shoots every film and cooks them a big meal.

As for me, when I stir the sauce, I tell it out loud that I love it. I smell it, breathing in deep, allowing the scent of tomatoes, garlic, and fresh herbs to travel deep into my bloodstream and transport me. When I cook at my parents' house, where I teach, my father sometimes walks into the kitchen during this process. "Who are you talking to?" he asks.

"The sauce." My father is perplexed. The man could not be less interested in cooking or the sensual qualities of food. He sees sauce on the stove and only cares how much oil went into it, worried about the cholesterol. "Dad, come here. Taste this."

No man, no woman, no human being is immune to the seductive power of fresh sauce. As he puts the wooden spoon in his mouth, a smile of childhood innocence overcomes him. With one taste, he's won over. The love is genuine.

This is why my sauce is so good. It tastes like what we all crave more deeply, more desperately than anything else in this entire universe: pure, unabashed love.

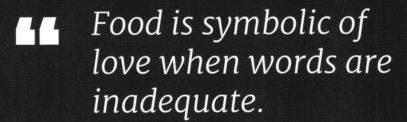

Food is symbolic of love when words are inadequate.

— Alan D. Wolfelt

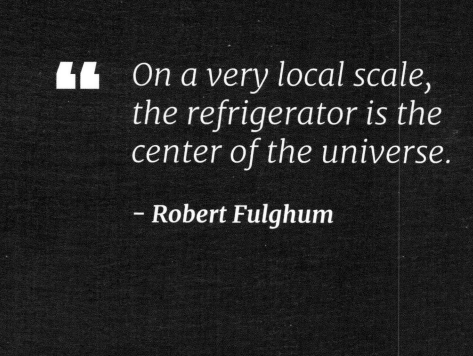

" *On a very local scale, the refrigerator is the center of the universe.*

– Robert Fulghum

Everything You Need to Become a Badass in the Kitchen

HALF THE BATTLE IN COOKING IS JUST HAVING THE RIGHT TOOLS and ingredients on hand. For example, you can walk into my house any day of the week, whether or not I've been to the market lately, and I can make you an authentic plate of pasta, a small cheese board, a salad, and a simple dessert. No, I couldn't roast you a rack of lamb or grill you a branzino—unless you caught me on the right day—but it's still delicious food. If you stock your fridge and pantry right, you can always make a meal.

How to Use This Book Like a Badass

This book is like a cooking class, carefully crafted to teach you how to become a badass cook. Here are few guidelines for using it, so you can navigate the most enjoyable and effective route possible:

1. GET IN BED

The most common mistake people make with cookbooks is that they open them up for the first time in the kitchen. They find a recipe, take out the ingredients, and follow the instructions step by step. Sometimes it works beautifully, and sometimes you burn the crap out of a meal because you're fumbling to figure out what the next step is while preparing the remaining ingredients. This has happened to everyone! When you treat a cookbook like the instruction manual for a washer-dryer, you sacrifice the spirit of the book. You lose the tone, the message, the feel of the recipes.

Instead, I suggest you curl up in bed or on the couch and allow yourself to enjoy this book before you take it into the kitchen. Read the spiels. These are the stories and insights I share in my classes before we start chopping an onion, and they're like red carpets laid out before each recipe, intended to inspire you to create your own stories, your own connection to cooking. From beneath the comfort of your duvet, flag the recipes you want to make. Get out a pen and write in this book. Underline stuff. Use it like a textbook. By the time you get into the kitchen with it, you'll have a much better sense of how to use it.

2. THE RECIPE LADDER

As best as I could, I ordered the recipes in each chapter from easiest to hardest. I actually don't think there are any truly challenging recipes in this book. However, the first ones will require less involvement and/or time than the last. This doesn't mean that the latter recipes taste better than the former—*assolutamente no!* I'm simply creating a way for beginner cooks to feel comfortable, to know a good place to start, and to gain confidence from the get-go. If you're a more experienced cook, feel free to start anywhere!

3. CLASSROOM CORNERS

As a cooking teacher, I field students' questions all day long—often the same questions. So I included them here, dispersed throughout the book, near the recipes they apply to. If you're like me, you might enjoy an afternoon of just reading these tips, geeking out to get some answers. For a complete index of Classroom Corners, see page 460.

- cheese board
- soup
- crostini - pecan
- chicken meatballs

radicchio
ribeye - babamic reduction - in frag
fennel salad -
...person ...person
...raveling

.com

STOP TRYING TO BE PERFECT and just cook!

By Elana Horwich

4. LIFE LESSONS THROUGH FOOD

I believe that cooking can teach us how to live. It can teach us to be mindful, grateful, passionate, and in the flow. Of course, it's not the only way—you can learn in classrooms, in therapy, in meditation—but cooking is the only way that guarantees us a nosh afterwards!

That's why I've included *Life Lessons Through Food* throughout the book. These lessons should help you open your spirit, so you can *feel into* the cooking, enjoy it immensely, allow for mistakes, release the need for perfection, and heighten your sensual connection to the food. So get off the therapy couch (only after your session is finished, of course) and get into the kitchen!

For a complete index of *Life Lessons Through Food*, see page 461.

5. A NOTE ON MEASURING

I developed this cookbook to help you to become an intuitive cook, and that means we are going to approach measuring a little differently than you may be used to.

My goal is for you to make your meals without measuring. Breathe, it's going to be okay. Most of these recipes don't require precision. Recipes can never be an exact science because things like potatoes and eggplants come in various shapes and sizes, and I can't tell you from my kitchen exactly how many granules of salt or thyme you'll need in yours.

So my recipes give you parameters: *about* a tablespoon, a *generous* cup, *about twenty grinds* of the pepper mill. Of course, my pepper mill may grind out less pepper than yours, so trust my guidelines, but remember that you are the badass of your kitchen, not me.

My recipes also instruct you to lick your fingers as you cook. Do it! Taste as you go, so you can experience the journey of the recipe as you make it. Do your *Rustic Olive Oil Mashed Potatoes* seem too thick? Add more broth. Does the *Eggplant Parmigiana* recipe leave you with leftover eggplant slices? Buy smaller ones next time. Do your *Little Italian Potato Sticks* taste bland? Add more salt. Flexibility is an important quality of a badass cook.

With some experience, I want you to be able to reach your fingers into a salt jar and just know how much your food needs, like Maria. I want you to be able to read a recipe that calls for ¼ teaspoon of salt or thyme and know what that feels like in your fingertips. And more than anything, I want you to not need recipes at all!

You can start with a mini homework assignment: pour a teaspoon of salt into your hand and see what it looks like, what it feels like in your fingertips—and then chuck the teaspoon. See if you can eyeball a teaspoon without measuring. Do the same with a tablespoon and ½ teaspoon, etc. Keep trying until you have a feel for it. It's not brain surgery. You'll learn sooner than you think.

6. KNOW YOUR ICONS

(S) Easy Enough for a Schlemazel (see Page 5)

(GF) Gluten-Free

(V) Vegetarian

(VG) Vegan

(P) Paleo-Friendly (no grain, no wine, no refined sugar, no cheese, no milk)

(DF) Dairy-Free

(▶) Video Tutorial: if you see this icon, you can watch me make this recipe on www.MealandaSpiel.com.

The Food Will Speak To You

Maria, the caretaker at Geggianello, the Tuscan villa where I first stayed in Italy, is the goddess on my kitchen pedestal and the inspiration for all of my cooking ventures. Everything she touches turns to gold, and just thinking about her makes me hungry.

Soon after I met her, I had the brilliant idea that I'd write a cookbook collecting the recipes and stories of the Italian *mamme* I knew, with Maria as the star of this bestseller. I started by asking Maria for the recipe to her soul-melting meat sauce. She obliged. I thought she'd go into a drawer and take out a piece of paper, but instead, she rattled off a couple sentences and expected that to be sufficient for me to know what to do. I slowed her down and demanded a list of specific ingredients.

The conversation went something like this—in Italian of course:

"Olive oil."
"How much?"
"To cover the bottom of the pot and then some."
"How big is the pot?"
"Elana…" (getting exasperated.)
"Okay, okay." (Note to self—pot size probably depends on how much sauce you're making)
"And then what?"
"An onion."
"Chopped?"
"Of course."
"Finely chopped?"
"Of course!"
"And then?"
"One or two carrots…"
"Which one?"
"Which one what?"
"One or two carrots?"
"One or two…"
"But if I'm going to write a cookbook, I need to tell people if it's *one* or *two* carrots. What is it: One or two?"
"One or two," she repeats, with absolutely no concern for my recipe dilemma.
Screeching halt.

How could I write a best-selling cookbook that would win me the accolades of my doctor-wanting parents and pave a passionate successful career among a worldwide community of creatives if I didn't know if Maria's meat sauce needed one or two carrots!!

What I understood years later is that Italian women don't cook by recipes. They cook by intuition.

Maria can look at her sautéed onions and the other ingredients before her and in that moment decide if the meat sauce needs one or two carrots. She couldn't explain that to me because it was too obvious for her to articulate; it was too intrinsic to her existence as a cook. In her mind, how could I *not* understand that the food speaks to us?

It may have taken me years, but *this* is what I teach my students: *there is a conversation between the cook and the food.* We need to start listening.

I've watched most of my students learn to cook intuitively because the food does actually speak to us when our hearts are open to loving it. It's an incredibly simple, yet powerful way to approach cooking.

If you're ever wondering what ingredient to use or how much of it is needed, just ask the food what *it* needs. Listen to your instincts. Cooking is a process of communication. It's a lifelong relationship. It's an opportunity to practice non-verbal love.

Discard all notions of perfection and aim simply to deepen the conversation.

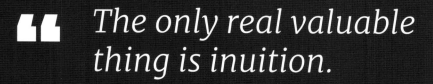

The only real valuable thing is inuition.

—Albert Einstein

What I Always Have in My Kitchen

In addition to the staples that everyone has in their kitchens—eggs, butter, baking soda, vinegar, etc.—I always keep the following ingredients on hand:

IN MY PANTRY

Extra-Virgin Olive Oil: Of all the ingredients necessary to make a successful, authentic Italian meal, this is the most important. Olive oil isn't just about greasing the pan. It's also about *flavor*. Olive oil lays the foundation for the entire dish by marrying itself to all the other ingredients, so you need to 1) use good oil and 2) use a lot of it. Probably more than you're used to. That said, I go through so much olive oil that I tend to choose a bottle that's good enough for drizzling but not so expensive that I can't use it for everyday cooking.

HOW TO CHOOSE AN OLIVE OIL

» **Only buy *extra-virgin* olive oil.** It's the least processed, which means it will have the best flavor and be the healthiest.

» **Don't ever buy *light* olive oil.** I've never seen it in an Italian home. I doubt it even exists in Italy. See above.

» **Always buy olive oil in dark glass.** Olive oil is light-sensitive (i.e. the light ruins it). Good olive producers know this and package their *olio* accordingly. Don't be swayed by cute, fancy labels; if it's in a clear bottle, ignore the temptation.

» **If you're looking for a higher end olive oil for drizzling on top of crostini, salads, or soups, choose an olive oil from a specific region.** Olive oil from Santa Barbara will likely be better than oil from the general state of California.. Similarly, olive oil from the hills of Siena will likely be more refined than Tuscan olive oil, which itself will be of higher quality than a generic Italian olive oil.

» **Smell your oil.** If you like the smell of a particular oil, then you'll likely enjoy the flavor. Smells like stale crayons? It's gone rancid, toss it.

» **Pay for it:** I spend about $16 dollars on a liter of extra-virgin olive oil. Sounds expensive? The only other way you're going to get Italian home cooking this good is to get on a plane to Italy and find a *mamma* to invite you to dinner. Don't skimp on your oil.

Quality Canned Tomatoes: Canned tomatoes are wonderful, particularly when fresh tomatoes are out of season. They offer a thicker, richer tomato taste than fresh tomatoes, and I use these all the time to whip up my *Simple Tomato and Basil Sauce* for pasta, *Spaghetti Squash Primavera*, *Roberto's Eggplant Parmigiana*, and more. I also add them to braised dishes like *Chicken alla Cacciatora* and *The Best Brisket Ever.*

HOW TO CHOOSE CANNED TOMATOES

Italians take their canned tomatoes seriously. Many jar their homegrown tomatoes in summer to use for the rest of the year, and city-dwellers learn to choose canned tomatoes wisely to add the best flavor to their cooking.

HERE ARE MY GUIDELINES FOR CHOOSING CANNED TOMATOES:

» **NEVER buy canned tomatoes with herbs and seasonings already added, unless you want your food to taste like cheap American spaghetti sauce.** YOU will be in charge of adding flavors to your recipes, not some factory. Always read the ingredients.

» **Always buy WHOLE peeled—not chopped—canned tomatoes.** Whole peeled tomatoes have better flavor than those that are already diced inside the can. You can use a blender or your hands to break up the tomatoes.

» **Choose Italian plum tomatoes when possible.** The top of the line are San Marzano. I like organic domestic varieties as well.

Pasta: If you want good pasta, buy brands that are imported from Italy, like De Cecco, Barilla, or Garofalo. Keep an eye out for artisanal Pasta di Gragnano, which is considered the best.

Gluten-Free Pasta: My go-to gluten free pasta is Tinkyada Brown Rice Pasta, which I've found readily available at Whole Foods stores throughout the country. You can also look for corn or other gluten-free pastas imported from Italy.

Salt-Packed Capers from Sicily (Capperi di Salina): Not all capers are created equal. Capers are essential to many Italian recipes, but I can't tell you how many cooking students thought they hated them until they tried my recipes with these special Sicilian treats. I too used to think of capers as the gross little green things found on the side of a bagel. It's true—American capers are gross! That's because of the way they're preserved, sitting in vinegar and citric acid for months or years before you buy them. Sicilian capers, on the other hand, are packed in a coarse sea salt that doesn't compromise the integrity of the caper's unique, indescribable flavor, recalling the rocky southern seashores of the Mediterranean. You can find them in Italian specialty shops or online. **Note:** Salt-packed capers must be rinsed before use. You can throw them into a fine mesh sieve, or put a small handful under the faucet and chide yourself when more than a few fall into the garbage disposal.

Tamari (or quality soy sauce): This is my little secret. Don't tell the Italians. I've been using this California-inspired trick of mine on them for years. A touch of tamari adds a hint of umami, a sweet saltiness, which in turn can harmonize salad dressings and accentuate the goodness of mushrooms.

Canned Italian Tuna: You likely already keep a can of tuna in the house, so consider buying Italian canned tuna in olive oil. I stock up whenever I go to Costco, so I can whip up my go-to pasta, *al tonno e capperi*, add some to a salad, or make *Jewish-Italian Tuna Toasts* (Page 100). If you can't find Italian tuna in olive oil, try albacore in olive oil or in water.

A Box of Good Crackers: In case guests spontaneously show up and you want to set out a cheese board. For brands I like, see my *Chic Cheese Board for Badasses.*

A Hunk or Bar of Good Dark Chocolate (at least 70%): In many gourmet shops and certain upscale supermarkets, you can find imported chocolate sold in rustic hunks of dark and dreamy goodness. Buy some and keep them on hand in case guests show up and you need dessert. Dark chocolate on a wood board, served up with a hefty knife so people can cut small bites at a time, epitomizes rustic chic. Nobody needs a fancy dessert. Chocolate makes people happy. If you can't find a hunk or block of chocolate, buy a few good bars to have on hand. My favorites: Valrhona, Green and Black's, and AlterEco.

Raw Honey: We aren't talking about the stuff that comes in plastic teddy bear squeeze-bottles. We are talking about the pure form of honey that adds the taste of love directly to your desserts and to your cheese boards. I prefer honey with a creamy texture and light color, and I encourage you to buy local varieties, not only to support local beekeepers, but because some studies have shown that local raw honey can treat pollen allergies.

Balsamic Glaze: This is essentially a thick, syrupy balsamic reduction that pairs well with cheeses and meats. Of course, the store-bought variety won't be as good as my homemade Rosemary-Balsamic Reduction, but if you're anything like my cooking students, you'll want to have some shortcuts, and store-bought glazes are often quite nice. I use them in my cooking classes which focus on quick recipes.

Box of Chicken Broth: I prefer to make my own broth and keep leftovers in the freezer, but in a pinch, I use a quality boxed broth in recipes that call for just a little bit (see *Cheater's Chicken Broth*).

Diamond Crystal Kosher Salt: This is the salt I use for basic cooking needs. It's kept in a salt jar, right next to the stove. Kosher salt has a better flavor than table salt and generic sea salt, and it's what all professional chefs use. It's less salty per teaspoon than table salt, so you might need a little extra. Diamond Crystal is not too coarse, as some kosher salts are, and has the perfect crystal size.

Finishing Salt: I also keep a good sea salt on hand, such as is Fleur de Sel, Maldon, or flaky Celtic salt. I wouldn't waste these salts in cooked dishes, but reserve them for a sprinkle on top of food before serving. Lots of recipes benefit from a quick a sprinkle of salt: crostini, salads, and chocolate bark, to name a few. This is a great opportunity to use a quality salt to really give your dishes a punctuation.

Pepper Grinder: I keep whole peppercorns in a grinder because freshly ground pepper is much sharper, more flavorful, and has better texture than the pre-ground variety. My recipes list pepper in twists of the mill rather than teaspoons, so get yourself a mill!

Tomatoes: Don't put them in the fridge! The cold will ruin your tomatoes, drain any sweetness, and turn the texture mealy. Let them sit on your counter, and if they begin to get soft and mushy, make sauce!

Onions and Garlic: These essential members of the allium family are a no-brainer, but like tomatoes, they shouldn't sit in the fridge, lest the cold kill their flavor and healing properties. Get a nice wooden or ceramic bowl or something that goes with

your kitchen style, and keep these out as a homey welcome to all who enter.

Lemons: A stocked Italian or California kitchen should always have lemons on hand. If you have the opportunity to plant a lemon tree, do it! Both the zest and the juice will be your best friends. The zest has a lemony flavor similar to what you would find in lemon candy, except without the sugar, and, hence, not surprisingly, is delicious in desserts. I also love it with the nutty flavors of quinoa and my *Pistachio-Crusted Salmon*. The juice you will use more often. It has a mild, acidic flavor, ideal for livening up salads, vegetables, meats, and fish. If you're ever in doubt about how to dress up a bland dish, just add olive oil, salt, and lemon before serving. It's an Italian secret that's not that much of a secret!

Oranges: Though not as important to have on hand as lemons, oranges can add an extra special touch. They keep for a while, so I always have a few on hand in case I want to spontaneously slice them up for a welcome prosecco, juice one into an *Aperol Spritz*, or zest one into a dessert.

Red Wine: There's always a leftover bottle of red wine on my counter. I let it sit there for months and use it as cooking wine for chicken, brisket, and reductions. I also keep a new bottle on hand in case guests stop by. I usually go for a Chianti Classico, Montepulciano D'Abruzzo, Nebbiolo, or California Cabernet.

IN MY SPICE DRAWER

I don't keep tons of dried spices in my kitchen, since most of the flavor in my food comes from fresh produce and herbs. But the spices you'll see again and again in this book are **Red Pepper Flakes** (from peperoncini, also known as Tuscan peppers), **Dried Thyme**, **Dried Rosemary**, and **Fennel Seeds**, along with **Cinnamon Sticks** and **Whole Pods of Nutmeg**—a secret flavor for sauces, which I grate on my microplane.

GOING ORGANIC

I buy organic ingredients whenever possible. They tend to be more expensive, but it's worth it to know that my food is free of harmful pesticides, chemicals, and hormones, and that it's raised without the cruelty of a factory farm. I also find that organic produce tastes better. Maybe most importantly, buying organic is better for the planet: it reduces pollution and maintains natural resources for future generations. Organic fruits and vegetables tend to be smaller than conventional ones, and the measurements in this book reflect that.

Parmigiano Reggiano is the king of all Italian cheeses. Parmesan is NOT the same thing! Parmesan is the American bastardization of this extraordinary Italian *formaggio*. Just like champagne comes from the Champagne region in France and Chianti wine only comes from the Chianti region of Tuscany, Parmigiano Reggiano is produced only in northern Italy, near Parma and Reggio Emilia—hence its name. It's made from milk from a unique type of cow, which feeds only on the high-nutrient grass of the region and gets milked at specific times of day, according to strict consortium regulations. Using Parmigiano instead of parmesan will up your cooking game a thousand-fold. Italians consider Parmigiano to have nutritional fortitude like red meat. "It makes you stronger," I've been told. If you insist on sticking to American parmesan, let alone the stuff in a green can, to make these recipes and no one goes totally bonkers over your food, you'll have only yourself to blame!

Pecorino Romano is a hard, aged sheep's milk cheese intended to be grated as a final touch. (*Pecora* means "sheep" in Italian, so any cheese made from sheep is a *pecorino*.) There is *Pecorino Toscano* from Tuscany, which is soft and rather creamy, *Pecorino Sardo* from Sardegna, which is medium-sharp, like a Manchego (sheep's milk cheese from Spain: *Pecorino Spagnolo*). Pecorino Romano comes from the farmland of Lazio outside the capital and may be the sharpest of all the *pecorini* available. I like to use it on pastas that either have a little spice or anchovy, like my *Spaghetti al Cavolo Nero*, or on soups that could benefit from a small, sharp kick.

A good piece of noshing cheese: Always have one well-chosen, well-wrapped, whole piece of cheese that can be opened for a spontaneous cheese plate in case unexpected guests visit. I prefer to keep cheese made from sheep or goat, since it's easier to digest and generally less agitating for those with allergies (namely me). See my *Chic Cheese Board for Badasses* for my favorite picks.

Carrots and Celery: Along with the onions you'll keep on your countertop, carrots and celery are used in traditional *soffritto* (sauté)—the base for soups, braised meats, and homemade broth—and are perfect for doctoring a box of store-bought broth for a last-minute risotto (see *Cheater's Chicken Broth*). Even when they get a little floppy sitting in your fridge, they're totally fine for cooking. Celery leaves are bursting with flavor, so don't leave them out! And if you buy organic, you don't need to peel your carrots.

Fresh Delicate Herbs: Don't underestimate the power of herbs to kick a dish up to the next level. Sometimes just sprinkling the right green herb, like fresh mint on my *Rigatoni al Tonno e Capperi*, can be a game-changer. Herbs contribute to an overall *leggerezza* (lightness) of a meal, as they boost digestion. When I go to the market, I make sure to grab a bunch of **flat-leaf parsley** (never the curly stuff!), **mint**, **basil**, **chives**, and **cilantro**, which isn't typical of Italian cooking, but my California self can't get enough of it. Whatever herbs I don't use, I chop up and throw into salads and eggs.

Hearty Herbs: Though **rosemary** and **thyme** are too bitter to be eaten raw, when added to juicy dishes such as soups, beans, braised meats, and roasted vegetables, their flavors permeate and lend an aromatic goodness reminiscent of a night in a Tuscan bed and breakfast. When crisped in a pan, **sage** is a wonderfully delicious garnish. These herbs are also easy to grow at home if you have a sunny spot in your garden, porch, or kitchen window!

Olive Oil Packed Anchovies: If you don't think you need anchovies to make good Italian food, or you're just generally grossed out by the little gray fishies, think again. But don't go and buy yourself the stuff in a can. Get quality anchovies packaged in olive oil. And for those of you true anchovy fans, go for the Italian salt-packed anchovies that you can find at certain specialty stores.

Almond Milk: I always have some almond milk on hand to make my *Lavender Latte* before bed.

Vin Santo: It's great to have a bottle of this traditional Tuscan dessert wine in the fridge to make *Cantucci Toscani* or *Maria's Crostini* or to serve as an after-dinner *digestivo*.

A Bottle of Prosecco: I always keep a bottle on hand in case guests spontaneously show up, and I want to feel like Martha fucking Stewart, Italian-style!

Master The Pieces

Every once in a while, clients that hire me for dinner parties or private cooking classes offer to save me time, and them money, by doing the grocery shopping themselves. I have to refuse. It's like asking Valentino to make you a dress for the Oscars with fabric chosen by Dr. Phil. It's like asking Michelangelo to carve the David with a piece of marble chosen by the Pope. If you're going to create a masterpiece, you have to be the master of *the pieces*.

If I don't carefully choose the quality of the ingredients, I cannot guarantee the quality of the meal. It's that simple. Shopping is as important to me as the actual cooking process. I start creating in the supermarket.

I spend a large portion of my classes discussing ingredients. For example, a tomato sauce topped with processed American parmesan cheese would be nothing, I mean NOTHING, compared to one topped with Parmigiano Reggiano. The specific ingredients I list in my recipes aren't *suggestions*. They're *THE* ingredients necessary to create the type of food that you want to eat, trust me.

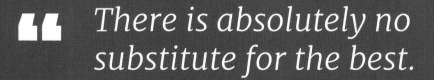

There is absolutely no substitute for the best.

—James Beard

Homemade Broth: I've gotten into the habit of making broth every so often and storing it in the freezer. That way, I can decide last minute to whip up a soup, a risotto, or a meat sauce and have it taste like Italy.

Ice Cream: I always have some non-dairy coconut ice cream on hand in case I decide to whip up *Flourless Chocolate Blender Cakes*, *Guilt-Free Blueberry Cobbler*, or *Caramelized Apples for Dummies*. My go-to is Coconut Bliss, which I've been able to find all over the country. But when I can get my hands on some artisanal vegan ice cream, my favorites are McConnell's and Van Leeuwen.

Tools I Can't Live Without

Every kitchen is different, with different sized drawers and cabinets, so I don't expect you to have every tool—not every home cook needs an ice cream maker or a sous vide. But I've listed the tools that will help you follow the recipes in this book and ultimately turn you into a badass cook. If you want to find them online, check out my shop at **www. MealandaSpiel.com**, which links to trusted retailers.

Salt Jar: If you learn just one thing from this book, I hope you'll learn to grab salt from a jar with your fingers instead of shaking it out or pouring it into a measuring spoon. A salt jar will make a difference in how you approach cooking, and ultimately in how your food tastes. (see *A Note on Measuring*, Page 34, and *Touch The Salt*, Page 98.)

Microplane Zester/Grater: This may be the best $14 you spend in your kitchen. Just ask any of my cooking students. One by one, they've been seduced by this wand. The microplane is a fine handheld grater which makes grating cheese easy and fun. There are different types of microplanes, but I'm in love with the long, skinny one known as a Zester/Grater. The microplane grates Parmigiano and pecorino into light, slender ribbons that taste so much better in pasta and soup than the pre-grated cheeses you buy in markets. The microplane effortlessly zests citrus (yes, lemon zest will no longer only be for fancy cooks!), grates fresh nutmeg for your meat sauces, and will allow you to finally throw away your garlic press, because it turns garlic and ginger into a pulp.

At Least One Good Sharp Knife: Almost all recipes require cutting or chopping, so using dull knives can make you hate cooking—or perhaps already has. Let's fix it. But before you go out and buy a whole new set of expensive knives, get the ones you already own sharpened professionally. (There are services for this. Google one in your area.) That said, I'm totally in love with my ceramic knives and so are my cooking students, who often buy their own after they try them in class. They're lightweight, extremely sharp, and affordably priced. Quality ceramic knives slice through tomato skin, which eliminates my need for a special serrated knife for this or any other purpose. If I were to tell you to get ONE knife, it would be a 6 to 7-inch stainless steel Santoku Chef's Knife. You'll use it for everything. Ideally you would have one in stainless steel, which can cut through harder foods (unfortunately the ceramic ones can chip), and then also a couple of ceramic Santokus, which will become your go-to's for everyday cooking. They are mine.

Wooden Spoons: The food you are making comes from the earth. Don't stir it with plastics and polymers. Plastic stirring spoons can melt into your pan if you're not careful, leaving you with carcinogenic sauce that tastes like chemicals. Wood spoons taste like love. Thank you trees. (Bamboo cooking spoons are another great, eco-friendly option.)

Tongs: I have lots of pairs of tongs in my kitchen. I use them for grilling and for turning meat, but mostly I use them for tossing long pasta into the sauce after it's cooked. You just can't toss spaghetti with a spoon. My favorite tongs have silicone tips, which just make them delightful to use.

Parchment Paper: It's a roll of paper that you line a baking sheet with so that food doesn't stick. To learn more, see *What is Parchment Paper For?* (Page 296).

Onion Goggles: A frequent cooking student finally got fed up watching tears flood down my face class after class and donated a pair of onion goggles to *Meal and a Spiel*. (Thanks Toni Corwin!) Since then, all of my students and I are obsessed. And if one of you decides to invent *prescription* onion goggles, you'll have a faithful customer in me!

LARGE Cutting Board: I cannot tell you how many times I've walked into people's kitchens to cater a meal and found that they only have tiny little cutting boards. No wonder they don't cook! Get yourself LARGE cuttings boards! The larger the better. Give yourself space to work and groove.

LARGE Baking Pans: Small baking pans are another reason why so many of my students find themselves stressed when they cook at home. With only small trays, you'll either crowd your food, which means it'll steam rather than caramelize, or you'll need to work in batches, which can mean uneven cooking. So for the love of God, measure your oven and get the largest possible baking pans. Your life will improve dramatically. Standard ovens can take 21 x 15-inch pans.

Blender: I have a Vitamix, which is an expensive, high-powered blender. I've found that it purees soup like no other blender. It's like velvet, and will marry the flavors really well, even if you messed up the recipe. I keep it on my counter and throw in a can of tomatoes for a quick pulse. I even grind my coffee in it. That said, a fancy blender is not necessary for making delicious Italian food. If you aren't ready for one, that's okay. But you should have some kind of blender or immersion blender on hand, and work your way up to a Vitamix when you're ready.

Spiralizer: A spiralizer allows you to make noodles from a variety of vegetables. With recipes like *Zucchini Linguine with Pesto Genovese* and *Sweet Potato Pasta all'Arrabbiata*, you'll be able to capture the sumptuous flavors of Italy with the calorie count of California. Not a bad combination!

Food Processor: With the press of a finger and without any tears, I can turn onions into coarse paste that makes my meatballs juicy. With the on-and-off-pulse of my same finger, I can instantly chop five different herbs together for my *Springtime Frittata* or my *Oy Veh, A Vegan Salad* in seconds. I can make rustic pestos and crostini toppings and other recipes that a blender just can't do right. I've led a lot of students across the sea of fear to the food processor promised land. Now I invite you to come along!

POTS AND PANS

Ramekins (about 5 oz each): These are little ceramic pots that are ideal for making personalized dessert servings, like my *Flourl Blender Cakes* or *Greek Yogurt Panna Cotta*. I find that people (particularly those under the age of 11) feel incredibly cared for when they're served a treat in an adorable ramekin. I also use them on my cheese boards for olives and honey.

Grill Pan: If you want delicious, healthy food made with minimal effort, you need a grill pan! Of course, you could just use an outdoor BBQ grill, but then you'd have to go outside and light it and wait in the cold and rain for it to heat up. Plus, grill pans are much easier to control. There's more room for error with a BBQ. My favorite brand for grill pans is All Clad. I find them really easy to use, even for beginner cooks. It's worth buying the larger one that fits over two burners. The smaller ones, with their long handles, take up awkward space in your kitchen drawers, and you'll grow out of them quickly.

Enamel Cast Iron Dutch Oven and Braiser: This cookware is best used for braising and for making soups and sauces. An oval **Dutch Oven** is ideal for foods that have some height or length to them, like a brisket or roast. It's also ideal for making large quantities of stews, soups, and sauces. The **Braiser** is more for everyday cooking. I use it for risotto, meat sauces, sautéed veggies, *Chicken alla Cacciatore*, *Italian Ski Chalet Chicken*, and the uber-juicy *Maria's Chicken*. My brand of choice is Le Creuset, but Staub is also top notch.

Ceramic Coated Pans: My go-to's. They're light, strong, and have a smooth, eco-friendly Thermolon coating that makes cooking *and cleaning* easy. My students who want to chuck their toxic Teflon non-stick pans but also want to avoid burning all their food, find themselves incredibly happy with these pans. I love my J. A. Henckels Spirit Pan.

HOW TO MAKE PEACE WITH YOUR FOOD PROCESSOR

There are two types of people in the world: Those who love their food processor, and those who fear them. If you fall into the first category, pat yourself on the back, you get a *Meal and a Spiel* A+. If you fall into the second category, don't worry. I've been there. I got my food processor from my Grandma when I was 25, and was too scared to use it until I was 30. I finally set it up, didn't do it right, and assumed I got a broken one that was too old to return. It wasn't broken. I was. Since then, I've learned the errors of my ways.

The reason so many people are terrified of their food processor is because it comes with multiple parts: the bowl, the blade, and the top—and if they aren't each attached to the base correctly, the thing won't work. I get it! Just relax. If there weren't these safety mechanisms, the blade could potentially spin out of control and chop off your nose. The manufacturers aren't trying to screw with you to make you feel like an incompetent cook. They're on your side!

Let me walk you through getting your food processor to work.

How to Create Menus That Flow

As I've mentioned, this book was designed to give you recipes that all fall into a very similar flavor palate, so you can mix and match as you like. That said—and this won't come as surprise—I have a few words of advice that can help you create menus that flow, in case you decide to entertain. (See: *Chill Out, It's Just a Dinner Party.* Page 66)

I ask you to think about the meal as a journey. Sometimes it's a very short journey. All on one plate. Sometimes there's a bowl followed by a plate. And sometimes there are a multiple bowls and multiple plates, one after the other. Envision the dishes. See yourself lining them up in a row, and see that this line of food has a beginning, a middle, and an end. This isn't just a meal. This is a journey you are leading people along.

Since food ignites all the senses, the journey of the menu is meant to be a sensual one. Think about how you might like to embark on a sensual journey into the unknown. Do you want to be bombarded, or do you want to be seduced? (Seduced!) Imagine a sip of something delicious and a light bite or two that say *hello* and *welcome*. And now, skip directly to the end of the meal. Do you want to end this sensual journey with a feeling of deep satisfaction, or do you prefer to feel like you have to go home and fucking die because you ate too much?

It's not generous to overfeed your guests! You're playing into people's lack of self control, including your own. Instead, consciously plan out a menu that leaves everyone just full enough, relaxed, and happy.

RULES FOR A BALANCED MENU

Don't overcarb. You can call out my Los Angeles roots here, but the truth is, no Italian would ever order pizza and then pasta, as Americans often do in Italian restaurants. In Italy, pizzas aren't even served in the same restaurants as pastas! One is ordered in a *pizzeria* and the other in a *trattoria*.

Carbs are sticky. They taste delicious, but eat too much and you'll enter a food coma. Think about how many times you serve carbs throughout the meal. I advise no more than twice. For example, if you serve crostini and then pasta, then cut the carbs right there, don't serve potatoes with your main dish, and choose a no-carb dessert. If instead you know you want to serve *cantucci* for dessert and bruschetta as a starter, then use a recipe from *I Can't Believe It's Not Pasta!* for your *primo*.

Go for smaller portions. Pasta in Italy is a three-ounce portion; that's less than a fifth of a box. If that's the main dish of the meal, you might serve more. But if you serve it as a *primo*, before a main course and perhaps after an appetizer or two, go with even smaller portions. The more courses or plates you serve, the smaller your portions should be. That goes for steak and fish and chicken and potatoes and dessert; don't force huge portions on people. We don't need to compensate for our grandparents' experience of the Great Depression anymore. Nobody can eat that much and still enjoy themselves afterwards, except maybe a boy of bar mitzvah age—and who wants to hang out with bar mitzvah boys?! Just chill out. There's going to be plenty of food.

Go plant heavy. Vegetables are light on the system, so serve plenty of them. I place the salads and the vegetable chapter before the mains, because they're as important as the meats. I love a huge salad next to a smaller piece of meat.

Use foods that aid digestion. As Hippocrates, the father of modern medicine, said, "Let food be thy medicine." Fresh lemon juice and zest help break down fats. Herbs aid in digestion. It's no coincidence that so many of my recipes have lemon and/or fresh herbs like parsley, mint, and basil. In case that's not quite going to cut it, have a *Caffè Corretto,* as both coffee and grappa are foods that aid digestion!

Things that grow together, go together. Italians are very conscious of topography when it comes to food. For example, they don't pair cheese and seafood, because for most of history, these weren't available in the same region. In Italy, cows come from the flat grasslands of northern Italy and that's where the best meat sauces come from, while the best seafood pasta comes from the rocky shores of southern Italy. So don't serve seafood followed by meats and cheeses, and vice versa. Mixing and matching too many types of ingredients will likely leave you bloated and overstuffed. Stick to one general region, like the seaside or the countryside.

SPECIAL OCCASION MENUS

This book is intended to make you a badass cook. Being badass isn't about how many dishes you can make at one time. It's about sharing your heart through food in a way that makes you just as happy as everyone you feed. So please, DON'T FREAK OUT about the size of the menus you see below. I do NOT intend that you make every dish listed. I just want to give you options. Some have more courses than others. For some, salads are served as side dishes. You can course these menus out or serve some dishes together. Pick and choose to help you design a journey that is all your creation.

DAMN-GOOD DINNER FOR DUMMIES

Main: Penne al Pomodoro
Salad Course: Tricolore Salad
Dessert: Hazelnut and Sea Salt Chocolate Bark

SUMMER DINNER PARTY

Cocktail: Sun-Kissed Aperol Spritz
Appetizer: Jewish-Italian Tuna Toasts
Primo: Linguine allo Scogllio
Main: Pesce alla Mamma di Edo
Side: Summer Escarole Salad
Dessert Cocktail: Sgroppino

MAKE AHEAD DINNER PARTY (GLUTEN-FREE)

Appetizer: Radicchio Arancini
Primo: California Ribollita
Main: No-Noodle Lasagna
Side: Oy Veh, A Vegan Salad
Dessert: Greek Yogurt Panna Cotta

MAKE AHEAD TUSCAN DINNER PARTY

Appetizer: Maria's Crostini
Primo: Un-Red Roasted Tomato Soup (perhaps without the bread)
Main: Maria's Chicken
Side: Tuscan Mixed Vegetables
Side: Celery Root Puree
Dessert: Cloud Nine Custard
Dessert: Cantucci Toscani
After Dinner Drink: Vin Santo

DATE NIGHT

Cocktail: Prosecco al Amore
Appetizer: Burrata Crostini with Honeyed Leeks and Basil
Primo: Bucatini con Bottarga
Main: Herb-Crusted Rack of Lamb
Side: Green Beans with Blistered Cherry Tomatoes
Dessert: Flourless Chocolate Blender Cakes

CAL-ITALIAN BRUNCH

Cocktail: Sun-Kissed Aperol Spritz
Appetizer: Tomato Bruschetta
Main: Springtime Frittata
Side: Oy Veh, A Vegan Salad
Dessert: Sfratti, served with coffee

LIGHT BUFFET

Lemony Quinoa Salad
Garbanzo Bean Tricolore
Oy Veh, a Vegan Salad
Grilled Endive with Arugula Pesto
Thyme Roasted Salmon
Guilt-Free Blueberry Cobbler

POOLSIDE PICNIC

Summer Fruit Sangria
Heirloom Tomato Gazpacho
Grilled Romaine with Lemon Cacio Pepe
Grilled Zucchini with Lemon and Mint
Authentic Caprese Salad
Olive Oil Potato Salad
Chicken Sorrentino
Andrea's Peaches in Moscato

Basic Recipes

Simple Tomato and Basil Sauce

A good tomato sauce cannot be made without good tomatoes. I like canned tomatoes for certain sauces because they're just as good in the winter as they are in the summer—unlike fresh tomatoes, which are only good in summer—and they lend themselves to a richer sauce, with very little work.

This sauce doesn't have many ingredients. It's the opposite of Emeril Lagasse's "BAM, BAM, BAM!" explosions of flavor. This sauce is about harmony, about letting the garlic and whole basil leaves gently infuse their flavors into the tomatoes. The carrots add natural sweetness, without sugar, and lend a mildly earthy flavor.

Makes about 2 cups

1 (28-ounce) can whole peeled tomatoes
(See Note)

¼ cup extra-virgin olive oil

3 large garlic cloves

½ teaspoon red pepper flakes

1 to 2 carrots, cut into matchstick pieces

1 to 1½ teaspoons kosher salt

10 to 15 fresh basil leaves
(no need to remove the stems)

Note: I prefer San Marzano tomatoes. Refer to page 40 to learn how to choose canned tomatoes.

1. Place a medium-sized heavy-bottomed pan over a medium flame for a couple of minutes.

2. Add the tomatoes and their juices to a food processor or blender and pulse into a thick pulp. You can also squeeze the tomatoes by hand, but be careful of the splattering!

3. Add the olive oil to the hot pan, followed by the garlic, red pepper flakes, and carrots. Watch as bubbles emanate from the garlic; this means the garlic is infusing its flavor into the oil. Don't let the garlic burn or even brown. You want it to stay translucent.

4. After several minutes, add the tomato puree. You will see olive oil coming up on the sides of the tomatoes; this is ok, the olive oil helps to transform the flavor of the tomatoes.

5. Add a good sprinkling of salt (about 1 teaspoon) and a large handful of basil leaves. Stir occasionally. The mixture will be done when it is no longer watery and the sauce has thickened, 20 to 25 minutes.

6. Taste for salt and add more if necessary. If you aren't sure if there is enough salt, there isn't. Add more.

7. Remove the carrots and use them as a side dish for another meal (see Variation). It's up to you if you want to remove the garlic and basil leaves or keep them in for a rustic feel.

Variation: If you'd like a sweeter, more nutritious sauce, remove the garlic and basil and puree the tomato sauce with about half of the carrots in a blender or food processor. It will be delicious (and a good way to hide vegetables from the kids).

Pesto

Pesto comes from the Italian verb *pestare*, to step on. In terms of food, a pesto is a paste or something made in a mortar and pestle. Pesto does not, by definition, have to include basil, as in the Pesto Genovese below. It can be made from almost anything. Pesto takes only minutes to make and tastes best if made last minute, right before using. If you need to make it in advance for convenience reasons, just add a thin covering of olive oil to your storage container to keep it fresh. Sometimes, if I find a dish needs more crunch, I will reserve some of the nuts before processing the pesto and sprinkle them on top at the end. Use leftover pesto on scrambled eggs, atop grilled fish, or mixed in with your favorite pasta.

Makes ¾ cup

Arugula Pesto

Extra-large handful wild arugula, about one cup

⅓ cup shelled roasted pistachios or untoasted pine nuts

¼ cup extra-virgin olive oil

½ to 1 teaspoon kosher salt (the amount will depend on whether or not your pistachios are salted)

Pesto Genovese

Sometimes pesto Genovese is deconstructed—which means some or all of the pine nuts are separated for texture.

2 cups basil leaves, compacted into your measuring cup

⅔ cup grated Parmigiano Reggiano (See Note)

⅔ cup grated Pecorino Romano (See Note)

⅔ cup extra-virgin olive oil

⅔ cup raw pine nuts

1 teaspoon salt

1. Add all the ingredients to a food processor. (See Note)

2. Pulse until well amalgamated. Depending on your taste, you can leave it with more or less texture.

Note: A microplane grater will create the right measurement. If your cheese is already grated or you're using a box grater, use ½ cup to start and add more if desired.

Rosemary-Balsamic Reduction

Homemade balsamic reduction adds a sweetness and depth of flavor to a range of dishes, from steak to *arancini* to cheese.

Makes about ½ cup

1 cup red wine vinegar

1 cup balsamic vinegar

¼ cup raw honey

2 large sprigs of fresh rosemary

1. Combine all of the ingredients in a small pot over medium high heat and stir until it boils.

2. Lower the heat to medium and let reduce until syrupy, 20 to 30 minutes.

3. Serve warm.

Make Ahead Prep: You can make these a few hours in advance. Place in glass that will fit in your freezer and cover with plastic wrap until ready to eat.

Grilled Eggplant

I love grilled eggplant because it can be used like a bread or pasta, but without the extra carbs. I love to wrap it around burrata for *Grilled Eggplant and Burrata Involtini*, use it in *Tamburello di Melanzane*, and layer it for *No-Noodle Lasagna.* Contrary to what many cookbooks will instruct you, I don't salt and drain my eggplant first. I've never found it necessary.

Makes 15 to 18 slices

3 large eggplants

½ cup extra-virgin olive oil

1. Light an indoor grill pan on medium high heat or place a heavy pan over medium high heat and let it get hot for 5 to 7 minutes.

2. Cut off the top and bottom of each eggplant so it can stand up. Slice the skin off of the right side and the left side. Now, one pair of the eggplant's opposing sides will have skin, and the other will not.

3. Cut the eggplant into vertical slices , ¼ to ½-inch thick, beginning where you have removed the skin, so each piece has a little skin on the sides.

4. Use a silicone brush to coat the front and back of each slice generously with the olive oil, and then place as many eggplants on the grill as you can without them overlapping.

5. Cook until the eggplant has beautiful golden grill marks and flip.

6. Once the eggplant has nice grill marks on the second side and is floppy when you pick a side up with your tongs, it is done. Remove from the grill and continue until you are finished with all the pieces.

Techniques

TOASTING PINE NUTS

Toasted pine nuts make a great garnish for a variety of dishes, from quinoa to *Spaghetti Squash Primavera.* Toast yours by heating a dry pan over medium heat, and then tossing raw pine nuts onto the pan. BE VERY CAREFUL: I tend to burn them regularly because I lose focus. Shake the pan every so often so they don't burn and so they toast evenly on both sides. They will take about 5 minutes to become golden brown.

SLICING BASIL

Stack about 6 large basil leaves on top of one another. Roll into a tight "cigarette," like a green California medicinal spliff. Cut horizontally into thin strips. Now do it again.

ZESTING LEMON

Grate your microplane against the lemon in long, smooth strokes until a yellow zest piles up like fresh snow. Be careful not to overzest and grate into the white pith. It's bitter.

PICKING PARSLEY

You don't need to pick parsley or cilantro leaves off the stems one by one. Just grab onto the bulk of leaves as best you can with your right hand, and grab onto the stems with your left. Now twist in opposite directions, like you're wringing a chicken's neck, but vegan-style.

PEELING GARLIC

Place a clove of garlic on a cutting board, curved side down, so you can get some leverage when you crack it open. Hold the blade of a wide chef's knife over the clove and place your hand on top of the blade. Push down—from your belly, just trust me—until the skin cracks. Now, you can easily remove the peel without getting smelly fingers!

Chill Out, It's Just A Dinner Party

The idea of throwing a dinner party can be intimidating. Even my most gifted students shudder to think that they'll be responsible for a culinary performance that will be judged by their closest friends and relatives. They think: How can I make sure the dinner party will be flawless? My home isn't set up for entertaining! How can I have everything done before guests arrive? How can I make it look effortless?

The short answer is: you can't. And you don't need to. The idea of throwing dinner parties to impress the neighbors is so 1950's. We live in a different time. We make our own rules. It's time for a new dinner party model.

The dinner party is simply an opportunity to share intimacy with new and old friends through homemade, love-infused food. It gives us a chance to share the vibes of our homes, and allows our friends to bring their warmth to us. We get to play music, let loose, maybe even get up and dance. It's also a time to exchange our most important ideas and connect deeply with our fellow human beings. But most fundamentally, you throw a dinner party to have fun.

That said, how do we throw a dinner party when the Stepford Wife model is still hanging over our heads? A few things to keep in mind:

1   **When it goes wrong, it goes right.** You can't make your dinner party flawless, so don't try to. The fun doesn't start until something goes wrong. Make it as elegant as you like, but don't make it fancy. Nobody likes a stuffy party. Everybody remembers the party where you blew a fuse and ate by candlelight.

2   **Invite your guests to pitch in.** Dinner parties don't need to look effortless. In fact, the fun is in the collective effort. Your friends want to help out! Get everyone involved, slicing bread, setting the table, lighting candles, serving prosecco to the newly arrived, passing appetizers or desserts. That way, they feel they own the party as much as you do, and the feel of the soirée will be less "you and them" and more "all of us," creating a magical evening together. There isn't a dinner party of mine when everyone doesn't applaud when we finally get the food to the table. The collaboration makes us proud and joyous that it's time to eat.

3   **Plan ahead.** You'll never have everything done ahead of time, but there are certain meals that you can prep early, so you can spend more time just relaxing with guests (see *Make Ahead Dinner Party* menus, Page 55). If you absolutely must, you can hire someone to help out during the party, but I personally prefer to have a staff-free evening so the gathering stays intimate. (However, I do love to have someone come to clean in the morning!)

4   **Your place is perfect!** You don't need a grand palace to entertain. Most Europeans don't live in the villas you see in the movies. In cities, they often have small apartments with galley kitchens. It doesn't stop them from eating together with friends. Light candles, play music, cook your heart out, and let the close quarters add to the intimacy and sexiness of the night.

Stop treating every dinner party like you're trying to impress your mother-in-law. She doesn't want to be impressed anymore. She wants to have fun!

" *If you really want to make a friend, go to someone's house and eat with him.... The people who give you their food give you their heart.*

—Cesar Chavez

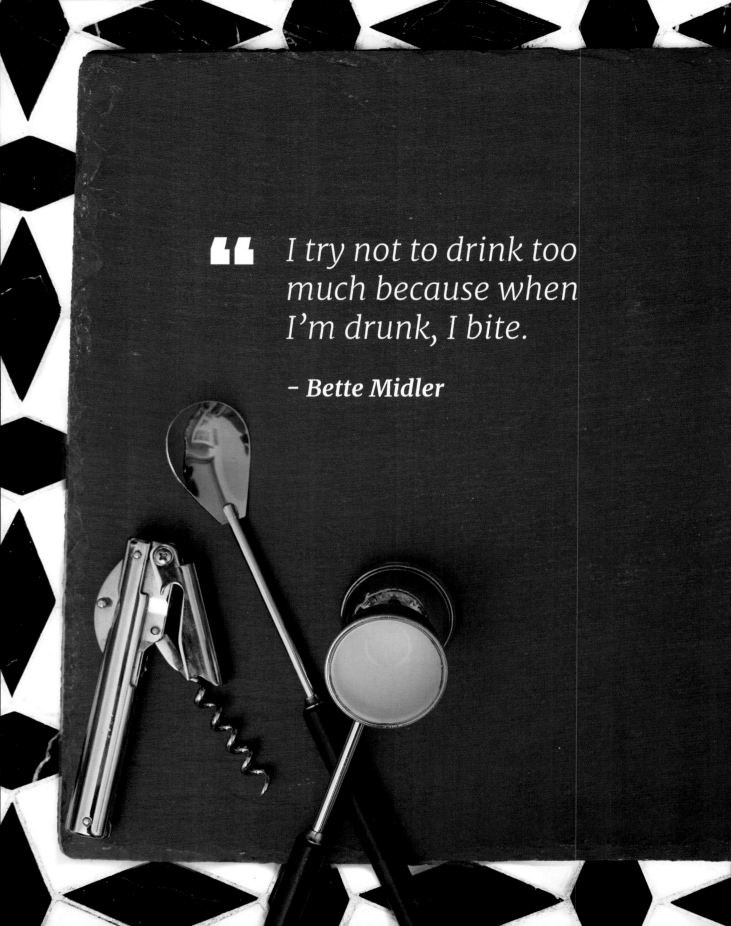

" *I try not to drink too much because when I'm drunk, I bite.*

– Bette Midler

Crafty Cocktails

PROSECCO AL AMORE

THE ROMAN STARDUST MARGARITA

SUMMER FRUIT SANGRIA

SUN-KISSED APEROL SPRITZ

VIN BRULÉ

SGROPPINO

Summer Fruit Sangria, page 76

THE FIRST THING WE DO IN MEAL AND A SPIEL CLASSES IS POUR ourselves a drink. I want everyone to feel comfortable, connected, and welcomed. A badass cook need not have a huge repertoire of cocktail recipes, but you should be able to pour a proper drink or two on the spot. Here are a few of my favorite go-to libations, all easy to make, low in sugar, well-paired with the cuisine in this book, and ideal for a party of any size, be it daytime, evening, summer, or winter.

Prosecco al Amore

The tone of a party starts right when people walk through the door. Your goal as the host is to make them feel comfortable. Whether you have just one guest or a hundred, nothing says welcome like a glass of bubbly, especially when the glass of bubbly has been adorned with the vibrant colors and flavors of fresh fruit and herbs. Plus, citric acid from the fruit helps with the digestion of the alcohol, so it will feel quite light, and the aromatic herbs will transport you to a Roman garden. Mostly, it will look absolutely fabulous.

Feel free to be creative. Mix up the herbs: try adding a bay leaf, a sprig of basil, or thyme. Experiment with the fruit: try lemon or kiwi, or add a slice of peach or watermelon in summer, or sprinkle in pomegranate seeds in the fall. Be inventive. Have fun.

Serve in champagne flutes, wine glasses, tumblers, or small mason jars.

Serves 6

1 orange

6 strawberries

6 3-inch pieces of rosemary

1 bottle prosecco, chilled

1. Cut the orange into 6 slices. Add one piece to each glass. Cut the slice in half if needed to fit.

2. Add one strawberry and one piece of rosemary to each glass.

3. Top with prosecco. EASY!

The Roman Stardust Margarita

If you want experiences that will shape the unique spiritual being that you are, it's imperative that at least once in your life you work nights for a raging alcoholic.

For me it happened at 21 and it happened in Rome. *Lo Stardust*, as the Italians called it, was an adorable jazz club in the artsy Trastevere section of the city, and Anna, 61, was the aforementioned alcoholic. She was thrilled to have a bartender who didn't like to drink much—so there would be no one to add to the losses she swigged down every night—and I was thrilled to have a job.

I welcomed the grotesque outbursts of anger and broken wine glasses as a departure from the nice-Jewish-Ivy-League-life I was molded for. Gone were the days of thesis statements and parental approval, and in were raw nights of untamed rage shrouded by the smoke of endless skinny cigarettes. Between drags and drinks, Anna dispensed invaluable advice: "Never use tongs to get ice from the ice-maker into a drink!" she advised. "Use your hands, it's sexy!"

Anna was a revolutionary of sorts. In the mid-90's, the cocktail scene in Rome was nonexistent. Bars served strictly wine, beer, and hard liquor straight up or on the rocks, which is why I was able to get a job as a bartender in the first place. But Anna decided to serve a margarita, shaken, in a martini glass. Salt on the rim, not an option. Where she got this idea, I have no idea. Mexican food was unheard of in Rome and guacamole unthinkable. But to this day, the Stardust Margarita is the best margarita I've ever tasted outside of Mexico.

Cheers, Anna!

P.S. This is a skinny, tart margarita. If you like it sweeter, try a touch more orange liqueur or tonic.

¼ cup tequila

2 Tablespoons orange liqueur (See Note)

Juice of 1 lemon

Large handful of ice cubes

Splash of tonic water

1. Pour the tequila and orange liqueur into a tumbler (whiskey glass). Follow with the lemon juice.

2. Add a large handful of ice and swirl it around.

3. Top with the tonic water and *Cin Cin! (That's "cheers" in Italian. Pronounced cheen, cheen.)*

Note: My favorite brand and first choice for orange liqueur is Combier but it's hard to find. I also recommend Cointreau.

The Trastevere section of Rome.

Summer Fruit Sangria

Sangria is tricky. Made well, it's an enlivening sensory experience formed by the perfect marriage of wine's earthy notes with the sweet acidity of juicy fruits. At worst, it's a hangover that doesn't quit. Trust me, I've been there.

The first sangria I attempted was for my own going-away party from Rome, circa 1997. Raquel, a Spanish friend of mine, gave me the recipe, which called for red wine, fruit, lemon soda, and vodka. My head hurts just writing those words. I have no idea if other Spaniards would agree with her recipe, but I learned a valuable life lesson from that experience: do not add sugar (or lemon soda, which is filled with sugar) or vodka to red wine.

In the vast hangover that followed that party, I made a secret pledge to bring forth a perfect sangria to share with the world. It took me 15 years, but here it is.

This sangria is perfect because it blends Moscato d'Asti, a favorite light bubbly Italian dessert wine, with a dry Vinho Verde to create a mixture that's just sweet enough and just strong enough. Its color reflects the summer sunshine, and once the fruit is added, you'll be serving a kaleidoscopic work of art.

As is true when preparing most dishes, let nature do the work. Choose the freshest fruit you can find, preferably at your local farmer's market. Just add the fruit to the wines and step back to let the quality of the ingredients radiate their innate goodness. You can't mess this up!

1 bottle Vinho Verde, chilled (See Note)

1 bottle Moscato d'Asti, chilled

Choose from the following fruit. You can use all the fruits, or as few as 4 of them. The amounts are a suggestion, not a rule:

1 orange, cut into ¼-inch rounds

3 apricots, cut into ½-inch cubes

3 plums, cut into ½-inch cubes

2 nectarines, cut into ½-inch cubes

2 peaches, cut into ½-inch cubes

1 pear, cored, cut into ½-inch cubes

1 apple, cored, cut into ½-inch cubes

2 handfuls grapes

10 cherries to garnish each glass, optional

10 strawberries to garnish each glass, optional

Fresh mint or basil leaves to garnish, optional

1. Place the fruit in a large pitcher, or in two smaller ones. Add the Vinho Verde and place in the fridge covered for an hour or more. Before serving, add in the Moscato d'Asti. We add it later because it has bubbles, and we don't want to lose them.

2. Pour the sangria into wine glasses garnished with cherries, strawberries, and herbs if desired. You can add some of the macerated fruit to each serving glass, or you can keep it in the pitcher and add more wine to it in order to make a second batch.

Note: Vinho Verde is a light, refreshing white wine. It is made from a blend of young (or "green") grapes in northwestern Portugal.

WHAT TO DO WITH LEFTOVER SANGRIA FRUIT

Don't throw it out! Make dessert! Here are a few ideas for it:

» Place it in a bowl with lemon sorbet on top, and garnish with fresh mint.

» Put it in a pan, add another "glug" of wine, cover, and cook over medium low heat for 45 minutes until soft and syrupy. Serve à la mode.

» Put it in a casserole, cover with the topping from *Guilt-Free Blueberry Cobbler*, and bake away until bubbly.

Sun-Kissed Aperol Spritz

Lo spritz (the spritz) is an Italian *aperitivo* that you can find throughout the peninsula, though it originates near Venice. In Los Angeles, it's become the drink of summer (and Instagram: #aperolspritz). The drink traditionally consists of prosecco, Aperol (a bright orange bitter), and a splash of soda. My mimosa spritz uses freshly squeezed orange juice, which makes it perfect as a wake-up cocktail for a boozy brunch or camouflaged against a glowing sunset.

Serves 1

1 cup prosecco

1 Tablespoon Aperol

Juice from one fresh orange—about 2 to 3 Tablespoons

A large handful of ice cubes

1 orange slice, for garnish

A splash of soda water, optional

1. Add the prosecco, Aperol, and orange juice together in a wine glass, tumbler, or mason jar.

2. Add ice and a slice of orange.

3. Add a splash of soda water, if desired.

4. Enjoy!

Vin Brulé

MULLED SPICED WINE

Italians have an expression: *"l'acqua fa male."* Water is bad for you. Clearly they don't actually believe this, but they'll say it to you if you're not drinking wine with dinner. Italians love peer pressure almost as much as they love their *vino*.

During winter, as cold weather takes over this otherwise hot-blooded peninsula, wine takes on a new form: Vin Brulé. A French term that literally means "burned wine," it's wine cooked in warming spices such a cinnamon and cloves. My Vin Brulé, sweetened only with a touch of raw honey instead of processed sugar, will warm not just your body, but also your heart. Some foods and drinks taste exactly like the inexplicable warmth of long lost love, and this is one of them. It's a drink that will nurture your spirit after a long year.

And it doesn't hurt that Italians use Vin Brulé as a remedy for the common cold.

2 oranges

1 lemon

1 bottle full-bodied red wine, like Chianti or Cabernet Sauvignon

1 red apple, cut into rounds vertically, avoiding the seeds

4 cloves

1 to 2 cinnamon sticks

⅛ of a whole nutmeg, grated

2 Tablespoons raw honey

1. Use a sharp knife to cut off the peel of one of the oranges and the lemon, being very careful not to include the white pith. It's ok if you get a little in there, but too much will make for bitter vin brulé. Set aside.

2. Cut the remaining orange into 4 rounds and place into 4 teacups or heat-proof glasses.

3. Add the wine, orange peel, lemon peel, apple, cloves, cinnamon sticks, nutmeg, and honey into a medium pot, stir in honey, and cook over medium high heat, uncovered, until it begins to boil.

4. Adjust the heat to medium low and simmer until the flavors have infused into the wine, about 15 minutes.

5. Taste and add more honey if desired.

6. Pour and serve. *Cin cin!*

Sgroppino

A CREAMY, BOOZY LEMON SLUSHY

Sgroppino comes from the verb *sgroppire*, to untie, and was invented in Renaissance Venice as a palate cleanser between courses. I serve *sgroppino* as a dessert cocktail, because it's light and delicious and keeps your buzz going at the end of dinner.

Viewing dessert as a cleansing of the palate, rather than as a sugary grand finale, is a revolutionary shift in culinary consciousness, and a good way to ensure that the end of your meal isn't the end of your evening. In fact, I used to eat it in Rome with friends on hot summer nights when we knew we were going to have a late one and didn't want dessert to hold us back. It's also great poolside on a sunny afternoon.

Some *sgroppino* recipes call for lemon sorbet only, while others call for lemon gelato. This recipe settles on the perfect compromise.

Serves 4

1 pint of lemon sorbet

½ pint of your favorite vanilla ice cream

1 cup cold prosecco

¼ cup vodka

zest of one lemon

Lemon slices and mint for garnishing, optional

1. Place the sorbet, ice cream, prosecco, vodka, and lemon zest in a food processor or blender and pulse until well mixed.

2. Pour the mixture into champagne flutes or small glasses.

3. To garnish, cut a little groove in each lemon slice so it can be placed on the edge of each glass. Top with a sprig of mint and serve.

Make ahead prep: *Sgroppino* can be made a few hours in advance. Place in a container that will fit in your freezer, and cover with plastic wrap until ready to serve.

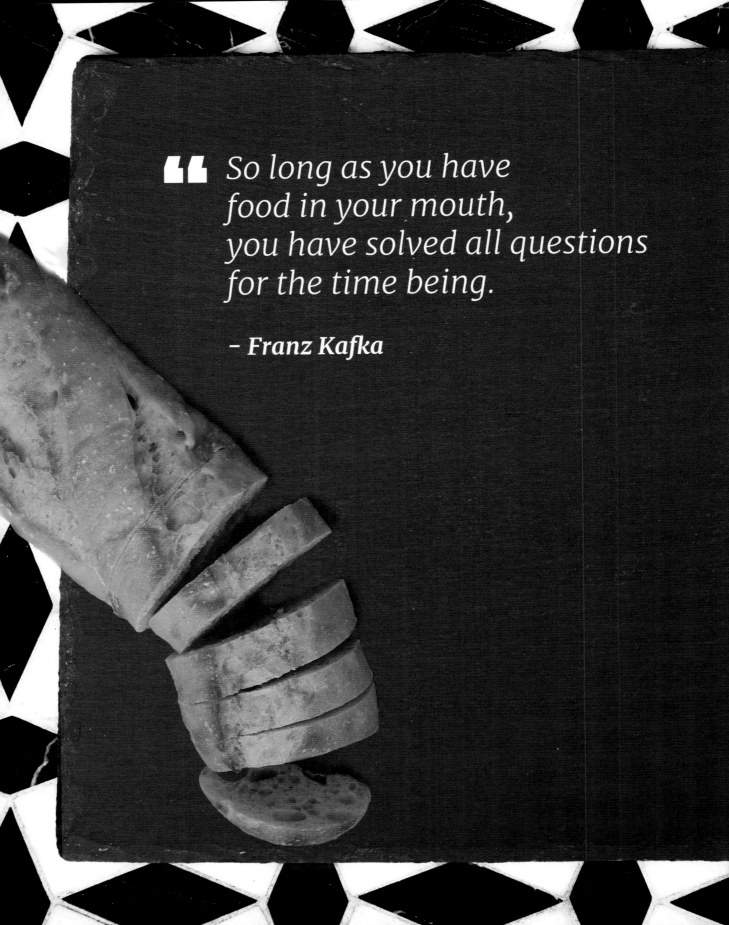

> **"** *So long as you have food in your mouth, you have solved all questions for the time being.*
>
> – Franz Kafka

Crazy for Crostini

BURRATA CROSTINI WITH ROASTED CHERRY TOMATOES

BURRATA CROSTINI WITH HONEYED LEEKS AND BASIL

ROSEMARY-SPIKED CANNELLINI CROSTINI

JEWISH-ITALIAN TUNA TOASTS

RUSTIC MUSHROOM CROSTINI

MARIA'S CROSTINI

TOMATO BRUSCHETTA

OLIVE OIL PIZZA WITH ROASTED ENDIVE
AND PESTO (GLUTEN-FREE)

OLIVE OIL PIZZA WITH LOX
AND ARUGULA (GLUTEN-FREE)

EASY TO ASSEMBLE AND FUN TO PREPARE, CROSTINI OFFER delicious flavors and textures in a small, handheld package. Everyone loves to eat decadent crostini while the bread is still right-out-of-the-oven warm. And while crostini certainly make ideal appetizers, most *Meal and a Spiel* cooking students agree that, along with a salad and glass of wine, a few crostini are enough for a light dinner. I've even included a couple of delicious gluten-free options at the end of the chapter.

Burrata Crostini with Roasted Cherry Tomatoes

Five minutes in the oven will turn ordinary cherry tomatoes into an act of love. And once placed on top of burrata on crusty bread and shoved into your mouth, they can be part of a life-changing experience. You could serve porridge all night afterwards, and everyone would still go home happy, talking about the appetizers.

This is not cooking. This is an assemblage of choice ingredients. Yet because it's so easy and so good, this recipe warrants a few *thank-yous:* Thank you to the cows who make the milk that becomes burrata. Thank you to the farmers who raise those cows. Thank you to the olive grove workers who harvest the fruit that gives us the life force of food—olive oil. Thank you God for tomatoes. Thank you to the bakers who wake up before the crack of dawn to make us bread and to the truckers who make sure it gets to our markets fresh. Thank you to all food producers who fervently believe in high quality. Our lives would not taste the same without you.

(Of course, no one who eats these will think about *that.* They'll just think you're a badass!)

1 pint cherry tomatoes

¼ cup extra-virgin olive oil, plus more for drizzling

1 teaspoon kosher salt, plus more for sprinkling

1 Tablespoon dried thyme

20 to 30 grinds of the pepper mill

8 ounces burrata

10 to 12 (½-inch thick) slices baguette

1 bottle prosecco, chilled

Note: If you have extra tomatoes, make more crostini. Add them to a salad or to an *aglio-olio* base for pasta (page 182).

1. Position the oven rack on the second rung from the top. Put the broiler on high and let the oven get hot for at least 5 minutes.

2. Place the tomatoes on a baking sheet, which can be covered with aluminum foil if desired. Drizzle the tomatoes generously with olive oil, a hearty pinch of salt, a hearty pinch or two of thyme, and the pepper.

3. Mix the seasoned tomatoes with your hands. Lick your fingers. You want them to taste good even if a bit oversalted and "over-herbed" because much of the flavor will burn off in the oven.

4. Put the sheet in the oven and cook for 5 to 8 minutes, opening the oven at times to give the sheet a shake to roll the tomatoes around. The tomatoes are done when the skins begin to bubble, burst open, and even burn. Let them cool for a couple of minutes before using.

5. Cut the cheese into thin slices, it will get messy. It's ok.

6. Toast the bread on a baking sheet by setting it under the broiler until golden, about a minute. Turn the slices over and toast the other side. Be careful not to let the bread burn.

Assemble the Crostini:

1. Top each slice of bread with a piece of cheese.

2. Sprinkle salt.

3. Place two or three tomatoes on top and crush down gently with a fork.

4. Drizzle with olive oil.

5. Pour yourself a glass of cold prosecco.

6. Eat. Sip. Eat.

7. Repeat.

Make Ahead Prep: Roast the tomatoes (be sure to leave them at room temperature) earlier in the day. Slice the baguette and cheese. Toast the bread and assemble the crostini as last minute as possible.

Variation: For a sweet touch, add a generous tablespoon of raw creamy honey to the tomatoes when you mix them up with the oil and thyme. Proceed with instructions. Top with sliced basil.

HOW TO PREP THE BREAD SO EVEN ITALIANS WILL BE IMPRESSED

CHOOSING AND CUTTING THE BREAD:

» **USE: French baguette, ciabatta, or a country loaf.** NOT sourdough, as its flavor is too pronounced.

» **CUT: into ½-inch slices.**

» **It's "skinnier" to cut the bread thin, but if it's too thin, you'll get a bagel chip.** That said, if you cut them too thick, people will have trouble tasting all the delicious toppings.

TOASTING IT RIGHT:

» **When you make crostini, you want the bread to be toasty on the outside and soft on the inside.** Using the broiler helps us achieve perfection in this department.

» **Place your oven rack on the second from the top rung.** Turn the broiler on high, and prepare your other ingredients while your oven heats up, at least 5 minutes.

» **Slice the bread and place it on a baking sheet.** Do not use any oil. It will change flavors in the oven and won't taste fresh anymore.

» **Put the bread in the oven until just golden on both sides.** Cooking times will vary depending on the strength of your broiler and how long it was pre-heated. This could take as little as 30 seconds or up to 4 minutes a side.

» **BEWARE: bread burns fast.** DO NOT LEAVE YOUR OVEN UNATTENDED! It's okay to leave the oven door a crack open while broiling so you can peek in easily. Set a timer on your phone if you're a forgetful type!

"GARLIC-ING" THE BREAD:

A touch of garlic rubbed on the bread gives a delicious kick to certain crostini and bruschetta. It's not intended to overpower the other ingredients and would never be used with something as delicately flavored as burrata. Once bread is toasted, rub a peeled garlic clove in a few quick sweeps across the bread. You won't see the garlic leave its residue, so don't overdo it. Pick up the bread to smell that the garlic has left its mark. Mmmm… Now continue preparing your crostini as instructed.

Burrata Crostini with Honeyed Leeks and Basil

This recipe is a perfect balance of sweet and savory, yin and yang, masculine and feminine, firm and creamy—basically, sex on bread.

And when I say sex, I mean delicious, loving, playful, consensual, expressive, connected, open-minded, exuberant sex.

You'll have to top your burrata with an extra touch of salt and olive oil, though. Don't think about it too much. Just enjoy it.

8 ounces burrata, cut into ¼-inch slices

3 large leeks, outer tough layer removed and cleaned

1 Tablespoon extra-virgin olive oil, plus more for drizzling

1 teaspoon kosher salt, plus more for sprinkling

30 grinds of the pepper mill, plus more for topping

½ to 1 teaspoon raw honey (yes raw is important for the flavor!)

1 bunch basil, thinly sliced (see *Slicing Basil*, Page 64)

10 to 12 (½-inch thick) slices baguette

DON'T FREEZE THE CHEESE

Cheese is one of the most nuanced foods that humans eat. If you eat it right out of the fridge, your tongue will miss the undertones and fine distinctions of its flavor. Cheese should be savored at room temperature. Whether it's burrata for crostini or goat Gouda for a cheese board, leave it on the counter a good hour before you serve it.

Makes 10 to 12 Crostini

1. Place the cheese on a plate and cut into thin slices, it will get messy. It's ok.

2. Place a medium pan over medium heat, and let it get hot for a few minutes.

3. Remove the dark green top and the root end of the leeks. Cut the white and light green part lengthwise into quarters, then cut those quarters crosswise into ⅓-inch slices.

4. Add a tablespoon of olive oil to the pan and then add the leeks. Stir.

5. Let the leeks cook until very soft, about 7 minutes, adding salt about halfway through. (You can add a couple of tablespoons of water if needed. Be careful not to let the leeks burn.) Remove from the heat.

6. Add the pepper and the honey to the leeks, and mix well. Begin with a ½ teaspoon of honey, and if you like it sweeter, add a bit more. You want enough sweetness to balance out the pepper.

7. Position the oven rack on the second rung from the top. Put the broiler on high and let the oven get hot for at least 5 minutes.

8. Toast the bread on a baking sheet by setting it under the broiler until golden, about a minute. Turn the slices over and toast the other side. Be careful not to let the bread burn.

Assemble the Crostini:

1. Spread a thin layer of the leek mixture on each piece of bread, and top with a spoonful of cheese to cover the surface.

2. Sprinkle with more salt, and drizzle a little olive oil.

3. Garnish with 4 to 5 slices of basil.

4. Serve immediately.

Make Ahead: Prepare the leeks (steps 3 through 6) and bring the burrata to room temperature before you begin to toast the bread and assemble the crostini.

Quickie Variation: I teach this version often in class when we're pressed for time. Forget the leeks. Just add light swipes of creamy honey to your bread, along with olive oil, and then top with burrata, salt, pepper, basil… and more olive oil.

WTF IS MY BROILER??

If you don't know what your broiler is, don't worry, you're not alone. Fortunately, the broiler is easier to find than your G-spot, so just chill out if this is new for you.

Assuming your oven was made after 1960, the broiler is a setting which makes extremely high heat come down from the top of your oven, like a torch. If you stuck an entire chicken under the broiler, the skin would burn, but the inside of the chicken would be raw. More delicate foods, however, like salmon, asparagus, and cherry tomatoes can be cooked under the broiler in very little time. The benefit is that the high heat will brown the foods (which means more flavor) and yet still keep them very juicy. I love to use my broiler to toast bread for crostini. I can do many at a time, and it's quicker than the toaster.

Hint: Turn your broiler on a good 7 minutes before using it so it will be at full force.

Warning: It is totally possible to burn things (like bread, specifically) when using the broiler, so don't go too far away. Set a timer on your phone, if you must, for as little as a minute at a time.

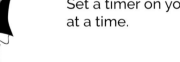

Rosemary-Spiked Cannellini Crostini

I became an expert at making this dish during my first years in Rome, when my pocketbook was always empty and my eagerness to experiment with Italian ingredients was always full. I shared an apartment with a rotating assortment of mostly French foreigners (who came and went as they fell in and out of love) and with a miraculous little pressure cooker. With that pressure cooker, I made the cannellini, starting with dried beans that I soaked overnight.

Naturally, using dried beans and cooking them for hours is optimal, but I've found that using a good can or—even better—a glass jar of store-bought cannellini is still quite good, much quicker, and far easier. Once it's atop a piece of good, crusty, toasted, garlic-rubbed ciabatta bread and doused with some fruity extra-virgin olive oil, your guests will never know you didn't slave away in the kitchen.

I usually serve this dish as an appetizer. But without the bread, the rosemary cannellini also makes a wonderful side for a grilled steak and green salad.

3 Tablespoons extra-virgin olive oil, plus more for drizzling

¼ teaspoon red pepper flakes

1 shallot, finely chopped

3 garlic cloves

2 to 3 (2-inch) pieces of fresh rosemary

1 ripe tomato, coarsely chopped

1 (15-ounce) can cannellini beans (See Note)

Kosher salt

20 grinds of the pepper mill

4 (½-inch thick) slices ciabatta or other crusty, thick Italian or country-style bread

Note: Undrained canned beans taste better. Drain and rinse them if you prefer less starch.

1. Light a medium flame under a heavy pan for several minutes.

2. Add the olive oil to coat the bottom of the pan. Add red pepper flakes, the shallot, and two cloves of garlic, making sure the garlic never burns or gets too brown.

3. Once the garlic and the shallot are translucent, about 5 minutes, add the rosemary and tomato, and mix to coat them well in the oil and juices for a couple of minutes.

4. Add the cannellini beans along with the liquid, a healthy sprinkling of salt, and a few generous grinds of the pepper mill.

5. Mix gently and regularly to make sure the beans do not stick to the bottom. They will be done when the tomatoes look cooked, most juices have evaporated, and the beans are hot and taste good to you, 7 to 10 minutes. Adjust seasoning accordingly with more salt or pepper.

6. Position the oven rack on the second rung from the top. Put the broiler on high and let the oven get hot for at least 5 minutes.

7. Toast the bread on a baking sheet by setting it under the broiler until golden, about a minute. Turn the slices over and toast the other side. Be careful not to let the bread burn.

8. Rub one side of each slice with the remaining whole garlic clove. No need to overdo it. Top with beans to fully cover the bread.

9. Plate the crostini and liberally drizzle olive oil on top. Serve and eat!

Make Ahead Prep: Prepare the cannellini, steps 1 through 5, earlier. Reheat before you begin to toast the bread, or serve at room temperature. Add a little water or broth if you need to loosen them up.

Variation: Try adding 4 ounces of canned tuna, along with the water or oil it came packed in, to the pan with the beans in Step 5. You'll have yourself crostini *al tonno e fagioli*.

HOW TO TURN WHITE BEAN CROSTINI INTO A SOUP

Add your crostini toppings to the blender with about a cup of homemade broth, *Cheater's Chicken Broth*, or water. Blend into a puree. Add more liquid as needed until the mixture reaches the desired consistency. Salt and pepper to taste. Top with a drizzle of olive oil.

Touch The Salt

I don't keep my salt in a little crystal granny shaker by the side of the stove. No, the salt is in its own jar with a mouth wide enough to fit a whole hand inside. No teaspoons or tablespoons in sight. I use my fingers to measure salt. When my cooking students see this, they sometimes panic. "But how will we figure out how to put exactly ¼ teaspoon of salt into this recipe?" they ask.

You won't.

Unless you're baking, you can abolish the rules of precision that impede your cooking process. Measuring salt does not require precise tools. Instead, you have to touch the salt. Get your fingers in there. Not just your index finger and thumb. You're not a four-year-old sprinkling fairy dust on a porcelain doll. You're a wild-haired conductor orchestrating a song of love. Use all five fingers and get in there with gusto! Salt is antibacterial, so no need to sterilize your fingers first.

You create a visceral connection with your food every time you touch it. When you put yourself directly into the food, that passion, that *chutzpah*, can be tasted.

Sophia, a beautiful, fashion-savvy, long-time *Meal and a Spiel* student, has bought everyone in her family a salt jar and tells them that they need to *massage the salt*. The cook is a sensual masseuse. Her word choice is precise. Feel the grains of salt on your skin. You are honoring the salt before you ask it to flavor your food. *The tactile experience you have with the salt will be remembered in your sense of touch.*

Have faith. Your hands know more than you do.

It's so beautifully arranged on the plate—you know someone's fingers have been all over it.

—Julia Child

Jewish-Italian Tuna Toasts

Jews have a long history in Italy. In fact, Rome has Europe's oldest Jewish community. When the Roman Empire conquered Jerusalem 2000 years ago, they sent the Jewish people from their holy land into the Diaspora, with different tribes settling in different regions. The Jews who settled in Spain are called Sephardic, while those who drew the short straw and ended up in Eastern Europe are known as Ashkenazi. Others went straight to Rome because, in that millennium, Rome was like New York—a big city with lots of jobs and great orgies. Most Jews went to Rome as indentured servants, working towards their freedom as they became integrated, upstanding citizens.

At various points in history, Jews from Spain came to live in Northern Italy via France, while other Spanish Jews made their way into southern Italy as merchants. The Jews contributed most notably to Italian culture in the mark they left on Italian cuisine. (You can learn more in my spiels for *Chicken Crack* and *Sfratti*.)

All this is to say that wherever you go in the entire world, Jews love a tuna sandwich!

This recipe is a lighter version of Joyce Goldstein's recipe for *Crostini di Spuma di Tonno* from her book *La Cucina Ebraica*. Its roots originate from the Jewish community in Padova.

Unlike American tuna salad, this is a whipped, fluffy tuna spread with butter and lemon. I know the concept of tuna whipped with butter is foreign to many of us, but *spalmata di tonno* is a delicacy in Italy. It's not *that* different from tuna salad with mayonnaise, only much more sophisticated. (If you want to make it even *more* sophisticated, you can throw some anchovies into your food processor when you whip the tuna—but I'm not even *that* sophisticated myself.)

Delicious on a summer day by the pool or as an outdoor lunch, these tuna crostini pair well with an *Aperol Spritz* and are ideally served before a meal that features seafood or as an afternoon snack.

1 (7-ounce) can Italian tuna in olive oil

3 Tablespoons unsalted butter, room temperature

Zest of 1 lemon

Juice of 1 lemon

10 to 20 grinds of the pepper mill, to taste

10 to 12 (½-inch thick) slices baguette

Extra-virgin olive oil, for drizzling

2 Tablespoons salt-packed capers, chopped

12 pitted green olives, roughly chopped

Small handful flat-leaf parsley, chopped

1. Place an oven rack on the second rung from the top and turn on your broiler.

2. Combine tuna (along with the oil in the can), butter, lemon zest and juice, and pepper in a food processor until it becomes a smooth paste.

3. Place the bread on a baking sheet and set under the broiler until golden, about a minute. Turn the slices over, and toast the other side. Be careful not to let the bread burn.

4. Drizzle oil lightly onto the bread and slather it with the tuna spread, as you would peanut butter. Top with the capers, olives, parsley, and extra pepper if desired.

Make Ahead Prep: Though it might lose some fluffiness, the tuna spread tastes even better the next day, in my opinion, so go ahead and make it ahead. Just be sure to bring it to room temperature for a couple of hours before using. Toast and assemble the crostini as close to eating as possible.

Gluten-Free Variation: If you would like a gluten-free option, replace the baguette with a gluten-free pizza crust mentioned in the *Olive Oil Pizzas* in this chapter. Cook the crusts as directed, with olive oil and salt, and then cut into tiny triangles before topping.

NOTE ON USING MULTIGRAIN BREAD

Italians would never make crostini or bruschetta on whole grain bread. But come on, no matter how good a fresh, crusty country loaf of ciabatta might be, white flour is just not that good for us. The point is to *eat* like Italians, not look like a fat old one. If you choose good bread, you might find that bruschetta made with multigrain bread will not feel like a runner-up to the original, but a winner all its own. I find that quality whole-grain tomato bruschetta pairs well as a side dish to frittatas.

Rustic Mushroom Crostini

The trick to making these mushroom crostini different and better than all other mushroom crostini is the addition of excellent quality capers, packed in salt, and preferably from Sicily. (That, and the few drops of tamari I add to all my mushroom dishes to bring out the umami.) As a result, the flavor simultaneously transports you to lush, green woods and the sun-blasted, salty seaside. Nature is amazing, especially when you can eat it.

Makes 12 or More Crostini

1 cup extra-virgin olive oil, divided

3 garlic cloves

¼ teaspoon red pepper flakes

2 pounds cremini mushrooms, stems removed and quartered

6 sprigs of thyme

1 to 2 sprigs of rosemary, optional

1 teaspoon kosher salt

½ teaspoon tamari or quality soy sauce

2 Tablespoons capers packed in salt, rinsed

40 grinds of pepper mill

12 (½-inch thick) slices baguette

Flat-leaf parsley, finely chopped for serving

1. Place a medium pan on medium heat, and let it get hot for a few minutes.

2. Add ½ cup of the olive oil to the pan, followed by the two garlic cloves and red pepper flakes.

3. Sauté the garlic until it becomes translucent—a couple of minutes.

4. Add the mushrooms and thyme. Add the rosemary if using. Stir. Add the salt and tamari, and stir. Let the mushrooms cook until soft and juicy, 10 to 15 minutes.

5. Add the mushrooms to the food processor, picking out the garlic cloves and herbs. Add the capers, pepper, and ¼ cup of olive oil.

6. Pulse until the mushrooms are very finely chopped and just a hint "creamy." You don't want to lose the texture so don't overprocess. Transfer the mushrooms to a bowl, and let them come to room temperature.

7. Position the oven rack on the second rung from the top. Put the broiler on high, and let the oven get hot for at least 5 minutes.

8. Toast the bread on a baking sheet by setting it under the broiler until golden, about a minute. Turn the slices over and toast the other side. Be careful not to let the bread burn.

Assemble the Crostini:

1. Rub each piece of bread with a couple of swipes of the remaining garlic clove so it leaves its essence on the bread.

2. Drizzle a little olive oil on the bread.

3. Top each piece with a large spoonful of the mushrooms to completely and generously cover the bread.

4. Finish with the parsley and, perhaps, another touch of olive oil.

Make Ahead Prep: Make the mushroom topping ahead of time if you like. Complete through step 6, up to 3 days in advance, and store in the fridge. Be sure to bring the mushrooms to room temperature before serving. This can take almost 2 hours. Taste for salt and pepper.

Maria's Crostini

WITH CHICKEN LIVER AND VIN SANTO

As a kid, I absolutely loved chopped liver, until I realized that chopped liver was actually the chopped *liver of a chicken*. I could no longer touch it. It broke my grandmother's heart.

Grandma Anne was a gentle and powerful matriarch, and her chopped liver was really good, but I have my Tuscan food mentor, Maria, to thank for restoring my love for the sensual magic of the chicken liver. Maria's crucial advantage over all the wonderful Jewish chopped liver recipes is simple: vin santo, the heavenly dessert wine of Tuscan vineyards. Vin santo is ambrosia, and Maria's chopped liver crostini tastes like the deepest oozing of love that food can transmit. *Mmmm* (hear the foodgasm rolling from my lips).

I hope Grandma Anne can taste it up in heaven, so she knows what I'm talking about. Maybe she can come back down here in another body, perhaps as my granddaughter, and I can share my love for her with chicken liver crostini cooked the Tuscan way, which is now *my* way—and soon will be yours too.

10 ounces chicken liver

½ large yellow onion, chopped

3 Tablespoons extra-virgin olive oil, divided

½ cup vin santo

1 Tablespoon salt-packed capers, rinsed

2 anchovy fillets, chopped

½ cup *No-Chop Chicken Broth* (Page 150) or *No-Chop Veggie Broth* (Page 153)

½ teaspoon kosher salt

Freshly ground pepper

1½ Tablespoons unsalted butter or duck fat

6 to 8 (½-inch) slices country loaf or ciabatta bread

Flaky sea salt, for finishing

1. Remove the filaments or "stringy" parts of the chicken liver. Rinse and dry.

2. Cook the onion in a medium pan over medium heat with 1½ tablespoons of the olive oil until very golden and even browning, about 12 minutes. Transfer the mixture into a medium bowl.

3. Increase the heat to medium high/high, and add the rest of the olive oil and the chicken livers to the same pan. You are searing the livers on the outside for flavor, so flip when each one is nice and browned, but not burnt.

4. Add the vin santo, then decrease the heat to medium, and add the onion back in. Stir and cook uncovered for about 15 minutes.

5. Place the contents of the pan, capers, and anchovies into a food processor and pulse until it is slightly creamy but still textured.

6. Put the contents back into the pan over a medium low flame. Add the broth and stir. Add salt and pepper and slowly stir. Taste for seasoning. If your broth is homemade, you may need more salt.

7. Add the butter or duck fat, and stir in until it becomes a nice paste.

Assemble the Crostini:

1. Position the oven rack on the second rung from the top. Put the broiler on high, and let the oven get hot for at least 5 minutes.

2. Toast the bread on a baking sheet by setting it under the broiler until golden, about a minute. Turn the slices over, and toast the other side. Be careful not to let the bread burn.

3. Top with the chicken liver puree, and drizzle with olive oil. Top with flaky sea salt if desired. Plate and serve!

Maria, the lady legend.

Make Ahead Prep: You can make the chicken liver topping ahead, even days in advance. You may want to add some broth as you heat it back up again.

Revere THE OIL

When I tell my Tuscan friends that some Americans fear olive oil, they roar with laughter. But for most of my first-time students, oil is no laughing matter. Using more olive oil—*much* more olive oil—than they're used to is their biggest hurdle in my cooking classes.

Americans associate olive oil with fat and fat, in turn, with heart disease and obesity—despite the well-known health benefits of extra-virgin olive oil, which has been shown to reduce inflammation, lower LDL cholesterol, and even decrease the likelihood of developing certain cancers. But still, somewhere in our cultural subconscious, we haven't adapted to using it abundantly like they do in the Mediterranean.

As a result, I often have to put my hands on my students' shoulders to calm their fears as I encourage them to begin to pour. I let them know that I'm by their side and that I'll stop them if too much comes out. Other new students look on, shocked that unmeasured olive oil is flowing freely and abundantly into the food. More seasoned students smirk and giggle. They remember being in this position not long ago.

For Tuscans, olive oil isn't just used to grease a pan; it's the life-force of food, *l'oro liquido:* liquid gold. Other forms of cooking oil exist in Italy, but when referring to extra-virgin olive oil, Italians simply call it THE oil: *l'olio*. There's no other oil in its category.

Nourished from above by sunshine and rain and from below by the minerals of Mother Earth, olive oil is used liberally, because whether cooked with food or drizzled on top, it makes everything taste and feel better. In the Bible, the olive tree symbolizes peace. So don't be scared of olive oil. Keep pouring. I'll tell you when to stop.

The olive tree is surely the richest gift of Heaven.

—Thomas Jefferson

Tomato Bruschetta

The word bruschetta comes from the Italian "bruscare," which means "to roast over coals." It refers to the *bread itself*, not the toppings. As opposed to the thin, small *crostini* on which the topping is the star, bruschetta is all about the bread. Rather large slices of bread are grilled, rubbed with garlic, then drizzled with olive oil. Stop right there. That simplicity is the traditional Tuscan bruschetta, also known as *fett'una*, or oiled slice. Bruschetta is often also topped with tomatoes and basil, though other toppings from meats to vegetables can be used.

Tomato bruschetta, like all Italian staples, comes with a set of rules. Unfortunately, many of these rules are broken regularly even in top establishments. I'm going to set it straight, right here, right now.

First off, it's pronounced *broo-SKETTA*, not *broo-SHETTA*.

Next, the tomatoes: *Tomato Bruschetta* is best in the summer, when tomatoes are sweet. Choose heirloom, if possible. The colorful batch of summertime heirlooms make for a beautiful presentation, if not also a more delicious treat. After heirloom, vine-ripened are your best choice. Try to find tomatoes that are already soft, and hence sweet, but still firm enough to the touch that they feel like they can be cut neatly-ish. When tomatoes aren't in season, use cherry tomatoes. They're quite good year-round.

Contrary to popular belief, neither balsamic nor any other kind of vinegar belongs in this dish. Chopped garlic has no place in this dish, either. As for the rest of the ingredients, go for quality. If there's ever a time to use really good olive oil, this recipe is it. Use fresh basil, sliced horizontally, not chopped, and good quality salt.

In terms of bread, sourdough and French baguettes are delicious, and so is olive bread, but they have NO place in bruschetta. Flavored breads are not permitted. Use the best ciabatta or crusty rustic country loaf you can find.

Makes 10 Bruschetta

2 pounds heirloom tomatoes, cut into ½-inch cubes (See Note)

A handful of fresh basil leaves, thinly sliced

½ to 1 teaspoon kosher salt

⅓ cup extra-virgin olive oil, plus more for drizzling

½ loaf ciabatta or crusty country bread

1 garlic clove

Make the topping:

1. Place the tomatoes, basil, salt, and olive oil in a bowl and gently stir.

2. Taste. Add more salt if needed. If it's not fantastic, you need more salt.

3. Cover with plastic wrap and let sit on the counter (NOT in the fridge) for an hour if you have the time. This allows the flavors to merge. If you don't have the time, add a little extra basil and assemble now.

Assemble the Bruschetta:

4. Cut the bread into ½-inch thick slices.

5. Position the oven rack on the second rung from the top. Put the broiler on high, and let the oven get hot for at least 5 minutes.

6. Toast the bread on a baking sheet by setting it under the broiler until golden, about a minute. Turn the slices over and toast the other side. Be careful not to let the bread burn.

7. Use the garlic clove to rub the top of the bread.

8. Spoon a tiny bit of the tomato juice onto the bread, followed by heaps of tomato pieces.

9. Drizzle with a generous amount of olive oil.

10. Eat immediately.

Note: Use a beautiful variety of colors—red, yellow, orange, dark purple. Choose tomatoes that are soft to the touch but firm enough to cut neatly-ish. Use cherry tomatoes in the winter.

HOW TO MAKE BRUSCHETTA FOR THE MASSES WHEN YOU ONLY HAVE ONE TOMATO

Make Poor Man's Bruschetta! Bruschetta is already considered *la cucina povera* (poor man's food), so this is the *very* poor man's version of poor man's food. That said, with a bottle of choice Tuscan olive oil, I've served this at chic Hollywood cocktail parties. It's easier to eat with a drink in hand than a full-blown bruschetta. Cut your tomato in half, and after you've rubbed the garlic on the bread, rub the tomato on there so it just leaves a light layer of tomato flavor. Sprinkle with salt and top with olive oil. *Ecco fatto!*

Olive Oil Pizza with Roasted Endive and Pesto

They say that necessity is the mother of invention, and when there's nothing in the house to eat, she's one hungry mother. This recipe hearkens back to a few years ago, when my fridge was empty except for some fresh arugula and endive, and I had a freezer full of gluten-free pizza crusts that had been sitting there since a disappointing encounter with tomato sauce a year earlier. I had a craving for crunchy, chewy carbs that a salad wouldn't satisfy, so I pulled a crust out of its icy abyss and thought, "Just because you're not good with tomato sauce doesn't mean you won't be good with olive oil." Might even be like a focaccia or what the Romans call *pizza bianca*...

Well, I was right. It was fantastic. I learned a valuable life lesson that day: let yourself get hungry enough to inspire creativity, but not so hungry that you can't think straight.

Fast-forward several years, and my gluten-free olive oil flatbreads are THE most popular request of my catering team for parties. We serve them on circular rustic wood boards, cut them into medium and very small pieces for appetites of all sizes, and circulate them around the party while guests indulge in cocktails and conversation. Most people never know the flatbreads are gluten-free. But for the gluten-sensitive among us, this little secret means everything.

1 (10-inch) frozen gluten-free pizza crust (See Note)

2 Tablespoons extra-virgin olive oil

2 large garlic cloves, finely chopped

½ teaspoon kosher or Celtic salt

2 endives, cut into ¼-inch strips

1 cup *Arugula Pesto* (Page 60)

1. Preheat the oven to 425°F.

2. Line a baking sheet with parchment paper or aluminum foil so the oil that drips off the pizza doesn't dirty your oven. Place it on the lower rack of your oven.

3. Brush the frozen pizza crust with the olive oil. Yes, it will seem like too much. The oil is what will create the chewy, crunchy texture.

4. Dot the oiled pizza with the garlic, and sprinkle the pizza generously with the salt. Use your fingers to even it all out. Top with the endive.

5. Bake until outer crust turns golden, 12 to 13 minutes.

6. Once the pizza is done, dot with the pesto. Cut into 8 pieces, and then cut some of those eight in half for smaller bites, if desired.

Note: Frozen gluten-free pizza crust can be found in the frozen section of many markets or can be ordered online. I prefer the Venice Baking Company brand. Udi's brand is available more readily throughout the country, but they are slightly smaller, so use less olive oil and decrease the cooking time by two minutes.

Garlic Bread Variation: Forget the endive and pesto. Just coat the crust with olive oil, salt, and garlic. Makes for fabulous garlic bread. This is a favorite of my nieces!

Olive Oil Pizza with Lox and Arugula

Going out for pizza in Rome is as integral to the culture as whipping up a plate of pasta is at home. It's a social occasion shared with boisterous friends (i.e. most Italians). *La pizza* is ideal when you don't want to spend a lot time (or money) on dinner because you have bigger plans on the horizon, like going to a concert, a movie, a dance club, or a stroll around town. Pizza is quick. In fact, many pizzerias don't even serve coffee or dessert, so they can shuffle you right out and bring new paying customers in.

When I used to go out for pizza in Rome, there was only one pizza I ordered: *Pizza al Salmone e Rughetta*, which is the word in *romanesco* (Roman dialect) for arugula. Smoked salmon is layered onto the tomato sauce, then covered with mozzarella, placed in the super-hot wood fired oven for just a couple of minutes until bubbly, and then topped with arugula right before serving, so that it wilts just a touch, yet still adds some crunch: Yummmm.

Seafood with cheese? Isn't that against the rules? While it's true that cheese and seafood are not common pairings in the Italian kitchen, there are many exceptions to this rule. In Sicily, for example, you will find swordfish wrapped around mozzarella on skewers or dusted in breadcrumbs and pecorino. Suffice to say, you will not be breaking any Italian culinary statutes with this pizza, in case you were concerned. (See *Pasta Faux Pas*, Page 232.)

This recipe is a less gooey, less gluten-y take on my Roman pizza addiction.

1 (10-inch) frozen gluten-free pizza crust (See Note)

2 Tablespoons extra-virgin olive oil

½ teaspoon kosher or Celtic salt

6 to 8 large cherry tomatoes, cut into VERY thin rounds

6 ounces smoked salmon, divided into thin slices

2 to 3 ounces shaved Parmigiano Reggiano

20 to 30 grinds of the pepper mill

A handful of wild arugula

1. Preheat the oven to 425°F. Line a baking sheet with parchment paper or aluminum foil so the oil that drips off the pizza doesn't get it dirty. Place it on the lower rack of the oven.

2. Brush the frozen pizza crust with the olive oil. Yes, it will seem like too much. The oil is what will create the chewy, crunchy texture.

3. Add the salt and use your fingers to evenly spread it around the crust.

4. Dot the oiled pizza with the tomatoes, and bake until outer crust turns golden, 12 to 13 minutes.

5. Once the pizza is done, lay down the slices of smoked salmon, the shavings of cheese, and ground pepper. You want to be generous with the pepper so it "combats" the saltiness of the salmon and cheese.

6. Scatter the arugula over the top.

7. Cut the pizza into 8 pieces, and then cut some of those eight pieces in half for smaller bites if desired. Serve immediately.

Note: Frozen gluten-free pizza crust can be found in the frozen section of many markets or can be ordered online. I prefer the Venice Baking Company brand. Udi's brand is available more readily throughout the country, but they are slightly smaller, so use less olive oil and decrease the cooking time by two minutes.

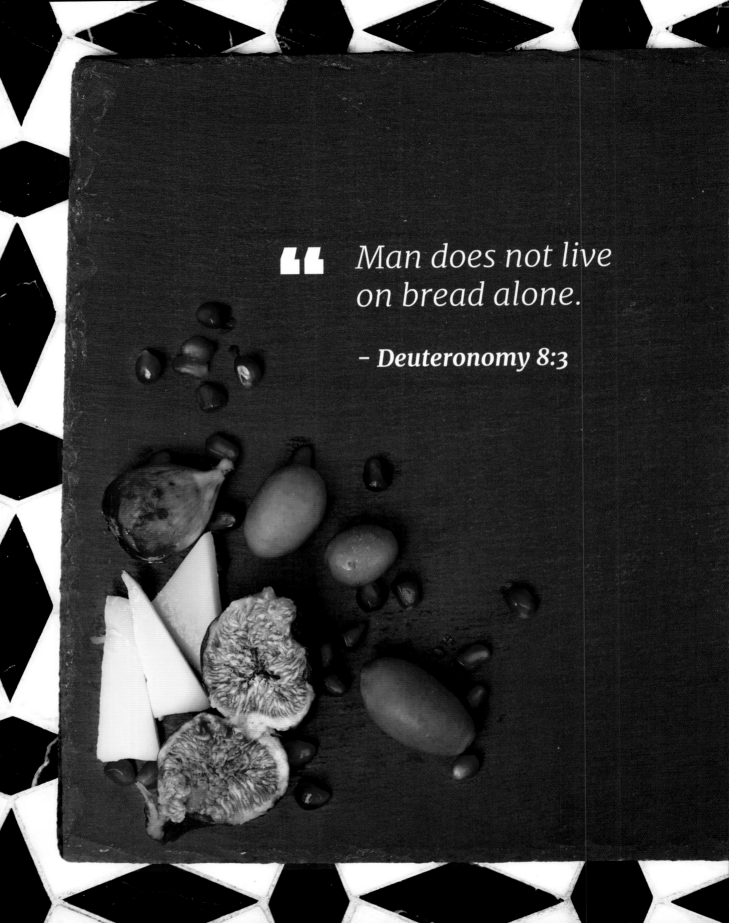

> **"** *Man does not live on bread alone.*
>
> – **Deuteronomy 8:3**

Appetizers Beyond Bread

FIG AND GORGONZOLA BITES

BRESAOLA BITES

HEIRLOOM TOMATO GAZPACHO

SWEET POTATO ROUNDS WITH PESTO

GRILLED EGGPLANT AND BURRATA INVOLTINI

POTATO LEEK LATKES

RADICCHIO ARANCINI

IN THE SPIRIT OF CREATING MEALS THAT ARE WELL-BALANCED, it's important to have a few bread-free appetizers in your repertoire. Apps that don't come on a slab of bread or in a phyllo dough package should be more common, especially if you're serving a carb-forward primo like pasta. The recipes that follow feature fruits, vegetables, and cheeses to open up the taste buds without filling up the stomach.

Fig and Gorgonzola Bites

WITH A BALSAMIC REDUCTION AND FRESH MINT

I'm a middle child, and like a lot of middle children, I was often ignored growing up. So I was forced to search the world for someone who would listen and connect with me. I found a tree.

Yes, one of my best friends was the fig tree in my backyard. It was a natural kinship: my name Elana means tree in Hebrew. I would climb up into the saddle-like seat between her two main branches and sit there cozily for hours, contemplating the meaning of life or picking my nose. And in between my deep thoughts and deeper nasal excavations, I noticed that my friend the fig tree had figs. Ones that I could eat.

That might seem obvious, but I was raised by city folk who weren't aware that food came from anywhere but a restaurant or a freezer. In fact, the yard was full of food. As a preschooler, I remember crouching down while no one was looking to eat the wild strawberries that grew around the border of our garage. And we had an avocado tree that produced tons of avocados that only Teresa, our Guatemalan housekeeper, would eat.

In fact, it was Teresa who taught me how to eat the figs. While my older sister made fun of me, as if only a bumpkin would eat directly from a tree, Teresa showed me how to pick the figs from the branches and laughed with me as we watched the little milky drop appear at the stem.

Later, I learned that the fig tree was the original life-source of the Garden of Eden. The Italians liken the fruit of the fig tree to the female reproductive organ, *la fica*. I wasn't aware of my tree-friend's legendary feminine energy as a child. But I know now that the fig, like a woman, must be prepared delicately and served with the intention to awaken the sublime and the sensual. Here is a recipe that does just that.

Makes 16 Bites

8 figs, halved

4 ounces Gorgonzola dolce

Rosemary-Balsamic Reduction (Page 61)
or store-bought balsamic glaze

Freshly chopped mint, for garnish

1. Place a knob of Gorgonzola on each fig half. Use enough to make its presence known, but not so much that it overpowers the fig or completely covers its pinkish beauty.

2. Drizzle a few drops of balsamic reduction on top.

3. Sprinkle with chopped mint leaves.

Make Ahead Prep: These can be made ahead of time. The sweetness of the figs will be tasted if they never touch the fridge. And as always, the cheese should also be served at room temp, so keep it out!

Bresaola Bites

WITH MANCHEGO AND ARUGULA

When I was living in Rome in my early 20s, I had a killer sandwich routine. Around noon (and not a minute after 1 p.m., as everything shuts down) I would battle the crowds and buy a warm piece of focaccia from the bakery *Il Forno* on the far corner of the Piazza Campo de' Fiori. If you don't speak Italian, you have to be a little pushy or you'll never get served. (And if you don't know how to be pushy, you're going to miss out on some of the best stuff in life, especially in Italy!)

I would always ask for "un pezzo di pizza bianca," aka focaccia. The guy would show me with his knife how much he wanted to cut off from the huge white pizzas, always trying to up-sell. I learned not to be guilted by his stern face while requesting a small piece. This man never smiled.

Once I got the prized bread, I brought it over to the old lady at the cheese and charcuterie cart in the middle of the piazza. One time, my visiting American friend Derek ordered a prosciutto and cheese sandwich and asked her to put olive oil on it. She nearly ran him out the piazza with a tirade on why olive oil had no place in that sandwich: there was already enough fat from the prosciutto, cheese, and *pizza bianca*. As traumatized as Derek was, her passionate spiel carved a lifetime of reverence and affection in me for her.

"Signora," I'd say, making a slicing motion to show her I wanted the focaccia sliced in half. "Un panino, per favore." A sandwich, please. She would utter something nearly incomprehensible, asking what I wanted in my sandwich.

"*Bresaola e rughetta e una caciotta (cah-chota) semi-stagionato.*" That's a semi-aged sheep's milk cheese to go with the bresaola and arugula. She handled the rest. Once I paid, I'd take my sandwich to the statue steps in the center of the piazza, look up at the ominous face of Giordano Bruno (who was burnt at the stake for heresy four hundred years ago, exactly where I was about to eat) and enjoy my delicious sandwich and the freedom to have been born in a country that allows me to openly tell my government to go fuck itself when needed.

That's also the freedom to lose the bread. These bites are the *inside* of my perfect sandwich, and they make delicious appetizers. They involve no cooking, which means that even a *schlemazel* could make them.

3 ounces manchego or other sheep's milk cheese

16 slices bresaola, sliced very thin (See Note)

A handful of wild arugula

1. Cut the cheese into ¼-inch thick matchsticks, about the length of the bresaola.

2. Place the cheese on the short-end piece of the bresaola.

3. Add a couple of leaves of arugula.

4. Roll it up. Press down on the closing flap to keep it "glued" together.

5. Stack on top of each other on a wooden chopping block or a simple rustic plate to serve. Watch them disappear.

Make Ahead Prep: These can be made several hours in advance and kept on your countertop.

Note: Bresaola can be found at Italian specialty stores or at a fine cheese shop. I have also found it at my local Trader Joe's. You can order it online at Amazon. Whole Foods carries a variation of bresaola called *mocetta*. It is slightly more difficult to pinch it into a roll that stays, though the flavor is good.

MORE BREAD-FREE APPETIZER IDEAS!

I love to use small portions of traditional mains as appetizers, particularly when I cater cocktail parties. My *Chicken Crack* makes the crowds go wild. We often serve my *Herb-Crusted Rack of Lamb*, sliced into individual chops and presented on a wood board. I've cut up steak into bite size pieces and topped each one with some arugula, a slice of Parmigiano, and a dab of balsamic reduction, holding them all together with a bamboo toothpick. I also love to offer tiny servings of *California Ribollita* or *Un-Red Roasted Tomato Soup* in espresso cups, topped with a burst of bright basil.

CHIC CHEESE BOARDS FOR BADASSES

Arranging food on a board can be just as badass as cooking.

As far as I'm concerned, it's fine to make a meal out of a cheese board and a bottle of wine, as long as you serve dark chocolate after. That said, don't make your cheese board a big deal. It's totally legit to have only one good, well-chosen piece of cheese, particularly if you're a small group with a meal ahead of you. Throw down what you have and snap your fingers like Sophia Loren.

WHAT YOU NEED:

A wooden board: The more rustic the better. But even if it's just a plain old cutting board, as I often use, it will look glamorously delicious once you get it all decorated with food.

One or more pieces of good cheese: Mix goat's, sheep's, and cow's milk cheeses for balance, and try to include one hard, one soft, and one semi-firm. I prefer goat's milk and sheep's milk cheeses because they're easier to digest and they taste like Central Italy to me. Here's a list of my favorite cheeses, commonly available at most supermarkets:

- » Manchego—*sheep's milk*
- » Midnight Moon—*sheep's milk*
- » Humboldt Fog—*goat's milk*
- » Naked Goat—*goat's milk*
- » Drunken Goat—*goat's milk*
- » Goat Gouda—*goat's milk*
- » Delice de Bourgogne—*cow's milk*
- » Sharp WHITE Cheddar (no orange cheddar!)—*cow's milk*

Fig jam and/or raw honey: A hint of sweet pairs well with cheese. I always make a few crackers with jam or honey topped with cheese and pass them around at the start so no one overlooks this special addition.

Olives with pits: From an olive bar, not a can. Large Cerignola olives and bright Castelvetrano are my two favorite varieties, and I personally prefer olives that aren't covered in oil and herbs. The pits preserve the flavor of the olive, and eating olives with pits is sexy, so put a little dish on the side for them!

Crackers: Most crackers work well on a cheese board, but some don't. If they contain hydrogenated oil (like Ritz or other crackers you loved as a child), they're a no-go. Look for thin, crispy, rustic-tasting crackers, perhaps infused with rosemary or black pepper. In the *Meal and a Spiel* world, it's chic to put out delicious, seed-rich, gluten-free crackers, like Mary's Gone Crackers or Jilz Crackers (which are paleo), since many people are sensitive to wheat or prefer a healthier alternative. Consider non-bread options like sliced pear or dried orange slices, which can easily be made by slicing oranges into ⅛ rounds and baking at 200 for 3 hours. Both make delightful vehicles for cheese.

Wine: Yes, please! You can rarely go wrong with a Chianti Classico or a Montepulciano D'Abruzzo. I also love a Nebbiolo on a cold winter night. For whites, try a Marlborough County Sauvignon Blanc, a Pinot Grigio, or a *Prosecco al Amore*.

Heirloom Tomato Gazpacho

WITH GRAPEFRUIT AND BASIL

Everyone says exactly the same thing when they taste this gazpacho: "Oh! My! God!"

They're right. This is indeed God's work. I can hardly take the credit. I didn't create the molecular perfection of sweet and succulent heirloom tomatoes, which grace us with their presence in summer and whose flavors shine through this gazpacho. I don't even know how to grow tomatoes. I do, however, know how to shop for them. If you don't make it a point to buy heirloom tomatoes in the summer, you should start. This is the perfect recipe to begin with.

Now, that said, let me tell you what I do get credit for:

One, I consulted my Spaniard friends for specific gazpacho recipe ideas. I learned to use sherry vinegar, which is delicate and adds only a mild zing. Second, I omit the use of bell peppers, which overpower the flavor of the sublime heirlooms and make other gazpachos hard to digest. Third, I use a food processor to puree half of the ingredients, and I finely chop the other half to create the perfect smooth-and-crunchy texture. Fourth, I chop the yellow tomato by hand to add a gorgeous bright color to the soup. Finally, I garnish with grapefruit and basil, a genius move, if I do say so myself. (And I do.)

Still, with all my self-praise intact, this gazpacho truly is God's work. Respect Her ingredients, and you'll create a gazpacho worth revering.

1 pound red or reddish-brown heirloom or 4 to 5 medium vine-ripened tomatoes

1 English cucumber, cut into 1-inch rounds

1 red onion, quartered

2 Tablespoons sherry vinegar

1 Tablespoon extra-virgin olive oil

1½ teaspoons kosher salt, divided

1 large yellow heirloom tomato, finely chopped

1 grapefruit

A handful of fresh basil leaves, cut into thin strips

1. Cut the red tomatoes in half and use a spoon to scoop out the seeds. (With heirlooms, you might need to be a little creative to get the seeds out. Just do it and don't stress. It's all good. You are on the way to making a delicious gazpacho.)

2. Put the red tomatoes, half of the cucumber, 1 of the onion quarters, the vinegar, the olive oil, and one teaspoon of salt in the food processor and puree. Pour into a large bowl or pitcher.

3. Add the rest of the cucumbers and 2 of the onion quarters to the food processor, and pulse until finely chopped. Do NOT overprocess or you will lose the crunch. (You will have 1 of the onion quarters left over.) See Note.

4. Add the chopped onion, cucumbers, and the puree to a bowl or a pitcher. Stir.

5. Add most of the chopped yellow tomatoes to the puree and the last ½ teaspoon of salt. Leave a small handful of the yellow tomato pieces for garnish.

6. Cover and chill in the fridge for an hour to allow the flavors to meld.

7. Use a knife to cut off all of the grapefruit peel including all of the pith, the bitter white inner skin. Cut the flesh of the grapefruit into ¼ to ½-inch pieces, avoiding the seeds and membranes.

8. To serve, place in small bowls or shot glasses and top with a few pieces of grapefruit, a few pieces of yellow tomato, a pinch of basil strips, and a small drizzle of olive oil, if desired.

Note: If you are still a schlemazel in the kitchen or simply a bit lazy today, you can throw all the ingredients in the blender. You will not get the same texture, but you will get great flavor.

Make Ahead Prep: This recipe can be made in advance. I prefer to make it fresh so it doesn't stay in the fridge too long, where it can lose its sweetness. That said, I have plenty of students who make weekly batches in the summer and drink a bit from the fridge every day.

Sweet Potato Rounds with Pesto

Here, you treat the sweet potato like a healthier, less-filling version of crostini bread, with its natural sweetness beautifully balanced by the sharp nuttiness of the topping.

If you'd like to serve sweet potatoes as a delicious and nutritious side dish, you can roast them with dried rosemary and thyme, and skip the pesto. It's a crowd pleaser from my *Trader Joe's To The Rescue* class.

Makes 25 Pieces or More

1 medium sweet potato

Extra-virgin olive oil

1½ teaspoons kosher salt

20 grinds of the pepper mill

Arugula Pesto (Page 60)

1. Turn the oven to 475°F and line 1 to 2 baking sheets with parchment paper.

2. Cut the sweet potato into very thin rounds, as close to ⅛-inch as you can. Don't worry if some slices are a bit thicker than others.

3. Place the slices of sweet potato on the parchment paper, brush both sides generously with olive oil, sprinkle with salt, and add pepper. Put them in the oven for about 25 minutes, flipping over after 15 minutes. You want your sweet potatoes with some browned edges.

4. Top with a small dollop of *Arugula Pesto*.

Variation with Cheese: Turn this into a sweet potato burrata crostini. Place a ball of burrata on a plate, and use a spoon to place a generous nugget on each round of sweet potato, enough so that it looks balanced. But don't put so much burrata on that you can't see the orange around it or can't eat the morsel all in one bite. Use your fingers to sprinkle each piece of burrata with some salt. Top with pesto.

Grilled Eggplant and Burrata Involtini

WITH HEIRLOOM TOMATO SAUCE

The best translation of involtini is "rollups." As in, this is an eggplant-burrata rollup. This is a bangin' recipe that I use all the time in class and for catering.

I love to teach it because even beginner cooks can master the vibrant and creamy flavors, and I get to witness the excitement on their faces. First they learn to make a simple four-ingredient tomato sauce. Then, while it simmers, they grill some eggplant. They assume the recipe gets a lot more complicated, but there's nothing fancy happening. We just roll the eggplant around the burrata and top with the sauce. It's this simplicity that literally blows their minds. Experiencing that lightbulb moment of self-empowerment alongside my students is what I love most about my job.

As for catering, everything can be prepped in advance, so it's an ideal dish when your hands are busy making other courses. And when we bring these to the table, people gasp.

In the summertime, make it with *Heirloom Tomato Sauce* for the full effect. Any other time of year, go with my *Simple Tomato Basil Sauce*.

Grilled Eggplant, room temperature (Page 63) You'll need 17 slices

Kosher salt

16 ounces burrata, cut into 16 equal pieces, 1 ounce each

Heirloom Tomato Sauce (recipe follows) or *Simple Tomato Basil Sauce* (Page 58), warm

⅔ cup *Toasted Pine Nuts* (Page 64)

8 basil leaves, to garnish

Assemble the Involtini:

1. Lay out a piece of eggplant to use as a tester. Use your fingers to sprinkle the whole side with salt. Taste it. Bland? You need more salt. Too salty? Adjust accordingly as you assemble the rest of the rollups.

2. Lay out and salt the next piece of eggplant. Place a piece of burrata on the narrow end of the eggplant. Sprinkle the cheese with some salt.

3. Use your fingers to roll up the eggplant so that it wraps around the cheese. Sprinkle with a little more salt.

4. Repeat.

5. Place two rollups per plate. Top with a few tablespoons of tomato sauce. Sprinkle on some pine nuts, and top with a basil leaf.

6. Let the rollups rest for about 10 minutes until room temperature.

7. Take a bite. Thank Mother Nature for making the act of nourishing our bodies so freaking delicious! Take another bite.

LEFTOVER GRILLED EGGPLANT? TRY THIS!

Salt the eggplant, and lightly spread some chopped garlic and freshly chopped mint on one side of each piece. You can keep them flat, or roll them into cigars. Drizzle lightly with red wine vinegar.

Make Ahead Prep: You can grill the eggplant and make the tomato sauce in advance. You can also make your rollups a day in advance, but be sure to bring them to room temperature before serving, allowing at least an hour. Top with warm tomato sauce.

Heirloom Tomato Sauce

When I teach pasta classes, as you will discover in Chapter 6, I start many of my sauces the same way: with garlic, red pepper flakes, and olive oil. But because this sauce is so delicate, I don't want even the slightest kick from the red pepper flakes. Don't get me wrong, they would be delicious, but this sauce was made for dishes far more delicate than pasta, like *Grilled Eggplant and Burrata Involtini*. The burrata flavor is so delicate, I don't want anything to overpower it. Hence, the trick to this sauce is to highlight only the sweetness of the tomatoes and keep it as simple as possible.

Does that mean I can't eat it with pasta? No! Of course you can. It's amazing with pasta. Top with Parmigiano Reggiano and some toasted pine nuts if you like.

What else can I eat it with? As far as I'm concerned, you can put it in a mug and drink it! It would be wonderful in an eggplant parmigiana or a lasagna. But as a sauce to top fish and chicken, I think it's too delicate, and you'd want a little more of a kick. But be inventive and try things out.

This sauce cooks slowly over a low flame to ensure the delicacy of the flavors. But if you're rushed, turn up the flame!! Sometimes we all have to speed things up—it'll still be a thousand times better than any sauce from a jar.

Makes 2 Cups

½ cup extra-virgin olive oil

4 garlic cloves

3 pounds assorted heirloom tomatoes, cut into ½-inch pieces

A handful of basil leaves, with stems

2 teaspoons kosher salt

1. Place a medium pan over medium heat for a few minutes.

2. Add the olive oil and garlic cloves to the pan.

3. Let the garlic infuse its flavor into the olive oil for a few minutes. Watch the bubbles. Don't let the garlic burn.

4. Add the tomatoes and stir.

5. Add basil and stir. Let cook for a couple of minutes.

6. Add the salt, stir, and let the tomatoes cook on medium low for about 1 hour, until the mixture thickens. When soft enough, smush the tomatoes down with a fork or with the back of wooden spoon. If you need the sauce to thicken faster, raise the heat.

7. Taste the sauce. If you want it to be thicker, cook longer, and add salt if needed.

Potato Leek Latkes

WITH CRÈME FRAÎCHE, POMEGRANATE, AND CHIVES

South Miami is a major stop on my East Coast cooking class tours, but this isn't a story about Miami Jews and latkes. I have a fun group of non-Jewish women that I see every time I'm there. A couple of years ago, they requested an appetizers class, and we went around and around in endless emails trying to choose just the right menu to fit everyone's tastes. But we couldn't reach an agreement until I mentioned the latkes that I normally reserve for my annual Hanukkah classes.

"YESSSSSS!!! YESS!!!!!! WE WANT LATKES!!!"

Everyone loves a latke! I mean, how can you not love fried potatoes?! Plus, latkes are fun to make. You can bring your guests into the kitchen to fry up these babies with you. That's right, show 'em the ropes and give them their own moment of kitchen badassery.

Wait, but is it healthy to fry in olive oil? Short answer: No. It's not healthy to fry at all! But if you're going to do it, then use nothing less than the best-tasting oil on the planet: extra-virgin olive.

Aside from the good oil, what makes these latkes so addictive is that they're not filled with too much egg and flour, which would make them taste like they came out of the freezer section. These latkes are crunchy and juicy. Instead of garnishing them with the traditional applesauce and sour cream, I pair them with crème fraîche, pomegranate seeds, and chives, for an updated version of the classic. But feel free to experiment: top them with lemon juice, lemon zest, black pepper, and ricotta salata, or, for a meatier variation, put a forkful of *The Best Brisket Ever* on the latkes and top with crème fraîche and parsley. Try not to faint from pure delight.

Latkes should be served when they're at their best, right out of the pan. By the time you get to the dinner table, your guests will plotz.

Makes 35 Latkes

2 pounds russet potatoes

1 yellow onion

2 leeks

2 Tablespoons potato starch or potato flour

1 egg

1 teaspoon kosher salt, plus more for sprinkling

30 grinds of the pepper mill

1 cup extra-virgin olive oil

8 ounces crème fraîche

½ cup pomegranate seeds

1 bunch fresh chives, chopped

1. Grate the potatoes into a large mixing bowl using the large holes of a box grater. (Using a food processor will not create the same texture and, hence, flavor!) Don't worry if your potatoes start to oxidize and brown. No one will notice once they're cooked.

2. Grate the onion using the small holes of the box grater. Add to the bowl.

3. Remove the outer layer of the leeks, and grate only the white and light green part on the small/medium holes of the box grater. You will lose some of the leek, but that's ok. Add to the bowl.

4. Add the potato starch/flour, egg, salt, and pepper to the bowl and mix with your hands.

5. Heat a heavy-bottomed skillet over medium high heat for 5 minutes, or until it's quite hot. Add the olive oil and let it get very hot. (Test the heat by dropping in a piece of potato. If it sizzles and browns easily, the oil is ready to go.)

6. Pick up a tablespoon-sized portion of the potato mixture. Squeeze it between your fingers to flatten and release the liquid. This is important. You want your latkes to be very thin and NOT in perfect circles—the potato gratings that stick out on the side will be the first to crisp—YUM. By using your hands, you will press out the water, which means less oil splatter. So get your fingers in there and get messy!

7. Add each potato latke to the hot pan, and fry until deep brown and crispy on each side. Transfer to paper towels.

8. Sprinkle with salt and top with a dollop of crème fraîche, a few pomegranate seeds, and chives. Serve immediately.

Radicchio Arancini

BAKED-NOT-FRIED RISOTTO CROQUETTES

When I was in my early twenties and living in Rome, most of my lunches consisted of two *arancini* (fried risotto balls), a Coca-Cola, and three cigarettes.

Bridget and Emily, my two anglophone partners in crime in the Eternal City, would ring my buzzer every day around 2 p.m., when I was just waking after a night of working in the neighborhood pub. We'd walk over to the nearby *pizza a taglio* (pizza-by-the-slice shop) to wait for *arancini* fresh from the fryer, so the mozzarella in the center would string itself out like a telephone cord. *Arancini* in hand (actually called *supplì al telefono* in Rome) we made our way to *Bar San Calisto* in the heart of Trastevere. Surrounded by the renegade left wing of Rome—artists, intellectuals, communists, laborers, Roman Jews, and ex-pats from all over the world—we ate, smoked, and worked on *The New York Times'* crossword puzzle. It was a daily routine made in heaven.

Well, times have changed. I don't drink sugary sodas anymore, I don't smoke cigarettes, and I very rarely eat deep-fried foods.

But I still crave the unforgettable sensation of holding a hot, crispy ball of risotto in my hands, biting into it, and finding the cheesy nugget of treasure in the center. Aside from baking instead of frying, I make them with radicchio risotto and smoked mozzarella for a more sublime take on the tomato-y classic. Below is a recipe that will bring back delicious memories of unhealthy habits, but without the diabetes and emphysema.

Makes 25 Arancini

Extra-virgin olive oil

2 cups (gluten-free) panko breadcrumbs

3 cups *Radicchio Risotto*, room temperature (Page 406)

1 cup grated Parmigiano Reggiano (See Note)

¼ cup grated Pecorino Romano (See Note)

20 grinds of the pepper mill

1 egg

2 to 3 ounces smoked mozzarella, or *scamorza*, cut into ¼-inch cubes

Rosemary-Balsamic Reduction (Page 61) or store-bought balsamic glaze

1. Preheat the oven to 500°F.

2. Line a baking sheet with parchment paper and drizzle a couple of tablespoons olive oil on it. Spread it out with a brush or your fingers.

3. Place breadcrumbs in a wide, shallow bowl or a pie plate. Set aside.

4. Place risotto, the cheeses, and the pepper in a large mixing bowl. Mix and taste. Want more cheese? Add it.

5. Add the egg, and mix it all together.

6. Take a heaping tablespoon of the risotto mixture, stick a piece of smoked mozzarella in the center, and form a 1½-inch ball. Place the ball down on the breadcrumbs, use your fingers to sprinkle the ball with the breadcrumbs, and then reform it into a ball. Repeat until you have used all of the risotto.

7. Place *arancini* on the baking sheet and bake for 15 minutes.

8. Let cool for a couple of minutes and serve hot with balsamic reduction drizzled on top.

Note: Using a microplane grater is preferred and will give you the right amount.

Variation: Of course, you can make *arancini* from any type of risotto, so feel free to substitute your favorite concoction. You may, however, want to consider substituting the smoked mozzarella for traditional mozzarella, depending on the flavors.

FACING PAGE: Left - Bar San Calisto on a spring day.
Right - Emily demonstrating the anglicized gesticulation of the Italian phrase "vaffanculo."

" Only the pure in heart can make a good soup.

– *Ludwig van Beethoven*

The Comfort of Soups

NO-CHOP CHICKEN BROTH

NO-CHOP VEGGIE BROTH

QUICK CAULIFLOWER SOUP

LUCKY LENTIL SOUP

LIGURIAN MINESTRONE WITH PESTO

UN-RED ROASTED TOMATO SOUP

SONOMA SQUASH SOUP

CALIFORNIA RIBOLLITA

Quick Cauliflower Soup, page 154

MORE THAN ANY OTHER FOOD, SOUP MAKES US FEEL NURTURED.
Around the world, it's encoded with nostalgia for grandmothers and cozy winter nights. It cures us when we're sick and fills our bellies just right. If we're aiming to heal the planet with food-love (spoiler alert: we are), then soup is a good place to start!

No-Chop Chicken Broth

Of all the recipes in this book, homemade broth might be both the easiest and the most life-changing. With just a couple of minutes prep and a few hours of unsupervised simmering on the stovetop, homemade broth will elevate your cooking into the upper stratosphere of top-bitch badassery.

You don't need to peel. You don't need to chop. You don't need to even be awake. If you can throw whole vegetables into a pot, cover them with water, and then go take a nap for a couple of hours, you can make broth.

There is no canned, cubed, or boxed substitute for what grandmothers around the world have always known: homemade chicken broth will change your life and bring deep, soul-filling satisfaction to everyone you feed. Go for it.

AS LONG AS YOU'RE MAKING BROTH...

You can use any root vegetables cooked in broth to make delicious side dishes! If you're making veggie broth, it would be a darn shame to cook all of those vegetables and then throw them out. If you're making chicken broth, throw in some whole root vegetables and you'll be halfway to a *Celery Root Puree*, mashed potatoes or a mixed root veggie puree (below). Plus, your broth will benefit from the added goods.

For a mixed root veggie puree, remove the cooked onion from your broth (being sure to discard the peel) and any other root veggies you choose to use. Puree them your in food processor along with olive oil and/or butter, salt, and pepper. You likely have to cut them into chunks first. Put into a casserole dish. Cover with foil and bake for 40 minutes at 350°F. Alternatively, add more broth to this puree and eat it as soup!

Makes three quarts

3 pounds chicken necks and backs (if you can't find necks and backs, use wings and legs)

2 whole onions

4 to 5 whole cloves

3 whole carrots

3 to 4 celery stalks

2 bay leaves

5 to 6 peppercorns

A large handful of flat-leaf parsley

Kosher salt

1. Place all the ingredients in a stock pot and add enough water to cover. (You don't need to chop anything, hence the name of this recipe!)

2. Bring the water to a boil, cover, and let simmer slowly for at least a couple of hours. Better yet, let it simmer all day long. Skim off any foam that doesn't look appealing.

3. Let it cool, as this process adds flavor.

4. Season well with salt. If it's not tasty, add more salt! (See Note)

5. Once cooled, it may be refrigerated. If desired, skim off the fat the next day.

Note: Broth has no flavor unless you add salt. And it takes more than you think. I tend to make a batch of broth and freeze it for future uses, without any salt. That way I just salt it as I use it, recipe per recipe.

Variations: Below I have added some possible add-ins and why you might choose to use them:

» Any other root vegetables, such as potatoes, turnips, and rutabagas, for richer flavor.

» Dill. This is a favorite with Jewish chicken soup makers.

» Parsnips. They add a sweet, earthy flavor. Parsnips were always in my grandma's soups. (Recommended if you are making matzo ball soup.)

» Beef knuckle marrow bones. They add depth of flavor.

I Don't Even Own A Peeler

If I had to peel vegetables every time I cooked, I don't think I would bother. What an absolutely unnecessary pain in the *tuchus*. I'm officially liberating all of you from this slavery right now!

First of all, buy organic produce so you can feel good about eating the skin, even if it has a little dirt on it. Second, the skin is usually the healthiest part of your produce (potato skins, for example, are full of nutrients), and there is no recipe I cook in which it would ever need to be removed. Whoever tells you differently is only trying to make your life difficult. If your response to that is, "Well, one time this important French chef told me blah, blah, blah," then you've proven my point.

To be obsessed with perfection and neatness is to risk creating a meal bereft of poetry, and cooking is a poetic endeavor: it requires the passion of the moment and faith in the unknown. What it does not require is peeling. Throw your carrots, potatoes, and onions WHOLE into your broth. Keep the skin on the fruit of your cobbler. Use whole branches of rosemary and thyme in your braised meats. Throw your peelers away and put Mother Earth into your cooking.

> **"** *Anyone who's a chef, who loves food, ultimately knows that all that matters is: 'Is it good? Does it give pleasure?'*
>
> **—Anthony Bourdain**

No-Chop Veggie Broth

If you're making a vegetarian broth, you're working at a disadvantage, so it's especially important to add lots of vegetables to create a rich flavor. You can thank my boarding school friend Jill van Berg, vegetarian, Fulbright scholar, and passionate "deadhead" for the addition of olive oil. She pointed out that adding some fat makes all the difference.

Makes 3 Quarts

3 onions

2 to 3 leeks, rinsed

3 to 4 carrots

3 to 4 celery stalks

1 head of garlic, sliced in half horizontally

¼ pound shiitake mushrooms

3 whole root vegetables, can be any a combination of parsnips, turnips, potatoes, sweet potatoes, yams, peeled celery root, or rutabagas

1 whole tomato

¼ to ⅓ cup extra-virgin olive oil

1 to 2 bay leaves

5 to 6 peppercorns

4 to 5 whole cloves

1 (4-inch) piece of kombu (See Note)

A large handful of flat-leaf parsley

Kosher salt

1. Place all the ingredients in a stock pot and add enough water to cover. (You don't need to chop anything!)

2. Bring the water to a boil, cover, lower heat, and let simmer slowly for at least a couple of hours.

3. Let cool, as this process adds flavor.

4. Season well with salt. If it's not good or lacks flavor, add more salt!

5. Once cooled, it may be refrigerated.

6. Store in individual containers in freezer for future use.

Note: Kombu is edible kelp that will add depth of flavor to your broth. It's widely available in Asian and health food supermarkets (Whole Foods, for example).

Variations: Optional add-ins are fennel, corn-on-the-cob, zucchini, and any other type of mushroom.

Quick Cauliflower Soup

WITH CRISPED SAGE AND POMEGRANATE SEEDS

I first taught this soup to a daytime cooking class of moms who were eager to learn kid-friendly meals. These are women who, before having children, kicked butt as professionals in all types of fields. I know this type well. They don't beat around the bush. They don't come to 10 classes in a row. They want me to lay it out for them quickly and directly, making it as straightforward as possible.

So I decided to teach these ladies to roast some cauliflower (See *Roasted Cauliflower with Lemon*), and then show them another way to use that same cauliflower in a soup that takes only minutes to make. Two birds with one stone, slam dunk, love at first sight: three metaphors and we're barely scratching the surface of their reaction to this soup.

In class, we did a group taste-test to find the best garnish. You can thank this maternal gaggle of kitchen badasses for choosing pecorino, crisped sage, and pomegranate seeds as your topping.

THE "INTERNATIONAL LANGUAGE" OF SOUP!

It's easy to make good soup, because it doesn't require precision. These are the soup principles you need to know:

» **Most soups start out in the same way:** with a *soffritto* (Page 158).

» **The quality of the broth** dictates the quality of the soup.

» **Low and Slow.** For soup, time = love. The lower the flame, and the slower the soup cooks, the more the flavors of the ingredients will meld together into one harmonious chord.

» **Next day is the best day.** Soup flavor increases after it stops cooking. Its flavor deepens even as it cools on your stovetop. Having guests over? Make your life easy and the soup better—make it one or two days in advance. Soup also freezes well.

» **The final touches.** A drizzle of good olive oil, a touch of freshly chopped herbs, and/or a grating of good cheese will elevate your soup to higher realms.

Serves 4

1 large head cauliflower, broken into medium florets

¼ cup plus 2 Tablespoons extra-virgin olive oil

2 medium leeks, thinly sliced, white and light green part only

1 cup *No-Chop Chicken Broth* (Page 150) or *No-Chop Veggie Broth* (Page 153)

1 to 1½ teaspoons kosher salt

20 grinds of the pepper mill

Crisped Sage Leaves (recipe follows)

Grated Pecorino Romano, for garnish, optional

Pomegranate seeds, for garnish, optional

1. Preheat oven to 450°F. Place the cauliflower on a parchment-lined baking sheet. Pour on ¼ cup oil, sprinkle the salt, and grind the pepper. Use your fingers to mix it all together evenly. Lick your fingers; if they taste quite salty and peppery, you have done well. The seasoning will burn off in the oven, so adjust now if you need more.

2. Heat a medium soup pot over medium heat for several minutes.

3. Add the remaining olive oil to cover the bottom of the pot. Add the leeks and let them sauté until soft and just beginning to take a golden color.

4. Add the roasted cauliflower and just enough broth to cover the cauliflower.

5. Throw in some kosher salt and grind that pepper. Bring to a boil, lower the heat to a simmer, and let it cook for at least ten minutes or up to an hour, if you like.

6. Let cool. Pour the contents into the blender or use a blender stick to puree until smooth, adding more broth if you prefer a thinner consistency.

7. Pour the puree back into the soup pot over medium low heat. Taste for seasoning.

8. When hot, serve into bowls. Top each with a couple of crisped sage leaves, a drizzle of olive oil, more pepper if you like, grated cheese, and pomegranate seeds, if using.

CRISPED SAGE LEAVES

8 large sage leaves

1 to 2 Tablespoons of butter or olive oil

1. Place a small pan over medium heat and add enough butter or oil to generously coat the bottom. Heat until the fat is just bubbling, though don't let it burn.

2. Add the sage leaves so they don't touch and let them crisp, about a minute or so on each side. Place the sage on paper towels when done.

Lucky Lentil Soup

WITH FENNEL SEEDS AND BARLEY

At the stroke of midnight, as one year staggers drunkenly into the next, Italians throughout the world partake in a time-honored tradition to gather good luck. They eat lentils. Sure, they also get plastered and act like imbeciles just like we do, but instead of stuffing their fat faces with whatever deep-fried abomination they stumble across on the way home, *à la* the Great American Partygoer, the Italians search out a frickin' *legume*. Why?

With its round shape and golden hue, each lentil looks like a small coin. So, for centuries, lentils have symbolized abundance. Basically, on New Year's, Italians eat to get rich.

Gotta love the Italians for their jubilant naiveté. In my lifetime the Italian economy has never been good. Could it be because the Italians manage to negate the lucrative potential of the nutritious lentil by cooking the New Year's version with *cotecchino*—thick, fatty sausages that come in long, vacuum-packed wrappings, so you can just squeeze the pork right out of them? No surprise to you, in the *Meal and a Spiel* vision for world perfection, there is nothing lucky about squeezable pork.

Please note, I do not keep kosher, and I will eat pork in the form of good salami, but to eat fatty ground pig out of a bag brings no *mazel* to this *madela* of meal.

Still, Italians love their *cotecchino* and love to complain about being broke, so it seems useless for me to try to address their longstanding economic crisis with one recipe for soup. Though let me tell you, I'm pretty sure *Lucky Lentil Soup* could do the trick. With its homemade chicken broth, fennel seeds, and bits of chewy barley, it's that good.

Try it and share a bowl with someone who could use a little extra *mazel*.

¼ cup extra-virgin olive oil

1 onion, chopped

2 carrots, chopped

2 celery ribs with leaves, finely chopped

2 garlic cloves, chopped, optional

½ teaspoon herbes de Provence

1 teaspoon fennel seeds

1 Tablespoon chopped flat-leaf parsley, plus more for garnish

1 Tablespoon chopped basil, plus more for garnish

1½ cups lentils (See Note)

½ cup barley pearls

8 cups *No-Chop Chicken Broth* (Page 150) or *No-Chop Veggie Broth* (Page 153)

1½ teaspoons kosher salt

Make the soffritto:

1. Place a heavy stock pot over medium heat for a few minutes.

2. Add the olive oil, onion, carrots, celery, herbes de Provence, fennel seeds, parsley, and basil, and let sauté for about 10 minutes. Feel free to lower the heat and let it go until nice and golden brown, another 10 to 20 minutes.

Finish the soup:

1. Add lentils and barley and sauté another minute or so, stirring to make sure they don't burn or stick.

2. Add the stock and salt. Bring to a boil. Reduce the heat to low, and cover until the lentils are soft, about an hour.

3. Let the soup rest to cool, as it will only make it more flavorful.

4. Add more broth if you like a thinner consistency. You can also puree a quarter of the lentil soup in a blender and pour it back in for a creamier texture.

5. Reheat to serve. Top with fresh herbs and a drizzle of olive oil.

Note: Use the brown or green variety of lentils. You do not need to pre-soak them for this recipe, but I have recently learned that soaking beans help to remove lectins, which essentially means that soaked beans are easy to digest. If you would like to try, just cover the lentils and barley in water overnight, or at least an hour. Drain water before using.

Variation: If you'd like a sweeter, more nutritious sauce, remove the garlic and basil and puree the tomato sauce with about half of the carrots in a blender or food processor. It will be delicious (and a good way to hide vegetables from the kids).

SOUP STARTS WITH *SOFFRITTO*

Soffritto literally means "the sauté" in Italian. It consists of sautéed aromatic vegetables—onion, carrot, celery, and often herbs—which provide the foundation of flavor for all the subsequent ingredients. It is also the key to slow-cooked meats, meat sauces, stews, and more.

It's so essential to cooking that many cultures have a name for it: the French call it *mirepoix*, the Portuguese *refogado*, the Germans *suppengrün*.

WHAT YOU NEED TO KNOW ABOUT A *SOFFRITTO*:

» A classic *soffritto* contains onion, carrot, celery, and something green, like some parsley. Variations exists, but onion is always present.

» Chop the *soffritto* ingredients into very small pieces, about ¼ inch square. Your *soffritto* is the flavor base, you don't want big chunks of it in your soup.

» Olive oil is my go-to fat for a *soffritto*, but you can use butter, duck fat, lard, or a combination of fats. You need enough oil to generously cover the bottom of the pan, so all of the vegetables get sautéed, not steamed.

» The longer you cook the *soffritto* on lower heat—without burning or browning it—the more the vegetables will caramelize and the better your entire dish will taste in the end. Get your *soffritto* going. Then prep all of your other ingredients while your *soffritto* cooks unrushed.

» The process of sautéeing veggies is so good for flavor that you should let each main ingredient sauté for a few minutes before adding the next and certainly before adding the broth.

Ligurian Minestrone with Pesto

Minestra is the Italian word for soup. *Minestrone* simply means a big soup, one with a lot of stuff in it. This is a lighter minestrone, as it doesn't have pasta or beans in it, as most Italian minestrones do.

Ligurian? That's simply the name of the region where Genova resides. Renowned for its riviera coastline and towns, such as the five that make up the Cinque Terre, Liguria is most famous, gastronomically speaking, for its pesto.

¼ cup extra-virgin olive oil

1 large onion, chopped

1 large carrot, cut into ¼-inch disks then into quarters

2 ribs celery, sliced down center and cut into ¼-inch slices

1 leek, cut into ¼-inch slices (white and light green parts only)

1 russet potato, cut into ½-inch cubes

1 endive, cut into ¼-inch slices

2 zucchini (one yellow and one green, preferably), cut into quarters lengthwise, then into ¼-inch slices

3 leaves of green chard, sliced down the center, then cut into ¼-inch slices, and then those slices cut in half

3 cups *No-Chop Chicken Broth* (Page 150) or *No-Chop Veggie Broth* (Page 153)

1 Tablespoon kosher salt

Pesto Genovese (Page 60)

Grated Pecorino Romano or Parmigiano Reggiano, for garnish

Make the soffritto:

1. Place a stock pot over medium heat, and let it heat up for a few minutes.

2. Add the olive oil, onion, carrot, celery, and leek.

3. Let it cook for at least 10 minutes, stirring occasionally. Feel free to lower the heat and let it go until nice and golden brown, another 10 to 20 minutes.

Finish the soup:

1. Add the potato, endive, zucchini, and chard one at a time, and let each sauté for a good three minutes before adding the next one. Add more olive oil, if necessary.

2. Add the broth and the salt. Bring to a boil, lower the heat to medium low, and cover. Let simmer until vegetables are soft, at least an hour.

3. Taste for salt. If you don't think it tastes good, add more salt! Let the soup rest to cool, as the process will only make it more flavorful.

4. Reheat to serve, and top with a healthy dollop of *Pesto Genovese* and grated cheese, if desired.

Variation: If you want this minestrone to be hardier, you have a few choices. I like to make a meal out of this soup by adding barley and chicken, but you can do one or the other.

» Add a chicken breast on the bone (about ⅔ pound) flesh-side down in the soup immediately after you have added the broth. Let it cook until done, about 30 minutes. Remove the chicken from pot. When it is cool enough to handle, shred the meat using your hands or a couple of forks, discarding fat and the bone. Place the shredded chicken back in the soup just long enough to get it hot before eating.

» Add ⅓ cup of pearled barley after you have added all of your vegetables. Let it sauté for a couple of minutes before adding the broth. You may need to add more broth towards the end to get the consistency you want.

Un-Red Roasted Tomato Soup

WITH "STALED" BREAD

Most tomato soup tastes like spaghetti sauce mixed with broth. Sometimes even really good spaghetti sauce mixed with broth, but still.

This is something else altogether.

Why? Because it uses only fresh tomatoes, with no tomato paste and no canned tomatoes. In fact, the color of the soup comes out more orange than red. I admit, when I first made it, I was disappointed that my tomato soup didn't look like Warhol's Campbell's iconography. What is tomato soup if not red?

What is it? Good. Light on your belly. Not acidic. Soothing. Sweet. Nuanced.

However, to make sure I wasn't fooling myself, I did a taste test. I made two versions of the exact same recipe, one with fresh Roma tomatoes and the other with really good canned ones, and I called my neighbors Judy and Martin.

Judy and Martin are upright professionals, a lawyer and a doctor respectively. But I have a feeling that before parenthood, they each took a few rides on the magic bus. In the past, when my late-night parties woke up their kids, this lovely couple asked only if I'd had a good time. No complaints issued. I think they may have wanted to be invited over for an un-parental puff.

Anyway, I brought over the two soups, each one poured over a piece of crusty bread and doused with excellent olive oil. I watched and waited and did everything in my power to keep my mouth shut while they tasted. The results were interesting: both Martin and Judy initially gravitated towards the red canned variety. But then Martin started reconsidering. "This one is growing on me. Judy, try it again," he said, as he continued to shovel spoonfuls of the fresh tomato version into his mouth. "It doesn't grab you at first, because it's not the tomato soup you expect."

He was right. Its goodness is in its subtlety. Judy soon followed suit and the red version was left alone. Their kids, lured from their homework dungeons by the commotion, were thrilled to participate in the food war. To my surprise, both boys immediately chose the *Un-Red Roasted Tomato Soup*.

And thus, so have I.

P.S. This soup tastes like the Tuscan *pappa al pomodoro*, which is a tomato bread soup. In alignment with my California approach to eating, we are only adding one piece of bread per serving. *Pappa al pomodoro* is made with leftover stale bread, so assuming you don't have old bread lying around, we will "stale" bread in the oven.

Serves 6 to 8

3 pounds Roma tomatoes (12 to 16 tomatoes)

½ cup extra-virgin olive oil, plus more for drizzling

1 teaspoon kosher salt, plus more to taste

1 onion, finely chopped

2 carrots, finely chopped

2 celery ribs, finely chopped

4 to 6 cups *No-Chop Chicken Broth* (Page 150) or *No-Chop Veggie Broth* (Page 153)

5 garlic cloves

1 cup chopped fresh basil, plus more for garnish

Pain rustique, ciabatta, or other country bread, optional

Roast the tomatoes:

1. Preheat the oven to 400°F.

2. Cut the tomatoes in half lengthwise and use a spoon to scoop out the seeds. (I forgot to do this for the photoshoot in the pic you see... oops!)

3. Place the tomatoes face up on a baking sheet covered with parchment paper.

4. Drizzle with ¼ cup of the olive oil and sprinkle with salt. Use your fingers to mix it all together. Lie the tomatoes back down peel-side up so that they're easier to remove once roasted.

5. Place the tomatoes in the oven and roast for 35 minutes.

6. When cooled, use your fingers to take off the peel. It's ok if some is left on here and there, we just want most of it off.

"Stale" the bread:

1. Cut the bread into ½-inch slices.

2. Place it on a baking sheet and bake at 350°F until "staled," 12 to 15 minutes.

3. Set aside.

Make the soffritto:

1. Place a heavy soup pot over medium heat for a few minutes.

2. Add the remaining olive oil, the onions, carrots, and celery. Let them cook for a good 10 minutes, stirring occasionally. Feel free to lower the heat and let it go until nice and golden brown, another 10 to 20 minutes.

Finish the soup:

1. Add the roasted tomatoes and 4 cups of the broth. (Keep the remaining broth in case you want to thin out the soup.)

2. Bring to a gentle boil, turn the heat to low, cover, and simmer for 25 minutes.

3. Add the garlic cloves and the fresh basil.

4. Pour the hot contents into a blender. Don't fill it more than halfway, and be careful that your lid is on tight. Puree. This might need to be done in stages. Or use a hand blender. Taste for salt and add more until flavorful.

5. Pour over "staled" bread and drizzle with your best olive oil.

6. Garnish with basil and serve.

Sonoma Squash Soup

For me, Tuscany is a place where time slows down and afternoons stretch out like golden pathways leading, inevitably, toward long, soul-nourishing meals. In the United States, my Tuscany is Sonoma County.

My friend Zepporah Glass first brought me to Sonoma. In 2002, before the dot-com revolution drove property values through the roof, she bought a tear-down on 40 acres outside the hippie town of Occidental, CA. Zepporah is 30 years older than me, but when it comes to friendship, I see her free spirit, not her age. She was born in Bergen-Belsen, Poland, to refugees who survived concentration camps, then moved to San Francisco with empty pockets and opened a liquor store that eventually became a thriving real estate business, which Zepporah eventually ran. Driven by her insatiable curiosity and empathy, Zepporah studies Arabic in her spare time to better communicate with the Syrian refugees she befriended while volunteering in Greece at the height of the migrant crisis.

I met Zepporah after leaving a Florentine graduate school with a Master of Arts in Italian Jewish Studies, a degree about as useful as a glass hammer. Zepporah was working on a short documentary about Jewish Italian partisans during WWII. Through Los Angeles circles, she met my mother, who, in turn, introduced me. With my knowledge of Italy's language and Jewish history, I helped craft the editing and ultimately presented the film to an audience in Turin. Our friendship has been one of the great blessings of my life.

For years, Zepporah has opened up her beautiful Japanese-style minimalist house in Sonoma to me as if it were my own. Some of this book was written in her light-filled living room, flanked by walls of windows that look out to majestic redwoods and the Pacific fog that creeps around them "on little cat feet," as the poet Carl Sandburg would say.

At Zepporah's Sonoma home, time stops. I never feel hurried or rushed. In other words, it's the perfect place to make soup. So when I saw a kabocha squash sitting on her counter, my usual hesitation to cook with this extra-hard-to-cut gourd vanished. I baked the whole thing in the oven until it was soft, and then scooped out the creamy orange flesh. It was so easy, I just needed to be in a calm state to try it. I omitted carrots for the *soffritto*, and piled on the cooling flavors of celery, leeks, green onions, and black pepper to temper the sweetness of the kabocha.

I've enjoyed adding different types of squash to the soup, such as delicata. But if you prefer, you can keep it simple. It tastes, as soup is supposed to taste, like love.

FACING PAGE: My view at Zepporah's house while working on this book.

1 medium kabocha squash

1 medium delicata squash, optional

¼ cup extra-virgin olive oil

1 medium yellow onion, finely chopped

2 large leeks, finely sliced, white and light green parts only

4 celery ribs, finely chopped

8 to 10 (one bunch) green onions, finely sliced, white and green parts only

2 large garlic cloves, chopped

4 to 6 cups *No-Chop Chicken Broth* (Page 150) or *No-Chop Veggie Broth* (Page 153)

1 to 2 teaspoons kosher salt

60 to 80 grinds of the pepper mill

Chopped flat-leaf parsley, mint, and/or cilantro, for garnish

Toasted Pine Nuts (Page 64) for garnish, optional

Roast the squash:

1. Turn oven to 350°F and throw the squash in there. You don't need to wait until the oven is hot. Place the squash on a baking sheet or a piece of aluminum foil so it doesn't drip onto your oven floor. Cook about an hour, or until they are both very soft. The delicata squash will be done first, so go ahead and take it out. Or leave it in there. It doesn't matter as long as nothing is burning! Let the squash cool.

2. Cut open each squash. Remove the seeds, and use a spoon to scoop out the flesh. Set aside.

Make the soffritto:

1. Place a stock pot over medium heat and let it get hot for a few minutes.

2. Add the olive oil, onion, leeks, celery, green onions, and garlic, and let sauté for at least 10 minutes, stirring occasionally. Feel free to lower the heat and let it go until nice and golden brown, another 10 to 20 minutes.

3. Add the roasted squash, and mix to combine.

Finish the soup:

1. Add the chicken broth to the pot. Start with 4 cups and add more as you go until you get the consistency you want. Use wooden spoon or potato masher to break up the pieces of the squash, if needed. You want it to be somewhat textured.

2. Add the salt and grind that pepper in there. Lots of pepper will temper the sweetness of the squash and harmonize the flavors. So don't be shy.

3. Cover and turn the heat to low. Simmer for an hour or longer, tasting for salt and pepper.

4. Let the soup rest to cool, as this step will only make it more flavorful.

5. Reheat to serve. Drizzle with olive oil, and garnish with cooling herbs and pine nuts, if using.

Zepporah and me on a kibbutz in Israel to film the testimonies of surviving WWII partisans.

HOW TO MAKE A SOUP FROM ANYTHING

Start with a *soffritto*. There's flexibility here. You need to chop and sauté one or more members of the onion family: yellow onion, red onion, shallots, leeks, green onions, and chives. Consider your flavors and decide whether you also want to add carrot, celery, garlic, and/or any herbs. Give it some time over the flame to get sweet.

   For a pureed soup *(the quick and easy route)* add big chunks of one vegetable and liquid to cover (water, *Cheater's Chicken Broth*, or homemade broth). Add salt and bring to boil until soft. If you're not rushed, let it rest so the flavors can meld, and puree in blender.

   For a textured soup add chopped vegetables or beans or hunks of meat, one by one to the *soffritto*. Let each one sauté in the oil for at least a few minutes if not longer. Add liquid to cover (homemade broth or *Cheater's Chicken Broth*). Add salt, minding the salt content of the broth. Grind in some pepper. Cover, and let simmer on low until it smells and tastes like love.

   Garnish with herbs, olive oil, and/or cheese.

California Ribollita

TUSCAN WHITE BEAN AND KALE BREAD SOUP WITHOUT THE BREAD

A good Italian vegetable soup is a work of art, and to create great art, you must first study with the masters. Italians do this in their mothers' kitchens. My mother was more of the Campbell's Soup type, so I had to live in Tuscany to train.

Years ago, I embarked on a journey of testing and experimentation in order to replicate and share the subtle genius of *ribollita*, the famed Tuscan bread soup. This recipe is far from a spontaneous creation on a cold and soupy night; I've been eating in preparation for this soup for 16 years. I've talked the ear off of enough Italian *mamme* to get glimpses of what makes their *ribollita* so incredible. I've fallen asleep many a late night with cookbooks scattered all over the bed, reading and re-reading recipes by trusted sources in the original Italian. And I have made enough variations on this *minestrone* theme to know that I have finally arrived.

This is the *minestra* to make *ribollita*. I prefer to make this California version of bread soup without the bread, because bread soup is for really skinny people, and I want a soup I can binge on. But if you want to throw in a slice of crusty carbs (one slice never hurt anyone!), see how to make staled bread with the recipe for *Un-Red Roasted Tomato Soup*.

Every work of art has a message. Mine is this: love every ingredient as you buy it, chop it, and add it to the pot, and it will love you back.

2 cups dried cannellini beans

3 teaspoons kosher salt, divided

1 sprig of rosemary

¼ cup extra-virgin olive oil, plus more for drizzling

1 large onion, finely chopped

1 carrot, finely chopped

1 celery rib, finely chopped

1 yam, cut into ½-inch pieces

1 russet potato, cut into ½-inch pieces

1 pound dinosaur or lacinato kale, stems removed and cut into ¼-inch slices

½ pound Swiss chard (green variety, not red), stems removed, cut into ¼-inch slices

2 Tablespoons tomato paste or 4 vine-ripened tomatoes, finely chopped

1 garlic clove, finely chopped

8 to 10 cups *No-Chop Chicken Broth* (Page 150) or *No-Chop Veggie Broth* (Page 153)

10 basil leaves

1 to 2 leeks, finely sliced, white parts only, optional

Grated Parmigiano Reggiano, optional

Make the beans:

1. Soak the beans in cold water for 12 to 24 hours, changing the water at least once. (If you forget to soak the beans, cover with water, bring to a boil, and then discard the water. Cover with more water, bring to a boil, and then simmer until done. The beans will take longer to cook than if soaked beforehand.)

2. Drain and place the beans, 1½ teaspoons of salt, and the rosemary in a medium pot covered with water by 3 to 4 inches.

3. Bring to a boil over high heat, lower the heat, and simmer uncovered until tender, 1 to 2 hours.

4. Take out the rosemary branch and remove two cups of the beans. Set aside.

5. Puree the remaining beans with the cooking water in a food processor. Set aside.

Make the soffritto:

1. Place a heavy soup pot over medium heat and let it get hot.

2. Add the olive oil, onion, carrot, and celery, and sauté for at least 10 minutes, stirring occasionally. Feel free to let the soffritto go for longer, until nice and golden brown.

3. Add the yam and potato, stirring occasionally. Let sauté for a few minutes. Add the kale and chard and stir. Give it a couple of minutes.

4. Add the tomato paste or chopped tomatoes and garlic, and stir until well mixed. Let caramelize with the vegetables for a couple of minutes.

Finish the soup:

1. Add 8 cups of the broth, throw in the basil leaves, add the remaining 1½ teaspoons salt, and bring to a boil. Lower the flame to low, cover, and simmer for at least 2 hours.

2. While the soup is still hot, add the whole and pureed beans.

3. Add the leeks. Stir and let sit to cool, as the flavor will only enhance with time.

4. Taste for salt and add more accordingly. Does it have flavor? Is it bland? Then it needs more salt!

5. Reheat to serve, drizzle with good olive oil, and top with grated cheese, if desired.

CHEATER'S CHICKEN BROTH

This lesson is dedicated to all of the women in my classes who refuse to make homemade chicken broth.

Lord knows, I've tried to instill in their taste buds the importance of the unparalleled flavor that only a homemade broth can bring to foods. It is liquid love. It is the secret behind the secret.

To their credit, these women have taken heaps of instruction of mine to heart, and not only want to feed their loved ones well, but actually do. They just aren't going to make broth from scratch.

I accept my defeat. It's me versus modernity. Someday, I pray, we'll return to homemade broth and handwritten love poetry. Until then, I insist that if you're going to cheat, at least make my *Cheater's Chicken Broth!*

HERE'S HOW:

» **Buy your broth in an organic box,** not a can. The quality will be much better.

» **Add "life" to the broth.** To erase the industrial flavor of pre-made broths and to add homemade flavor, choose at least three of the following "live" ingredients and boil them in your boxed broth covered for 20 minutes, if not more: a carrot or a baby carrot, a piece of celery or celery leaves, a bay leaf, a sprig of parsley, a piece of onion or its skin, a sprig of thyme, the dark green top of a leek, or the skin of a potato.

Use this Cheater's Chicken Broth for making risottos, meat sauces, braised meats or—gulp—in a soup.... BUT DO NOT expect this to hold up in actual chicken soup. If you make fresh matzo balls, for example, and serve them in a broth that's not homemade (Nancy Pritikin Ruttenberg, I'm talking to you!), you'll cause legions of dead grandmothers to rise from the dead in exasperated anguish. And when these zombie grandmothers close in on you, demanding to know why you served mediocre broth and why you're wearing ripped pants, the rest of the *Meal and a Spiel* community and I will sip homemade chicken soup surrounded by the light of fluttering angels whose every wing-beat sings *I told you so!*

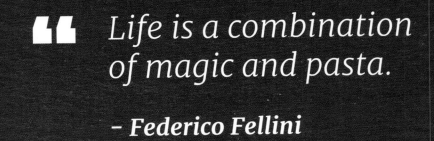

Life is a combination of magic and pasta.

– Federico Fellini

Pasta That's Better Than a Restaurant

AGLIO OLIO

BUCATINI CON BOTTARGA

PENNE AL POMODORO

PENNE WITH MUSHROOMS AND THYME

SPAGHETTI AL CAVOLO NERO

RIGATONI AL TONNO E CAPPERI

PASTA FRANCESCA

PASTA DI FARRO CON GLI ASPARAGI

LINGUINE ALLO SCOGLIO

TAMBURELLO DI MELANZANE

TURKEY "BOLOGNESE"

RAGÙ DI CARNE

MY PASTA CLASSES ARE MY MOST POPULAR, BECAUSE EVERYONE wants to know how to whip up an amazing Italian plate of pasta in 20 minutes. But my students are sometimes surprised to find that I don't give them recipes: I teach a *process*, called *aglio olio*. We apply this process to different pasta dishes. With just a single lesson, even the greenest beginners become confident kitchen badasses, whipping up meals like Italians do every day. It's life-changing. Furthermore, I don't teach them to make fresh pasta noodles. It's not my style. It requires precision and it makes a mess—plus, most Italians aren't sitting at home rolling spaghetti on a Tuesday night. If you want to learn to make fresh pasta, there are great cookbooks for that, and I'll be happy to come over sometime to taste your work. In the meantime, you're going to learn the rules that all Italians follow for pasta. Perhaps the most important one is: You gotta eat it when it's hot!

THE *AGLIO OLIO* PROCESS NO ONE TOLD YOU ABOUT

Whenever I tell Italians that I teach the *aglio olio* process—certain that this will earn their respect—they always chuckle. *"Ma di che!"* Who cares, they say. "Everyone knows the *aglio olio* process."

"No they don't!" I retort. "Nobody in America has any idea what it is! I can't believe some Italian hasn't made a fortune teaching this."

To which they pause, then silently nod their heads, giving just a hint of a smile that shows their surprise. But I can tell from the glint in their eyes that what they really want to say is, "Woman, you are doing God's work."

HERE'S THE SECRET:

Ninety percent of the pasta sauces that Italians whip up daily start in the exact same way: *aglio, olio, peperoncino.* Garlic. Olive oil. Red pepper flakes. In short it's called *aglio olio.*

This is the foundation of vegetable-based pasta sauces, just like *soffritto* is the base for soups, except it's a much quicker process. We're simply flavoring olive oil with garlic and red pepper flakes. This olive oil then flavors the other ingredients that we put into the pan to make the sauce. It's that simple.

HERE IS HOW YOU DO IT:

1. **Put a wide-bottomed pan over medium heat.** As you get more comfortable and efficient with this process, move to a **medium high flame.** Let the pan heat up as you prepare your garlic.

2. **Add olive oil to generously coat the pan.** Now add a bit more. Olive oil is flavor.

3. **Add peeled garlic cloves to the pan.** Anticipate two large cloves per sauce for four people (for peeling tips, see Page 64).

4. **Add a dash or two of red pepper flakes.** The size of your dashes will depend on the strength of your *peperoncino* and the level of spice you want to create in the dish. (For example: *Aglio Olio* takes more heat, *Penne al Pomodoro* takes less. Plan on topping the sauce with cheese? Use less *peperoncino!*)
    Note: *Don't pinch or touch the red pepper flakes, because, if you touch your*

eyes, nose, or any other delicate part of your body afterwards, you'll feel the burn. I sprinkle them into the bottle cap and then into the pan.

5. **Watch the little bubbles form around the garlic**. This is the garlic infusing its flavor into the olive oil. Don't grab your phone. Stay present. This is an act of love.

6. **Lift the pan to an angle so the garlic is fully submerged in the oil.** Through your hands on the handle, feel the process that's happening in the pan. Become one with the garlic. Commune with it. Love it. I'm not joking. I make my students do this. It works.

7. **DO NOT LET THE GARLIC BURN!** You want the oil to pull out all of the goodness from the garlic without it browning. This process takes about three minutes on average, depending on the heat of your pan. Once the garlic begins to have a translucent, slightly blistered look, it's done. A little golden brown is okay, but no more. Add your next ingredients to stop the garlic from cooking further. They will most likely be vegetables—tomatoes, mushrooms, broccoli rabe—which are water-based and prevent burning. **Note:** *If you **almost** burn the garlic, just throw your vegetables in there fast. But if you **actually** burn the garlic, wait for it to cool and then pour the whole thing into the trash, take a paper towel to wipe out most of the oil and remaining bits of peperoncino, and start over from the top. You've lost a few minutes, but it's better than tasting burnt garlic in your sauce.*

8. **Add your sauce ingredients.** You're now letting your primary pasta sauce ingredients—tomatoes, mushroom, or kale, etc.—get flavored by the delicious *aglio-peperoncino*-scented olive oil you've just created. Stir your ingredients with love into the oil.

9. **Now add salt.** Now add a touch more. Come on, be generous. You're becoming an Italian. Stir.

10. **Let your sauce cook until it's done.** Timing will depend on the ingredients. See the recipes that follow. In general, you want just enough liquid to coat the noodles, but not so much that you have watery pasta. If more liquid is ever needed, add some pasta cooking water to the pan.

11. **Add the pasta.** As soon as your pasta is cooked *al dente* (see *Rules for an Al Dente Pasta*, page 194), drain it, and throw it into the sauce over a lively medium high flame, a *fuoco vivace.* Toss it all around until evenly coated in sauce and serve immediately.

Aglio Olio

WITH GARLIC AND RED PEPPER FLAKES

Aglio olio isn't just a life-changing process, it's also the recipe Italians make when they have nothing in the house to eat—nothing, of course, but spaghetti, olive oil, red pepper flakes, and salt. (Those staples are the Italian equivalent of ketchup in the door of the fridge.)

Because it requires so little prep and so few ingredients, *Aglio Olio* is also the go-to, 4 a.m. binge food after a night at the discoteca. If you add enough *peperoncino*, it helps you sweat out the alcohol.

Perhaps because there are so few ingredients, this is one of the hardest pasta dishes to perfect. Like a haiku with only three lines, or a country album with only five subjects (trucks, prison, trains, Mama, gettin' drunk), the restrictions inspire the art. Every aspiring pasta cook should start here for two reasons: first, you'll be surprised how much you like it, and second, this dish will teach you to fully understand the importance of the flavor base used for the rest of the sauces.

Because *Aglio Olio* originates from the spicy seaside city of Naples, if you top it with anything but cooling parsley—like cheese for instance—a Neopolitan might attack you for breaking the culinary prohibition against consuming spicy food with cheese. That said, Florentine friends of mine, far enough away from Naples to escape its culinary decrees, are known to top an *Aglio Olio* with some sharp Pecorino Romano. Hence, I offer it as an option for you to try as well.

¼ cup extra-virgin olive oil

2 garlic cloves

½ to 1 teaspoon red pepper flakes

Kosher salt (See Note)

½ pound spaghetti

Chopped flat-leaf parsley

Grated Pecorino Romano, optional

1. Place a medium pan over medium heat and let it get hot for a few minutes.

2. Add the olive oil, the garlic, and the red pepper flakes, in that order.

3. Let the garlic infuse its flavor into the olive oil for a few minutes. Watch the bubbles. Don't let the garlic burn. As it just begins to take a faint golden hue, remove the pan from the heat.

4. Bring a large pot of water to boil over high heat. Throw in a generous handful of kosher salt (See Note), followed by the pasta. Stir, and cook al dente.

5. Drain and add the pasta to the sauce over medium high heat. Toss until all of the noodles are coated in the flavored oil. Adjust the seasoning to your taste by adding more salt or more red pepper flakes, for example.

6. Top with the parsley and cheese, if using.

Note: Because this "sauce" doesn't have any salt in it, you will need to add more salt to the pasta water. That's right, more than the normal handful you add. Trust me. Remember, this is all practice until you get it right.

Bucatini con Bottarga

PASTA WITH DRIED FISH ROE

So this is where your new *aglio olio* trick gets crazy. You're about to take the simplicity of *aglio olio* to a whole new level, from the most basic home cooking to the heights of restaurant haute cuisine. You'll use the exact same cooking process as the last recipe, except you're going to sprinkle on a few more ingredients, most importantly—*bottarga*.

Referred to by Italians as poor man's caviar, *bottarga* is dried, cured fish roe, usually of mullet or tuna. It has the subtle taste of the sea. If you like fresh seafood, fish soup, or uni (sea urchin) sushi, you'll love *bottarga*. You can buy it as a "bar/filet," which you'll grate onto your pasta, or in a jar, pre-grated. It's hard to choose which is better. The freshly grated is more sophisticated and delicate, but the pre-grated is richer in flavor. Since the *bottarga* "bar" has a milder flavor, you'll have to use more, meditatively allowing the fresh flavors of the sea to take hold of your tongue. The pre-grated is less expensive, and you won't use as much.

When I tested the recipe on my editor Seth and his wife, Lauren, we couldn't decide which we preferred. Though when given the choice to keep one type of bottarga over the other, they chose the jarred stuff, and I chose the fresh. Ultimately, what you use will likely depend on what's available. (Though through many sources on the Internet, including my online shop, you can get either.)

If you've never tried bucatini, you're in for a treat. It literally means "little holes," referring to the needle-sized tunnels running through what looks like thick spaghetti. The texture is quite fun in your mouth, and with juicier toppings like tomato or meat sauce, you'll find sauce in the middle of your noodles. Yum!

½ cup extra-virgin olive oil

4 medium garlic cloves

1 to 2 teaspoons red pepper flakes

1 pound bucatini pasta

Kosher salt

½ cup grated or ¼ cup jarred Bottarga di Muggine (See Note)

2 Tablespoons chopped flat-leaf parsley

Zest of 1 lemon

Flaky sea salt, optional

1. Place a large pan over medium heat and let it get hot for a few minutes.

2. Add the olive oil, the garlic, and the red pepper flakes, in that order.

3. Let the garlic infuse its flavor into the olive oil for a few minutes. Watch the bubbles. Don't let the garlic burn. As it just begins to take a faint golden hue, remove the pan from the heat.

4. Bring a large pot of water to boil over high heat. Throw in an extra-large handful of kosher salt because the "sauce" is very mild, followed by the pasta. Stir. Cook al dente.

5. Drain and add the pasta to the pan over medium high heat. Toss until all the noodles are coated in the flavored oil.

6. Add three-quarters of your bottarga to the pan (all but 2 tablespoons of the freshly grated or all but 1 tablespoon of the jarred). Toss until the bottarga is spread evenly throughout the noodles. Serve onto plates, and top equally with the remaining bottarga, parsley, lemon zest, and flaky sea salt, if using.

Note: Bottarga di Muggine may be purchased online or in gourmet grocery stores. Make sure you can see somewhere on the packaging that it comes from Sardegna. It keeps indefinitely in the refrigerator.

IS IT SAFE TO COOK WITH OLIVE OIL?

With the growing concern about the carcinogenic oxidation of oils at high temperatures, this is a common question I get in class. This is my answer: I teach cooking classes for the Barbra Streisand Women's Cardiovascular Center at UCLA. In those classes, the cardiologists, including my sister Tamara, warn students not to let any oil get to its smoking point. As long as it's not burning in the pan (turning color and smelling bitter), there isn't a problem. Remember, you're not cooking the oil alone. You're adding food to it, and food slows down the heating process of the oil. Plus, plant food is mostly made of water, so it's also tempering the fire, so to speak. When your veggies are roasting at 450°F, for example, the oil is not getting up to that temperature. Got it? And then, I always add at the end of this spiel: as long as the long-living, gorgeous, thick-haired Italians keep cooking with olive oil, then so will I!

Penne al Pomodoro

PASTA WITH FRESH CHERRY TOMATO AND BASIL SAUCE

Adding cherry tomatoes and basil to your *aglio olio* base is so simple, yet so good that it will become one of your absolute go-to's. In my class, this is the recipe that makes people say, "Wow, this is better than at a restaurant!" Of course it's better than at a restaurant! Home-cooked food, made in small quantities, with love, and eaten as soon as it's ready, should *always* be better than a restaurant's. Restaurant prep cooks can't add the love you can. They're at *work*.

You'll notice that I throw the basil leaves in whole, with the stems attached. It's the easiest way to get great flavor.

This recipe serves 2 to 3 people, so you can practice with a smaller portion. But feel free to double it to serve more or hungrier people.

WHAT DO I DO WITH WHOLE PIECES OF GARLIC IN THE PASTA?

Do what I do, and leave them in there. In Italian homes, it's normal to be served a plate of pasta and find a clove of garlic in there or a sprig of cooked basil. You just eat around it. If you prefer, you can remove the garlic and herbs from your sauces before you add the noodles.

¼ cup extra-virgin olive oil

2 large garlic cloves

½ teaspoon red pepper flakes

1 pint cherry tomatoes, halved

2 large sprigs of basil leaves

1 teaspoon kosher salt, plus more for pasta water

½ pound penne rigate

Grated Parmigiano Reggiano, for garnish

1. Place a medium pan over medium heat and let it get hot for a few minutes.

2. Add the olive oil, the garlic, and the red pepper flakes, in that order.

3. Let the garlic infuse its flavor into the olive oil. Watch the bubbles. Don't let the garlic burn.

4. Once the garlic has just taken on a slightly golden color, add the tomatoes and stir. Throw in the basil, stems and all. Add salt and stir. Let the tomatoes cook for about 10 to 15 minutes.

5. When soft enough, smush the tomatoes down with a fork or with the back of a wooden spoon. Taste the sauce. If you want more flavor, add more salt.

6. Once you can swipe your spoon across the bottom of the pan and it "parts like the Red Sea" for a moment before oozing its way back to the center, you are done. If you want it to be a little thicker, cook for a few minutes longer. Remove the pan from the heat.

7. Bring a large pot of water to boil over high heat. Throw in a handful of kosher salt, followed by the pasta. Stir, and cook *al dente*.

8. When the pasta is nearly done, turn the heat under the sauce to medium high, a *fuoco vivace*, a lively flame.

9. Drain and add the pasta to the sauce. Toss until all the noodles are coated in the sauce.

10. Serve and top with the grated Parmigiano.

Variation: Top with *Toasted Pine Nuts* (Page 64) and sliced basil.

Respect The Tomato

Every so often one of my cooking students, inspired by the utter simplicity of a good tomato sauce, gets carried away by the urge to enhance it: "Oh my goodness, this is so easy, I can just throw in chicken and peppers and broccoli... Whatever I want! My family will love this!"

I hate to squash her enthusiasm, but teaching people to replicate the worst of American restaurant cuisine is not my job. Lots of restaurants try to maximize their tomato sauces by filling them with every ingredient they've got, from grilled chicken to salmon to buffalo tofurkey, in an attempt to convince diners they're getting more for their money.

Italians, on the other hand, don't just throw a bunch of arbitrary ingredients into a tomato sauce—or into any dish for that matter. Cooking is an act of respect for the unique properties of the foods themselves. The key is learning to heighten the flavor of the primary ingredient. If they want to add more vegetables or protein to their diets, that's what side dishes (*contorni*) and main courses (*secondi*) are for.

Of course, the tomato is not always the star. For example, seafood is the primary ingredient in my sauce for *Linguine allo Scoglio*. I add a couple of fresh tomatoes, though, just to balance the taste of the sea.

The primary ingredient is not white paint to which you add colors wantonly. In fact, adding a bunch of colors to white paint gets you nothing but muddy brown. The primary ingredient *is* the color, it *is* the source, it *is* the essence, the center, the guest of honor, the bride, if you will, of the dish. The other ingredients used in a tomato sauce (garlic, onion, basil, parsley, etc.) are there *only* to respect the tomato.

For Italians, thyme complements lamb, lemon enhances fish, Parmigiano supports eggplant, and basil exalts tomato. Be it Indian, Thai, Mexican, or Moroccan cuisine, the truly well-flavored meal respects the integrity of the ingredients. It's a song played with instruments chosen to create perfect harmony in your mouth.

" *He who distinguishes the true savor of his food can never be a glutton; he who does not cannot be otherwise.*

*—**Henry David Thoreau***

Penne with Mushrooms and Thyme

By adding mushrooms to your *aglio olio* base, you will create a flavorful coating for your pasta. It's not quite a "sauce" as you'd expect it, so be sure to finely chop your mushrooms so you can eat them with every bite of every noodle.

Serves 2 to 3

¼ cup extra-virgin olive oil

2 large garlic cloves

½ teaspoon red pepper flakes

1 pound cremini mushrooms, stems removed and finely chopped (See Note)

3 large sprigs of thyme

½ teaspoon tamari or quality soy sauce

1 teaspoon kosher salt, plus more for pasta water

½ pound casarecce or penne rigate

Grated Parmigiano Reggiano, for garnish

1. Place a medium pan over medium heat and let it get hot for a few minutes.

2. Add the olive oil, the garlic, and the red pepper flakes, in that order.

3. Let the garlic infuse its flavor into the olive oil for a few minutes. Watch the bubbles. Don't let the garlic burn. Once the garlic has just taken on a slightly golden color, add the mushrooms and thyme (stems and all), and stir. Let them sauté for a couple of minutes.

4. Add the tamari and the salt. Stir and let the mushrooms cook over medium heat until soft and juicy, about 15 minutes. Taste for salt, and remove the thyme branches if desired (I leave them in for a rustic look and because I'm lazy). Remove the pan from the heat.

5. Bring a large pot of water to boil over high heat. Throw in a handful of kosher salt, followed by the pasta. Stir and cook *al dente*.

6. When the pasta is nearly done, turn the heat under the sauce to medium high, a *fuoco vivace*, a lively flame.

7. Drain and add the pasta to the sauce and toss until all the noodles are coated with the mushrooms and oil.

8. Top with grated Parmigiano.

Note: You may also use a mixture of mushrooms including oyster, portobello, and porcini.

RULES FOR AN AL DENTE PASTA - FROM START TO FINISH

INGREDIENTS:

1 box (1 pound) for 4 people

A large pot of water

A handful of kosher salt

A timer/stopwatch to help you stay on task

1. **Always use a big pot of boiling water,** even if you are making pasta only for one. The pasta needs to "breathe" while it cooks, and using a big pot guarantees that the temperature won't drop drastically when you add the pasta.

2. **Once water boils, throw in a full handful of kosher salt.** Yes, a handful. Just do it.

3. **Put in the pasta all at once,** i.e. don't put in one handful after the other or you will mess up cooking times.

4. **Stir pasta vigorously a few times at the beginning** to make sure it doesn't stick. Spaghetti and all brown rice pasta needs extra stirring. Get your tongs in there to separate the strands!

5. **YELL TO FAMILY AND FRIENDS: "Butto la pasta. I am throwing in the pasta."** This lets them know they have about 10 minutes to finish up whatever they're doing and to get ready to be at the table the moment the pasta is served. Just an FYI, Italian teenagers are never late to the table.

6. **Don't leave a wooden spoon or metal tongs in the pasta water while it's cooking.**

7. **Put the colander in the sink now, early.** If you fumble for it later, you risk mushy pasta, which is punishable by law in certain parts of Italy.

8. **Do NOT get distracted while your pasta is cooking.** Again, you're risking mushy pasta. And your imaginary Italian friends will notice and comment.

9. **If you must step away from the pasta, set a timer** for 4 minutes before the pasta is said to be ready according to the package instructions.

10. **Start testing pasta for doneness** 3 minutes before it's supposed to be ready according to the package instructions.

11. **If your sauce has been turned off, turn the flame on** again to medium to make sure it's heated through and ready for the pasta.

12. **All crunchiness in the pasta should be gone,** and the intense chewiness should just be giving way to a softer texture. Stop. You are done.

13. **Thirty seconds too much or too little DOES make a difference.** (When in doubt: better to undercook a tad than to overcook.)

14. **Drain pasta.**

15. **DO NOT RINSE THE PASTA.** The starch on the pasta is what marries the sauce to the noodles.

16. **YELL TO FAMILY AND FRIENDS: "La pasta è pronta! The pasta is ready!"** This is when they need to come to the table.

17. **Raise the heat under the sauce to a "fuoco vivace,"** a lively flame (medium high to high), and pour the drained pasta into it.

18. **Use tongs or two big forks or wooden spoons to TOSS** (not mix) the pasta and sauce together.

19. **Serve onto individual plates,** and top with freshly grated Parmigiano Reggiano, Pecorino Romano, or fresh parsley or mint if the dish calls for it.

20. **THE FINAL AND MOST IMPORTANT RULE: the pasta is to be eaten IMMEDIATELY.** You don't let it sit until you're ready to eat. If you are not ready, **do not go past step 1.** The pasta is a demigod in Italian culture. *Its* readiness dictates *your* readiness. If someone is late to the table, you do not wait for them to eat. The pasta is ready. Eat it now!!

 Everything you see I owe to spaghetti.
– Sofia Loren

HOW TO EAT SPAGHETTI LIKE A PRO

The true beauty of spaghetti, and all pasta, is its texture in your mouth, which you can only experience by wrapping it around itself on your fork. Nobody expects you to do this without a little pasta hanging out here and there, so don't fret. Savor your noodles the Italian way. Here's how:

1. Position your fork over to the side of the plate, towards the edge of your mound of spaghetti. Stab your fork in at a 90 degree angle. (The usual issue for non-Italians is that they stab the pasta at the top of the mound and then they get too much pasta on one forkful and don't know what to do.)

2. Then—and you don't need to stay at the 90 degree angle—keep the tips of the fork touching the plate and just twirl the pasta round and round until it's mostly all on there. Lift fork. A few stray pieces will hang down.

3. Bring the fork to your face, stick it in your mouth, pull out the fork and inhale the low-hanging strands of pasta into your mouth without making any noise. Yes, I am serious. This isn't a joke. Even Sophia Loren said, "Spaghetti can be eaten most successfully if you inhale it like a vacuum cleaner."

Spaghetti al Cavolo Nero

BROWN RICE PASTA WITH KALE

Though kale is sometimes derided as a staple of the California/vegan/ hippie diet, the darker, comparatively flat-leaved variety is actually a cherished ingredient in Tuscan cooking. It is called *cavolo nero*, which literally translates to "black cabbage." (That's also the name of my favorite vegan heavy metal band.) When prepared right, *cavolo nero* will transport you to the rolling countryside of Siena, as this recipe does.

Chopped anchovies add a savory umami note to the preparation. You can swap out the kale for sliced-up broccoli rabe when it's in season.

I love to make this recipe with a good brown rice pasta, so I can invite both my discerning Italian friends and my picky health-nut peeps over to the same dinner party. Everybody is happy and feels loved by the food.

EWWWW, DO I HAVE TO USE THE ANCHOVY??

Whenever I mention anchovies in my beginners' classes, half my students freak the fork out: "Anchovies?? Ewww!! I hate anchovies!"

I, too, was once anchovy-phobic. Highly. That said, I always kept a bottle of anchovies packed in olive oil in my fridge, because for years in LA, I only hung out with Italians, and I knew all Italians did. I just never opened mine. That is, until one night, when everyone was over, and Cinzia went into the kitchen to whip up dinner for ten of us—in twenty minutes, like I teach you to do in this chapter. She found all the ingredients for *Tonno e Capperi*, my go-to pasta. She served it up, and it was better—WAY better—than mine.

What had this woman done? I drilled her step-by-step on how she made it. Her secret? She sautéed anchovies with garlic at the start. I still don't like plain anchovies. I don't want to see them on top of a salad or on a pizza. However, I love them in small doses, and I like to chop them super fine so they disintegrate into the olive oil, which adds a delicate, umami, sea-salty goodness that you just can't get in any other way.

Do you have to use anchovies? Short answer: Yes. The end.

1 bunch lacinato or dinosaur kale

¼ cup extra-virgin olive oil

2 garlic cloves

½ to 1 teaspoon red pepper flakes

1 large anchovy fillet, finely chopped

1 teaspoon kosher salt, plus more for the pasta water

12 ounces brown rice spaghetti (See Note)

Grated Pecorino Romano, for garnish, optional

Freshly ground black pepper, optional

1. Cut off the thick bottom part of the kale (at least 4 inches) and discard. Cut the remaining bunch of kale in half vertically and into thin ¼-inch slices. You want the kale to be thoroughly dry because otherwise it can splatter when you put it in the hot oil. Personally, I buy organic and don't wash my kale.

2. Place a large pan fitted with a lid over medium heat and let it get hot for a few minutes.

3. Add the olive oil, the garlic, and the red pepper flakes in that order.

4. Notice as the garlic lightly bubbles. It is infusing the olive oil with its flavor. Make sure it does not burn, as this will add a bitter flavor to your whole dish.

5. Add the anchovy to the pan, stirring so it dissolves in the oil.

6. Just as the garlic becomes translucent and slightly golden brown, toss the kale into the oil (use tongs if you have them) until it is all coated.

7. Let the kale sauté for a couple of minutes, and then add 1 teaspoon of salt and ½ cup of water. Turn the heat to low, and cover the pan.

8. Cook until the kale is very dark and tender, about 20 minutes. It should fall apart in your mouth when you taste it. Check every so often to make sure it does not burn. If it looks dry, add a bit more water. Remove the pan from the heat.

9. Bring a large pot of water to boil over high heat. Throw in a handful of kosher salt, followed by the pasta. Stir, and cook *al dente*.

10. When the pasta is nearly done, turn the heat under the sauce to medium high, a *fuoco vivace*, a lively flame.

11. Immediately add the pasta to the pan with the kale and toss the pasta, using tongs or two forks, until the kale is evenly distributed around the spaghetti.

12. Divide onto plates and generously add freshly grated Pecorino and freshly ground pepper, if desired.

13. *A tavola*, to the table!

Note: I prefer the Tinkyada Brown Rice Pasta, Spaghetti Style. It's a whole-grain pasta that's gluten-free and kosher certified. One package is smaller than a normal box of pasta. This recipe reflects that.

Rigatoni al Tonno e Capperi

PASTA WITH TUNA AND CAPERS

All Italians have a signature pasta dish they claim to make better than anyone else. It's usually something they regularly whip up in the kitchen even when there's nothing in the house to eat. This is called *l'arte d'arrangiarsi* or the art of making something out of nothing. Every single Italian keeps a few special ingredients on hand so he or she can *arrangiarsi* at the drop of a hat. You can always find a slab of pancetta in my friend Adolfo's fridge. His signature dish: *Spaghetti all'Amatriciana*. Federico makes the best *Burro e Parmigiano* (butter and parmigiano), for which he melts the butter in a pasta bowl that he places over the pasta water as it boils. Andrea will make a pasta out of anything, and then drizzle a few drops of white truffle oil on top; he's a bit fancier than the rest of us.

My signature pasta is *Pasta al Tonno e Capperi*. All of its ingredients have a long shelf life, so even when I haven't gone to the market and am too lazy to move, I can still root around in my kitchen to find garlic and onion, anchovies and Kalamata olives, along with several years' supply of capers packed in salt that I brought back from the Aeolian Islands off Sicily. I can also usually find a can of tuna and a can of tomatoes in my pantry. But even when I can't, I've made this exact pasta without those two key ingredients and it was delicious.

Of course, if you make this without the tuna, you're making *pasta puttanesca*, which literally translates to "slutty pasta," as *puttana* means "whore." Theories diverge on what makes this pasta slutty: one professor says it's because "you throw a bit of everything in her." (Pasta being feminine in Italian.) Most pasta sauces use either garlic or onion, *puttanesca* takes both. Another theory posits that this was the dish commonly served in Italian *bordelli* (whorehouses).

Whatever the case, I've impressed quite a few gentlemen with my ability to whip up a *Tonno e Capperi* or *puttanesca* out of "nothing." A sprinkling of parsley—or even better, mint—which does require that at least something be fresh in your house, takes this pasta over the edge.

1 (14-ounce) can whole Italian tomatoes

¼ cup extra-virgin olive oil

2 garlic cloves

½ to 1 teaspoon red pepper flakes

1 shallot or ¼ of an onion, finely chopped

1 anchovy, chopped

2 Tablespoons salt-packed capers, rinsed and chopped

6 pitted Kalamata olives

1 (5 to 7-ounce) can albacore tuna, packed in water or olive oil

Kosher salt, for pasta water

1 pound rigatoni

A small handful fresh mint, chopped

1. Briefly pulse the tomatoes in a food processor or blender. Or crush them well with your hands. Set aside.

2. Place a large pan over medium heat and let it get hot for a few minutes.

3. Add the olive oil, the garlic, red pepper flakes, and the shallot or onion, in that order. Be careful they don't burn or brown.

4. Once the *soffritto* is translucent (in a few minutes), add the anchovy and stir until it has mostly dissolved.

5. Add the capers and olives. Let them sizzle for a couple of minutes, and then add the tomatoes, stirring to combine.

6. Let the tomatoes cook for a moment before adding the canned tuna and its water or olive oil. Break up the tuna. The water or olive oil of the tuna will add flavor as the sauce reduces. Let the sauce cook until it has thickened and is no longer watery, about 15 to 20 minutes. Remove the pan from the heat.

7. Bring a large pot of water to boil over high heat. Throw in a handful of kosher salt, followed by the pasta. Stir, and cook *al dente*.

8. When the pasta is nearly done, turn the heat under the sauce to medium high, a *fuoco vivace*, a lively flame.

9. Drain and add the pasta to the sauce, and toss until all the noodles are well coated.

10. Serve and top with freshly chopped mint.

Pasta Francesca

WITH EGGPLANT, OLIVES, MINT, AND RICOTTA SALATA

Here's an example of why I love Italians: One Monday morning, I called my friend Francesca, and asked her if she could meet for coffee. "I am so busy, I can't do it," she said—an odd response for an Italian. Italians in general are not a busy people.

"Wait, wait," she interjected. "If you want, I will make a sauce and bring it to your house, and we can have a pasta for lunch." A far more appropriate response—even in the most strenuous times, Italians always find time to eat well and share the goods.

"I ate the most amazing pasta last night!" Francesca explained. (I can't tell you how many times I've heard that exact statement come out of an Italian's mouth. They love to talk about what they ate, and they remember every meal in sensuous detail, as though they're describing love making. This may be why Italians have a reputation as such skilled lovers. I did live in Italy for awhile, and—no comment.)

In any case, Francesca was inspired by the delicious pasta she'd eaten the night before at *Mozza* in Hollywood. "I paid very close attention to the ingredients while I was eating," she explained. "I want to try to make it." So she prepared a sauce with eggplant and ricotta.

Francesca is an amazing cook, but lunch that day was not quite amazing, so the recipe below is not quite the pasta we ate that day. It had *fresh* ricotta, which to me drowned out the flavor of the sauce, and she'd cooked the mint in the sauce, rather than sprinkling it generously on top. (Fresh mint, in my opinion, is what takes this pasta into a totally different realm.) She had used only a very little bit of tomato, and though I don't use much more, I like how the tomatoes add a light freshness of flavor, reminiscent of the shores of southern Italy.

Needless to say, I would have never have thought of combining eggplant, olives, and mint had it not been for my stunning and talented friend. Voila! *Pasta Francesca!*

P.S. If you'd like to see Francesca, watch the hit series *The Assassination of Gianni Versace*—she plays Versace's mother.

1 (14-ounce) can whole Italian tomatoes

¼ cup extra-virgin olive oil

4 to 5 Italian eggplants, cut into ¼-inch rounds (See Note)

3 to 4 garlic cloves, cut in half lengthwise

¼ cup Greek green olives, roughly chopped

1 teaspoon kosher salt, plus more for pasta water

¾ teaspoon red pepper flakes

2 basil leaves

1 pound rigatoni

½ cup chopped fresh mint leaves

2 ounces ricotta salata, grated, optional (See Note)

1. Briefly pulse the tomatoes in a food processor or blender or crush them well with your hands. Set aside.

2. Place a large pan with a cover over medium heat and let it get hot for a few minutes.

3. Add the olive oil, followed by the eggplant and two of the garlic cloves (four halves). Using tongs or a slotted spoon, stir the eggplant to make sure all the rounds are coated in olive oil.

4. Add the olives, sprinkle with salt, and cover the pan.

5. Every few minutes, uncover the pan, mix to make sure the eggplant rounds each get their turn on the bottom and to make sure the garlic does not brown. Continue with this process until the eggplant is cooked and is beginning to fall apart, about 20 minutes.

6. Add the tomatoes, the remaining garlic, the red pepper flakes, and the basil leaves. Keep the pan covered, and continue to check and stir every so often to make sure nothing is sticking to the bottom, 12 to 15 minutes until done. If the sauce seems a little liquidy, keep it over the heat uncovered until it thickens. Remove the pan from the heat.

7. Bring a large pot of water to boil over high heat. Throw in a handful of kosher salt, followed by the pasta, stir, and cook *al dente*.

8. When the pasta is nearly done, turn the heat under the sauce to medium high, a *fuoco vivace*, a lively flame.

9. Drain and add the pasta to the sauce. Use tongs to flip pasta over itself until it is completely coated in the sauce.

10. Serve onto plates and generously top each one with the fresh chopped mint and ricotta salata.

Notes:

Italian eggplants are smaller than the more familiar Western eggplant. They're lobed and shaped like a teardrop. If you cannot find Italian eggplants, use one medium-sized "regular" eggplant. Slice it into ¼ inch rounds, and then into quarters.

Ricotta salata, which I suggest as a topping, literally translates to "salty ricotta." It is an aged version of the mushy ricotta you know from cannoli or from American versions of lasagna. It can be found at gourmet grocers, has a delicate flavor, and will look like beautiful snow once grated with a microplane. Try it on roasted vegetables and salads.

SHOULD I BE USING THE PASTA WATER IN MY SAUCES?

First of all, I don't discuss this in my introductory pasta class. So if you're a beginner, go ahead and skip this classroom corner until you're ready for it.

The starchy and salty pasta water can be a great addition to a sauce. Here's the low down: if you undercook the pasta to pre-*al dente* status, and add it to your sauce along with some pasta water, you can finish cooking the pasta right there in the pan. The noodles will absorb the delicious liquids, creating a creamier coating for each noodle, no matter what sauce you use. That said, you have to be an expert to to know exactly how much to undercook your pasta and how much pasta water to use to get it right. Watery pasta is a big no-no for Italians.

If you want to experiment with this process, try *Pasta di Farro con gli Asparagi,* or read the *spiel* and follow instructions to my *Linguine allo Scoglio*. It'll give you a good sense of how it works. Otherwise, try undercooking pasta by two minutes, add it to your sauce with a cup of pasta water, and stir on a high flame. If the water evaporates and the pasta still isn't done, add more.

WHAT PASTA GOES WITH WHAT SAUCE?

This is a long conversation, and I'm sure every Italian you encounter would love to wax philosophical on this topic. Here's the scoop, as I understand it: You want to make sure that your choice of pasta can properly "carry" the sauce, and heighten its flavor. For example thin angel hair cannot take the weight of a meat sauce, and a simple *aglio olio* cannot be appreciated with the thickness of a *penne*. Tomato and other vegetable-based sauces are often paired with *pasta corta* (short pasta) like *penne rigate*, *rigatoni*, or *strozzapreti*. Meat sauces are usually paired with *pasta lunga all'uovo* (long pasta made with egg), such as *tagliatelle* or *pappardelle*, while a seafood pasta is usually found with *linguine* or *spaghetti*. The moral of the story: pay attention to the unique marriage between the sauce and the texture of the pasta with it, and make your choices from there.

Pasta di Farro con gli Asparagi

SPELT PASTA WITH ASPARAGUS, LEMON, AND NUTMEG

When I cater a dinner party, I take the crafting of the menu very seriously. Of course, I invite my clients' input, but ultimately *I* get the final word. That's because a meal should flow smoothly from one course to the next, taking diners on a journey to a place of gustatory contentment. The client might want to serve lasagna, steak, potatoes and ice cream, but if I overstuff the guests with heavy rich foods, they won't be content. They'll be bloated. There's a difference.

This task can be tricky when you want to fit a pasta into the mix. For a recent dinner party I catered, we had decided on *Grilled Eggplant and Burrata Involtini* as a sit-down appetizer and *Pesce alla Mamma di Edo* as the main dish. I needed a pasta that didn't have a tomato-based sauce like the *involtini*, didn't have olives like the fish, and that could take us from the cheese-y intro to the seaside palate of the main. Asparagus would be perfect, I thought! With its bright flavor and color, asparagus pairs well with cheese or fish, making it a perfect bridge. Only, I had never made asparagus pasta.

If I'd been in Tuscany, I might've asked Maria for advice, but since I was in Los Angeles, I used the traditional Italian method known as *googleare* (verb, infinitive: *to google*), sitting at my computer and searching through dozens of Italian recipes for *pasta ai asparagi.* What I encountered took me by total surprise. Many of the asparagus pasta recipes used nutmeg, which I never would've thought to use since asparagus is a springtime flavor and nutmeg evokes winter. Others called for lemon, which sounded delicious, but I'd never made a pasta with lemon and wasn't sure how to approach that.

I decided I wanted the pasta to be creamy, but without the added heaviness of actual cream. To achieve the right texture, I pureed half of the asparagus after cooking, leaving the other half its crunch. I also decided to char the tips of the asparagus and to serve them on top the pasta, creating three different textures with the same vegetable. I pair the asparagus with *pasta di farro* (made from spelt) because I find the whole grain grounds the flavor of the verdant asparagus. Needless to say, this recipe was an enormous hit at the dinner party, and now I'm proud to add it to my repertoire.

Serves 4 to 6

2 pounds asparagus

½ cup extra-virgin olive oil, divided

2½ teaspoons kosher salt, plus more for pasta water

Freshly ground pepper

2 garlic cloves

½ cup finely chopped shallots

Zest of 1 lemon, plus more for serving

½ of a whole nutmeg, grated

1 pound whole wheat spelt or semolina pasta (See Note)

Ricotta salata or Parmigiano Reggiano, for grating, optional (See Note)

1. Heat the broiler on high.

2. Remove and discard the bottom third of the asparagus. Cut off the tips, and set aside. Slice the remaining stalks into ¼-inch thick rounds.

3. Place the asparagus tips on a foil-covered baking sheet and drizzle with ¼ cup of the olive oil, a scant teaspoon kosher salt, and 60 grinds of the pepper mill.

4. Mix the asparagus with your hands, and lay the tips down so that they're flat. Place them under the broiler until they sizzle and look a bit charred, about 5 minutes. Set aside.

5. Place a large pan over medium heat, and let it heat for a few minutes.

6. Add the remaining oil to the hot pan followed by the garlic and the shallots. Let them sauté until translucent, 3 to 4 minutes.

7. Add the asparagus rounds, lemon zest, nutmeg, and 40 grinds of the pepper mill. Sauté for a few minutes, then add 1½ teaspoons kosher salt. Continue to sauté until the asparagus is soft, another 8 minutes or so. Remove from the heat.

8. Remove the garlic. Puree about half of the asparagus rounds in a blender until smooth (if you need to add some hot water to get it to puree smoothly, that's fine). Place it back in the pan.

9. Bring a large pot of water to boil over high heat. Add a handful of kosher salt, toss in the pasta, and stir. When the pasta is 2 minutes from being al dente, place the sauce over medium high heat and use a mug to scoop out some pasta water.

10. Drain the pasta a minute earlier than *al dente*, and put it in the pan along with ½ cup of the pasta water. Keep tossing the pasta until the water has evaporated and the pasta is fully cooked *al dente*. If the water has evaporated and it's still not *al dente*, add more and keep tossing. You're a pro.

11. Plate the pasta and top with the roasted asparagus tips. Garnish with grated cheese and lemon zest (for beauty) if desired.

Notes: You can use spelt or regular semolina pasta.

Ricotta salata, which I suggest as a topping, literally translates to "salty ricotta." It is an aged version of the mushy ricotta you know from cannoli or American versions of lasagna. It can be found at gourmet grocers, has a delicate flavor, and will look like beautiful snow once grated with a microplane. Try it on roasted vegetables and salads.

Linguine allo Scoglio

PASTA WITH MUSSELS AND CLAMS

Before I tell you how to make this dish that will transport you to the sun-kissed, azured-sea, rocky-shored, hot-and-gorgeous-sunbather-laden isle of Ponza, off the coast of Rome, I would like to issue a complaint. It's a *kvetch* necessary for the *spiel*.

For many years I cooked what I considered a masterful *pasta con le vongole* (pasta with clams) without using the precious juices released by the clams as they cook. I knew Italian chefs considered the juices the secret to this dish, but I didn't know what to do with them and certainly wasn't going to allow my pasta to sit in a watery plate of clam juice—that goes against every Italian culinary principle in existence.

Despite researching dozens of Italian recipes and Youtube videos of Italian chefs, I couldn't find anyone who properly addresses the steps in between cooking the clams, which creates an abundance of liquid, and then having a precisely *al dente pasta* with a sauce that perfectly coats each noodle with no run-off on the side of your plate. What are these chefs doing that they are not telling us?

Some recipes add wine, some don't. Some add tomato, some don't. Most recipes call for covering the pan when cooking the clams, which allows for no evaporation of liquids. Furthermore, most encourage you to save water from the pasta pot in order to add even more liquid to the sauce once the pasta is done. Where the hell does all that water go? Maybe because Italian clams are smaller, less water is produced in the cooking process? So I consulted American cookbooks, which brought me to Mario.

Ah, Mario Batali, you ginger genius, lately undone by your own appetites (particularly your alleged appetite for inappropriate groping). Your restaurant *Mozza* is one of my favorites in LA, so I went straight to *Molto Gusto* for guidance. Unfortunately, your recipe for *Linguine with*

Clams—closed lid, wine, extra water from the pasta—led to another watery disaster. Mario, there's a secret step in that recipe that you are not telling us!

Finally, I found another recipe of Mario's online that finally set this pasta right. He left the mollusks uncovered and undercooked the pasta so he could finish cooking it in the pan. Aha!!!

SO HERE'S WHAT YOU NEED TO DO:

1. **Cook the clams over a lively heat UNCOVERED.** Aside from allowing the juices to condense, this will also slow down the time it takes for them to open and help you synchronize the timing with the cooking of the pasta.

2. **Undercook the pasta by two minutes.** If you don't know what two-minute-undercooked-pasta tastes like, this recipe is not for you. Yet. Practice with more forgiving recipes first.

3. **Finish cooking the pasta with the clams.** It will soak up all their precious juices, flavoring every bite without leaving a puddle on your plate.

Okay, *kvetch* complete! Now go make this pasta and imagine yourself on Ponza, surrounded by those gorgeous sunbathers. Slurp slurp!

¼ cup extra-virgin olive oil

4 garlic cloves, sliced in half vertically

1 teaspoon red pepper flakes

2 vine-ripened tomatoes, chopped

1 teaspoon kosher salt

1 pound linguine

1 pound clams

1 pound mussels

½ cup or a "glug" of dry white wine

¼ cup freshly chopped flat-leaf parsley

Notes: The flavors of this pasta are too subtle for cheese, so don't even try it! See Page 204 for culinary statutes. If you feel it needs a little something, add some flaky salt.

1. Read the headnote above. It's necessary for the proper execution of this recipe.

2. Bring a large pot of water to boil over high heat.

3. Place a large pan over medium heat, and let it get hot for a few minutes. Choose a pan that's deep enough to hold the clams and the mussels along with all of the pasta once cooked.

4. Add the olive oil, the garlic, and the red pepper flakes, in that order.

5. When the garlic is translucent, a minute or two, add the tomatoes and stir.

6. Add the salt to the tomatoes, which will help them release their water.

7. Cook for about 5 minutes or until the tomatoes have begun to form a sauce and the liquid has begun to tighten.

8. At this point, add a handful of kosher salt and the pasta to the boiling water. Stir. And jump immediately to the next step, 9.

9. While the pasta is cooking, put the clams and mussels in with the tomatoes, and add the wine. Shake the pan and stir gently at times to create space for the clams and mussels to open. Let them cook for about 7 minutes. At this point, the pasta should be about 2 minutes short of al dente. Drain it, and throw it into the clam and mussel sauce to finish cooking.

10. Toss with care for the next couple of minutes, until the pasta has soaked in the juices and has become al dente.

11. Sprinkle with parsley and serve!

Tamburello di Melanzane

EGGPLANT PASTA "TAMBOURINE" WITH BURRATA

Allie, a friend and reluctant cooking student, stopped by one evening in a particularly bad mood. She was emotionally distraught, depressed, and in no state to be consoled. Fortunately for Allie, I was cooking my first *timballo*.

Timballo is a baked Italian dish usually filled with pasta or rice. The word itself means drum, as it's shaped like a kettledrum. But because I cook mine in a simple springform pan, so it looks more like a tambourine, I call it a *tamburello*. Whatever it's called, for Allie that night, my tomato, basil, and burrata pasta-cake, wrapped in grilled eggplant, meant *love*.

By the end of dinner, Allie was laughing and talking about exciting possibilities for her professional and personal life. I pointed out her change of mood and asked if she thought the *tamburello* had anything to do with it. "Oh my God, yes!" she said. "I never realized this before, but good food, made with love, has the power to change a person. It could change the whole world!"

In my head, I was steaming; I'd been telling her this FOREVER!! I say those *precise* words in a video on the homepage of my website. Was she not paying attention?

In all fairness to Allie, it's not something you learn from words. It's something that must be felt. Tasted. And my *tamburello* led her there.

Lead someone there yourself with this recipe.

Special equipment: 9-inch springform pan

Kosher salt

1 pound penne rigate, or any other tubular pasta

1½ recipe *Simple Tomato and Basil Sauce*
(Page 58), warmed

1 pound burrata, cut into very small pieces

1 bunch basil, thinly sliced

Extra-virgin olive oil

Grilled Eggplant (Page 63)

Grated Parmigiano Reggiano, to serve

Make the pasta:

1. Bring a large pot of water to boil over high heat. Throw in a handful of salt, and cook the pasta until it's 4 minutes away from being al dente, or a little over half the cooking time suggested on the box. Drain the pasta.

2. Mix the hot pasta with the tomato sauce in its pot or in a large mixing bowl. Add the burrata and ½ teaspoon of salt. Stir to melt. The sauce should look creamy from the added cheese. Add the basil, and mix to combine. Set aside.

Build the tamburello:

1. Preheat the oven to 350°F.

2. Line the springform pan with the roasted eggplant. Your goal is to create an "eggplant bowl" that you will fill with the pasta. In order for the eggplant bowl to hold the pasta, it can't have cracks. So you need to overlap each piece of eggplant to make sure there are no openings. Here's how to do it:

3. Use a little olive oil on a paper towel to lightly oil the springform pan.

4. Use a few slices of eggplant to mostly cover the bottom of the pan. Be sure to overlap the edges.

5. Begin to lay the eggplant up the sides of the pan, and let the pieces hang over the top edge. Each eggplant slice must slightly overlap the one next to it and must overlap the one below it on the bottom of the pan.

6. Go around until you have a "bowl" made of eggplant.

7. Fill your eggplant bowl with the pasta, pushing it down to make sure all spaces are filled. Flip over the eggplant side flaps and cover the pasta with remaining eggplant slices, overlapping of course.

8. Bake in the oven for 30 minutes. (Since the oil may seep through the cracks of the cake pan, I usually place a baking sheet on the bottom rack of the oven to catch it.)

9. Remove and let sit for about 10 minutes. (The longer it sits, the less messy it will be when cut.)

10. Place a large serving plate on top of the pan. Holding onto the plate and the pan, flip them over carefully so that the plate is on bottom.

11. Remove the springform pan.

12. Use a large sharp knife to cut and a spatula/ cake knife to serve.

13. Top with freshly grated Parmigiano

Turkey "Bolognese"

Let me be very upfront about the title of this dish, lest I draw the ire of the Bolognese people: I know this isn't a *bolognese!*

Some background: *bolognese* refers to Bologna, a northern Italian city in the Emilia Romagna region, known for its extreme left-wing politics, portico-covered sidewalks, its thousand-year-old university, and of course, its food. From the nutrient-rich grassy countryside of Emilia Romagna comes prosciutto di Parma, Parmigiano Reggiano, along with many of the best butters, creams and other cheeses. This makes for a deliciously rich cuisine.

Every region of Italy has its own *ragù di carne* (meat sauce), made from local ingredients. In Bologna, that means pork, milk, and butter. A *bolognese* meat sauce uses very little tomato, cooking the meat in milk for hours. Chefs in Tuscany, Piedmont, and Naples don't make their *ragù* that way, and, in fact, a Neapolitan chef might throw a pan at you if you call his bright red meat sauce, laden with local sausage, a *bolognese*—as if Bologna invented meat sauce! Unless it's made in the traditional style of Bologna, meat sauce is NOT *bolognese*.

Unfortunately, *bolognese* has become the American shorthand for meat sauce. So for years, my cooking students have requested a "turkey *bolognese*" recipe. I've held them off, explaining the etymology, trying not to let my blood pressure rise as I hear about how they've gone ahead and substituted turkey for beef in my meat sauces. Turkey has a flavor of its own, I explain, and requires its own techniques and spices.

However, in recent years, I found out that even Italians have been cooking *ragù di tacchino* (turkey meat sauce).

So I gave up! I invented a recipe, using woodsy herbs such as rosemary, sage, and thyme to accentuate the forest-y flavor of wild turkey and only using the dark meat—use light meat and you'll end up with dry, grainy sauce. I also accentuated the flavor with chicken sausage.

This is a *ragù in bianco*, which means "in white"—in other words, meat with broth that coats and penetrates each noodle, instead of tomatoes. This will not look like the meat sauce you expected, nor will it taste like it. It will be better.

This recipe took me completely by surprise. In struggling to create a meat sauce with turkey instead of beef, I've ended up creating something utterly delicious and unexpected. After testing this recipe, my nieces, my brother-in-law, and my father all had seconds and thirds. No one could stop talking about how good it was. It tastes a lot better than it looks. It tastes like home.

2 Tablespoons extra-virgin olive oil

2 Tablespoons unsalted butter or duck fat

1 small onion, finely chopped

1 medium carrot, finely chopped

1 stalk of celery, finely chopped

2 teaspoons finely chopped thyme leaves

2 teaspoons finely chopped rosemary leaves

7 large sage leaves, finely chopped
or 1 teaspoon dried sage

1½ teaspoon fennel seeds, roughly chopped

1 pound ground dark meat turkey

½ pound mild Italian chicken sausage, casings removed

¾ cup dry white wine

1 cup *No-Chop Chicken Broth* (Page 150)

¾ teaspoon kosher salt

25 grinds of the pepper mill

Grated Parmigiano Reggiano

Chopped flat-leaf parsley, for garnish

1 pound rigatoni

1. Place a heavy-bottomed pan over medium heat and let it get hot for a couple of minutes.

2. Add the olive oil, butter, onion, carrot, celery, thyme, rosemary, sage, and fennel. Stir and let cook until softened, about 15 minutes.

3. Add the ground turkey and chicken sausage. With the side of a wooden spoon, "cut" the two meats until they are well mixed and have been incorporated into the *soffritto* mixture. Cook until the meat no longer looks raw, about 7 minutes. In this step the meat will take on the flavors of the *soffritto*.

4. Add the wine and let it evaporate.

5. Add the broth and the salt. Grind in the pepper. Cover the pan with a lid, and decrease the heat to low. Cook for an hour. Taste to adjust the seasoning. If it lacks flavor, add more salt.

6. Bring a large pot of water to boil over high heat. Throw in a handful of kosher salt, followed by the pasta, and stir.

7. When the pasta is nearly done, turn the heat under the sauce to medium high, a *fuoco vivace*, a lively flame.

8. Drain the pasta when it's just a touch before *al dente*, and toss it in with the sauce for a couple of minutes, letting it complete its cooking in the juices.

9. Plate the pasta. Top with grated cheese and chopped parsley and any leftover broth remaining in the pan.

Make Ahead Prep: If you choose to make the sauce a day or so in advance, or even freeze it, you might need to add more broth when you heat it up again so it can soak into the noodles for full flavor.

WHEN CAN I PUT ONIONS IN THE FOOD PROCESSOR?

The answer an Italian woman will give you: never! They would use a *mezzaluna*, a half-moon-shaped, hand-held knife, to cut onions finely. Fortunately for you, I'm not actually an Italian woman, and I'm willing to take the easy route when I don't think it damages the quality of the food. For example, it's okay to use the "pulse" button on your food processor to turn your onion into little pieces if you're making meatballs. Just remember, the machine makes the onions lose liquid, so if you're pan frying, the water from onions will make your oil splatter. And do NOT use the food processor when you're making a *soffritto* for meat sauce or soup, because with the extra liquid, you'll be simmering your onions instead of browning them, which means you'll miss out on all the flavor. So get yourself a pair of onion goggles and a sharp knife, and chop in the name of food that tastes like love.

WHAT DO I SERVE PASTA WITH?

NOTHING! Pasta is not a side dish. It is its own course. It's considered a *primo* in Italian cooking. Though that means "first course," it comes after the *aperitivo* and *antipasti* (starter cocktails and appetizers), but before the *secondo*, the meat dish. When Italians eat at home, pasta is often the main or only dish of the meal, sometimes with a salad or some veggies to follow. Italians never serve pasta as a side dish. It's too hard to digest alongside other foods, so keep it on its own.

Ragù di Carne

A NO-PORK, RELATIVELY QUICK MEAT SAUCE

Ragù, in Italian, means meat sauce. When I was a kid, my family made *ragù* by dumping a jar of Ragú Spaghetti Sauce on top of ground meat that had been mixed with a seasoning packet labeled *Italian*—as if Italy has one flavor! Once plated, we shook a green canister of parmesan over it.

I loved it. How could I not? My young palate was addicted to the MSG in the seasoning packet and the high fructose corn syrup in the Ragú.

Since then, my palate has matured, and I've read about what processed food does to your metabolism. I've often wondered if the maternal notion of food-as-love skipped a generation. Of course, times were different. My mother chose feminism over the kitchen, and even though our family's food didn't nourish me emotionally, I wouldn't have gained the *chutzpah* to tackle the shortcomings of the American food philosophy without her. And along the way, I learned that feminism and cooking aren't at odds; in fact, my work in the kitchen is an expression of my ambitions and aspirations as a woman.

A good meat sauce isn't something you dump out of a can or whip up in 20 minutes. It's an act of love that takes time. Here is a meat sauce that can be done in 2½ hours—a short time for a meat sauce. And except for 30 minutes of this time, you can be enjoying a glass of wine or taking a nap.

Note: Most Italian *ragùs* are made with pork. This recipe isn't. I don't keep kosher, but I rarely eat pork and never cook with it. This recipe, however, does contain lots of love, which makes up for what we aren't putting in with pancetta or sausage or prosciutto or ground pork loins.

2 cups homemade or store-bought
chicken, veal, or beef broth

3 carrots, divided

3 celery stalks, divided

1 Tablespoon chopped parsley
plus one whole sprig

1 large or two small onions, finely chopped

¼ cup extra-virgin olive oil

2 bay leaves

1 sprig thyme

1 veal shank with marrow bone,
approximately ¾ pound

10 ounces boneless beef chuck in one piece

1 cup wine

1 (28-ounce) can Italian plum tomatoes

1 Tablespoon kosher salt

40 grinds of the pepper mill

½ whole nutmeg, grated

½ stick unsalted butter or
2 tablespoons duck fat, optional

1 pound tagliatelle

Parmigiano Reggiano, for grating

1. Heat the broth in a medium pot over medium low heat and throw in the whole carrot, the whole celery stalk, and the sprig of parsley. If you kept the outer part of the onion, add that too. Let it simmer until it's reduced by half. Remove and discard the vegetables. Set aside.

2. Finely chop the remaining carrots and celery stalks. Cut the meat away from the marrow bone of the veal shank.

3. Place a large pot or Dutch oven on the stove and turn it to low. Add the olive oil, chopped onions, chopped carrots, chopped celery, bay leaves, chopped parsley, and the sprig of thyme. Add the marrow bone. Cook for at least 30 minutes, until the *soffritto* is nice and golden.

4. Increase the heat to medium high. Add the veal shank meat and beef chuck, scooching the *soffritto* to the side to make room for the meat. Let the meat brown well on both sides until it sticks a little to the bottom of the pan— this is good. It means flavor!

5. Decrease the heat to low while you complete the next step, 6.

6. Take the meat out of the pot, and finely chop it by hand or in the food processor. (Do not overprocess and end up with ground meat!) Add the chopped meat back to the pot.

7. Increase the heat to medium high. Add the wine and cook until it evaporates, leaving just a touch of moisture around the meat mixture.

8. Briefly pulse the tomatoes in a food processor or blender.

9. Decrease the heat to low, add the tomatoes, broth, salt and pepper, and nutmeg. Cover, and cook for about 2 hours, or longer if you have time. If the sauce has not thickened, cook uncovered until it does.

10. Add the butter (or duck fat), and let it melt.

11. Remove half the sauce and set it aside for leftovers. If you like your pasta with a lot of sauce, leave more in the pot.

12. Bring a large pot of water to boil over high heat. Throw in a handful of kosher salt, followed by the pasta. Stir, and cook *al dente*.

13. When the pasta is nearly done, turn the heat under the sauce to medium high, a *fuoco vivace*, a lively flame.

14. Drain and add the pasta to the sauce. Toss to coat noodles. Serve with grated Parmigiano.

PASTA *FAUX PAS*

When I go to authentic Italian restaurants here in Los Angeles, the waiters are surprised by my command of the language, seasoned as it is with quips in Roman dialect. They thank me for teaching women to cook, praying my influence will reach the Americans they date. Mostly, they're deeply relieved to discuss the horrific culinary state of the union with a local who understands their culture.

Trust me. I know exactly why your Italian waiters are laughing at you. Here are some *faux pas* that will earn you the derision of your *carmeriere* when he returns to the kitchen:

» **You add a topping to your pasta.** Innovation is not the power of Italian cuisine. Respecting tradition is.

When you ask for shrimp to be added to your carbonara, you're disrespecting tradition. Adding a delicate seafood to a pasta that has creamy egg and fatty bacon is nonsensical. Eggs, pancetta, and shrimp don't come from the same earthscape. The first two are of the land, the latter of the sea. It's geographical culinary idiocracy.

Nor does chicken go on pasta. When people in my family do this, I lower my head in shame. I know exactly what the waiters are thinking. If you need protein in your meal, order the grilled chicken breast (something that Italians don't eat, to begin with, because it's considered the dry, flavorless part of the bird) as a *secondo*. A hunk of meat on pasta dampens the flavor of the sauce and ruins the texture of the dish.

» **You order pizza and pasta in the same meal.** Italians think a lot about digestion. Too many carbs in one sitting is a recipe for bloat. If you get up from a meal and feel sick, they consider it a poor reflection on the cook. But if you order food that overloads your stomach with improperly matched dishes, that's a poor reflection on you. And yes, your waiter notices.

» **You ask for cheese on a spicy pasta.** Again, this is about digestion. I'm telling you, Italians really think a lot about digestion, which could be why they can eat liberally and still stay thin. The combination of hot peppers and cheese is a recipe for curdling acid and gas. Furthermore, cream dampens the fire of spice, so flavor-wise, this is an incompatible pairing.

» **You put cheese on a seafood pasta.** You are essentially putting a cow's baby food on shellfish, and eating it. I don't think I need to elaborate on this further.

» **You eat bread with your pasta.** Again, adding carbs to your carbs is laughable to Italians. Pasta is a revered course. It's meant to be eaten immediately and quickly, while hot. The pasta is about texture as much as flavor. Adding bread to the mix disrespects the pasta itself and indicates someone who can't appreciate the subtle delicacy of the *primo piatto*.

That said, it's totally acceptable to *fare la scarpetta*. Swiping your bread along the plate of leftover sauce, after the pasta itself has been finished, is a way to let nothing go to waste, to fill your belly in hard economic times, or simply to enjoy every molecule of the love-filled sauce.

» **You cut your spaghetti.** Not only will this make an Italian waiter laugh at you, it might give him heart failure. *Lo spaghetto*, the singular of spaghetti, is perhaps the single most apotheosized entity of Italian culture, in close competition with the Ferrari. To take a fork or knife and cut the spaghetti (or break it before boiling) is a flippant act of irreverence. But, "why, why why," the waiter will ask himself, "did you order spaghetti if you only planned to hack it apart and desecrate its most sacred quality?" That is, its length. The beauty of the *spaghetto* is its specific texture, twirled and shoved into your mouth. Eliminating the twirling in spaghetti-eating defeats the purpose of spaghetti.

If you are a victim to any of these pasta *faux pas*, don't worry; recognizing the problem is the first step to recovery.

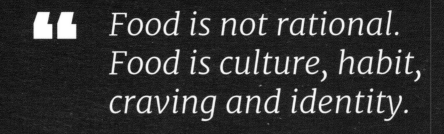

> *Food is not rational. Food is culture, habit, craving and identity.*
>
> *– Jonathan Safran Foer*

I Can't Believe It's Not Pasta!

ZUCCHINI LINGUINE WITH DECONSTRUCTED PESTO

ONE-PAN SWEET POTATO PASTA ALL'ARRABBIATA

CAULIFLOWER MAC N' CHEESE AI QUATTRO FORMAGGI

SPAGHETTI SQUASH PRIMAVERA

NO-NOODLE LASAGNA

IN A PERFECT WORLD, EATING LOTS OF PASTA WOULD TAKE inches off our waistlines, enrich our cells with nutrients, reduce bloating in the gluten-sensitive, and rejuvenate our skin to boot! Alas, we do not live in a perfect world. As much as I love pasta, it's a high-carb food that most of us can't eat every day. However, we can eat spaghetti squash and zucchini every day, and just because they're healthy doesn't mean we can't dress them like an Italian would pasta. So here's a chapter that does just that. It is full of recipes that replace pasta with vibrant vegetables that can satisfy our deep cravings for Italian dishes while surprising us with delightful new textures and flavors. Maybe this is a perfect world after all.

Zucchini Linguine with Deconstructed Pesto

I'll be honest with you, making noodles out of vegetables with a spiralizer wasn't my idea. I hadn't even caught wind of it until my cooking student, nutritionist Shira Lenchewski, MS, RD and I decided to teach a class together. She basically gave me the menu. "Elana, you need a zucchini noodle pasta." A what? "Trust me. Look it up, and make the best one ever."

Believe it or not, I like taking orders, particularly when given by people who actually know what they're doing. And Shira does. As the author of *The Food Therapist*, Shira's specialty is helping people bridge healthy relationships with food, with indulgence and mindfulness as core values. Since I had to recreate my own relationship with food years ago, I understand this. And for me, the key to balanced eating is creating conscious, nutritious, healthy meals that have the flavor of sin.

This zucchini pasta is just that. I mean, if we're making noodles out of squash (zucchini is a member of the squash family), then why not put a totally authentic pesto *Genovese* on top?!

You'll notice only some of the pine nuts are mixed into the pesto. The rest are left whole, to give a crunchy texture and some bite. And be careful not to overcook the zucchini, as that will make it watery. It's not the worst thing, but strive for the vegetable equivalent of *al dente*.

Serves 2

Special equipment: Spiralizer

4 zucchini

1 Tablespoon extra-virgin olive oil

Pesto Genovese, partially deconstructed (Page 60)

1. Use your spiralizer to turn your zucchini into "pasta noodles." You want them to be of medium thickness, if possible.

2. Place a heavy-bottomed pan over medium heat, and let it get hot for a couple of minutes.

3. Add the olive oil, followed by the zucchini. Toss until all of the "zoodles" have had a chance to be on the bottom of the pan.

4. Cook until the zucchini noodles are "al dente," 5 to 7 minutes, depending on their thickness. If you see water coming out your "zoodles," they are done! Turn off the heat.

5. Toss immediately with the pesto, and garnish with extra pine nuts.

One-Pan Sweet Potato Pasta all'Arrabbiata

In Italian, *all'arrabbiata* means "in an angry style," and with its feminine conjugation, it literally means "in an angry woman's style." Culinarily speaking, this refers to the spiciness of this tomato sauce. In the Jewish culture I grew up in, when a woman is angry at her husband, she nags or screams. Not particularly sexy. In Italian culture, when a woman is angry with her man, she tries to poison him with chili peppers. That's hot!

The yams pair well with the piquant sauce, a flavor reminiscent of sweet potato french fries with spicy ketchup. The noodles are hardier than zucchini or spaghetti squash, and because they cook directly in the sauce, it has the richness of a meat sauce. Of course, this flavor profile is not traditionally Italian, but I'm okay with that. And you better be too, or I'll be very *arrabbiata*.

P.S. If you ever happen to drink a little too much, consider this a fabulous and nutritious meal for a hangover. That said, if you're really dragging, you might have to get someone else to make it for you!

Special equipment: Spiralizer

1 (14-ounce) can whole peeled tomatoes

¼ cup extra-virgin olive oil

2 large garlic cloves

1 to 2 teaspoons red pepper flakes (See Note)

4 cups spiralized sweet potatoes, from two medium sweet potatoes

1½ teaspoons kosher salt

1 cup green olives, pitted or unpitted

Freshly chopped mint or flat-leaf parsley, for topping

1. Briefly pulse the tomatoes in a food processor or blender. Or crush them well with your hands. Set aside.

2. Place a heavy-bottomed pan over medium heat and let it get hot for a couple of minutes.

3. Add the olive oil, the garlic, and the red pepper flakes, in that order. Let the garlic infuse its flavor into the oil, until it is just golden.

4. Add the sweet potato noodles, toss with the tongs to fully coat the noodles with the oil, and sauté for several minutes.

5. Add the tomatoes along with the salt, and toss the noodles so that they're fully coated in the sauce.

6. Add the whole olives and mix them into the saucy parts. Taste. Add more red pepper now if you like. The sauce will be much less spicy once eaten with the sweet potatoes, so push yourself to add as much heat as you can.

7. Let cook for about 30 minutes, tossing only intermittently, being careful not to break the noodles. Be sure to flatten the noodles into the sauce so they cook evenly in the liquid of the tomatoes. When the noodles are cooked *al dente* (the exact timing will depend on the thickness of your noodles), plate and serve with mint or parsley.

Note: *Attenzione!* Not all red pepper flakes have the same heat. Younger flakes tend to be much spicier than older ones. So start with a teaspoon, then add more as you taste your tomatoes. I use 2 teaspoons with the bottle I have at home.

Cauliflower Mac N' Cheese ai Quattro Formaggi

Quattro formaggi refers to the famous "four cheeses" of Italian pizza and pasta. While there's variation in exactly which cheeses to use, most pastas also include milk and flour to create a base of *besciamella* (white sauce). However, in order to avoid using any carby flour or gluten in this dish, I choose creamy and slightly sweet mascarpone as the first of our four cheeses, layering it with three more, each one a bit more pronounced than the last: fontina, Parmigiano, Gorgonzola. The pepper and nutmeg act as a spice undertone that holds all the flavors together.

Serves 4 to 6

2 heads cauliflower (about 2 pounds each)

2 Tablespoons extra-virgin olive oil

2 teaspoons kosher salt

Freshly ground pepper

⅔ cup mascarpone

1⅓ cup grated fontina (See Note)

1 cup grated Parmigiano Reggiano (See Note)

⅔ of a whole nutmeg, grated

3 ounces Gorgonzola dolce

A small handful of basil leaves, cut into thin strips

1. Place an oven rack 6 inches from the top of the broiler, and turn the broiler on high.

2. Cut the cauliflower into extra small, small, and medium florets, and place them on a foil-lined baking sheet.

3. With a pastry brush, lightly coat each piece of cauliflower with just a glistening of oil. (So unlike me!) Toss with salt and 40 grinds of the pepper mill.

4. Place in the oven until the toasty spots are visible in most places, for 7 to 8 minutes. Remove from the oven and set aside.

5. Turn the broiler off and turn the oven to 375°F.

6. Put the mascarpone, ⅔ cup of the fontina, ⅔ cup of the Parmigiano Reggiano, 40 grinds of the pepper mill, and the nutmeg in a large mixing bowl. Mix with a fork. Taste. It should have a kick. If not, add more pepper or nutmeg.

7. Add the cauliflower to the cheese mixture and gently mix until each floret is covered in the pasty coating. (Don't worry, it will get velvety and creamy once baked.) Place into a 9 or 10-inch square casserole pan.

8. Spread the remaining fontina and Parmigiano on the cauliflower. Use your fingers to place small nuggets of the Gorgonzola dolce across the top surface.

9. Bake uncovered until bubbly, about 30 minutes.

10. Remove from the oven, top with the basil, and serve.

Note: If you're grating your own cheese, use the large holes of a box grater for the fontina cheese and a microplane for the Parmigiano Reggiano. If your Parmigiano is already grated, use about ¼ cup less.

Variation for Kids: Gorgonzola dolce might be a little strong for some kids. Try substituting a sharp white cheddar. Paired with the mascarpone and fontina, its strong flavor will be tempered. Kids love it! Also, kids love anything served in a ramekin. So, if your prefer, bake individual portions in ramekins.

Spaghetti Squash Primavera

WITH VEGETABLES AND PARMIGIANO

Topped with a delicious tomato and basil sauce, toasted pine nuts, roasted broccoli, sautéed peas and onions, and Parmigiano Reggiano, this dish will make you feel like you're in Italy at the height of spring, while still fitting into all the fabulous clothes you bought at that infamous Prada outlet outside of Florence.

But the fact is, pasta primavera—which means pasta in the style of springtime, with spring vegetables—isn't actually an Italian dish. It originated forty years ago in New York, made famous by Le Cirque restaurant, and became one of the signature developments of New York cuisine in the 1970s. So this primavera, made with spaghetti squash rather than pasta, is even less authentically Italian, but in my opinion, just as delicious.

The roasted broccoli adds tremendous flavor and depth to this dish. The key to roasting any food: Olive oil. Salt. Pepper. Broccoli has a tendency to brown and crisp, so you might worry that you ruined it, but fret not. You're adding a little taste of "potato chip" to the green giant of superfoods.

The roasted broccoli and sautéed peas make excellent side dishes, and you can make them on their own. Truth be told, you don't have to wait for spring. Even Maria, my Tuscan cooking mentor superhero, regularly uses frozen peas. No one needs to know!

1 large or 2 small spaghetti squash

Simple Tomato and Basil Sauce (Page 58), heated

Roasted Broccoli (recipe follows)

Peas and Onions (recipe follows)

½ cup *Toasted Pine Nuts* (Page 64)

Freshly grated Parmigiano Reggiano, for garnish

1. Preheat oven to 375°F.

2. Prick the spaghetti squash with a sharp knife being very careful not to hurt yourself.

3. Place the squash in the oven directly on the rack, and bake until it's soft to the touch when you squeeze it with an oven mitt on your hand, about an hour. Remove the squash from the oven, and let it cool for about ten minutes.

4. Cut the squash in half, and remove the seeds with a spoon.

5. Using a fork, scrape out the insides so it forms "spaghetti" and add to a large serving bowl or to individual plates.

6. Top with *Basic Tomato Sauce, Roasted Broccoli,* and *Toasted Pine Nuts.*

7. Garnish with lots of cheese on top, so it resembles a snow-capped mountain atop spring veggies. *Mangia, mangia, che ti fa bene!*

Make Ahead Prep: The peas and onions and tomato sauce can easily be reheated, so make them in advance.

Quickie Variation: Though it won't be a traditional primavera without the vegetables, you can simply top the spaghetti squash with tomato sauce, toasted pine nuts, and grated Parmigiano for a simple spaghetti meal.

"Baked Ziti" Variation: After removing the "spaghetti" from the squash, mix it together with *Ragù di Carne* (Page 253) and place the mixture into the squash shells. Top with more sauce, grated Parmigiano Reggiano, and some sliced mozzarella or burrata. Bake at 375°F until hot and the cheese is bubbly.

ROASTED BROCCOLI

3 heads broccoli

¼ to ⅓ cup extra-virgin olive oil

2 teaspoons kosher salt

Freshly ground pepper

1. Preheat the oven to 425°F

2. Cut the broccoli into extra small, small, and medium florets and place them on a parchment-lined baking sheet.

3. Drizzle with the oil, enough to lightly coat each piece. Sprinkle with the salt and pepper. Use your fingers to mix it all together. Lick your fingers; if they taste quite salty and peppery you have done well. Seasoning will burn off in the oven, so you want it to taste extra salty and peppery.

4. Place in the oven until soft and slightly charred, 11 to 15 minutes.

PEAS AND ONIONS

3 Tablespoons extra-virgin olive oil

1 small red onion, finely chopped

1 pound fresh or frozen shelled peas

1 teaspoon kosher salt

20 to 30 grinds fresh pepper

Chopped fresh mint, optional

1. Place a heavy-bottomed pan over medium heat and let it get hot for a couple of minutes.

2. Add the olive oil and the onion. Let sauté. The longer you cook, the sweeter the onion will become. Try 10 to 15 minutes, or until you see some golden or brown caramelization.

3. Add the peas and stir. After a couple of minutes, add the salt and pepper, and stir. Let the peas cook until they are tender and have taken on the caramelization of the onion, about 10 minutes. If the pan seems dry and the peas are not getting tender, add a touch of water or chicken broth to complete the cooking.

4. Top with chopped mint, if using.

HOW TO TURN PEAS AND ONIONS INTO PEA SOUP!

I made a couple of men really happy with this one. Once your peas and onions are finished and are well caramelized, transfer them to a medium stock pot and add some broth to just cover. Cook covered on low for 30 minutes. Remove half of the peas while you puree the rest of the peas and broth, and then add the reserved peas back in. This provides great texture. If you want to make pea soup from the start, add a leek or two to your *soffritto*. See *How to Make a Soup From Anything*, Page 171.

No-Noodle Lasagna

WITH EGGPLANT, MEAT SAUCE, AND MASCARPONE

I developed this recipe for "I Can't Believe It's Not Pasta," my first online cooking class, and I wonder how on earth I lived without this recipe before. It's the perfect meal for the meat sauce lover. You get all of the rich goodness of an Italian *ragù di carne* without any of the heavy feeling afterwards. That said, I leave it up to you how much mascarpone you add. More mascarpone means more richness, while less means a lighter belly. Believe me, the first time I made this, I only used a touch of mascarpone, and it was still one of the most delicious things I had ever eaten. If you want to bulk it up and you don't have dairy sensitivities, like I do, then by all means, add more.

Ragù di Carne (Easier Variation), see facing page

⅓ to ½ cup grated Parmigiano Reggiano

4 to 8 ounces mascarpone

Grilled Eggplant (Page 63)

1. Preheat the oven to 350°F.

2. Spoon a quarter of the sauce on the bottom of a medium casserole dish. Lightly sprinkle the grated cheese from end to end, and dot with a quarter of the mascarpone. Now cover with a single layer of the eggplant.

3. Repeat that same pattern until you have 3 total layers of eggplant and 4 total layers of meat sauce. (Remember to save the last quarter of sauce, some Parmigiano, and mascarpone for the top!)

4. Add the remaining sauce, grated cheese, and mascarpone to the top layer.

5. Bake in the oven, uncovered, until the oil has begun to bubble on the edges, about 45 minutes.

6. Remove from the oven and let cool. Eat while warm or at room temperature. Store leftovers in the fridge.

Ragù di Carne (Easier Variation)

2 Tablespoons butter

3 Tablespoons extra-virgin olive oil

1 medium onion, finely chopped

1 large carrot, finely chopped

1 celery stalk, finely chopped

1⅓ pounds ground beef (around 85% lean, 15% fat)

¾ cup red wine

1 (28-ounce) can whole peeled tomatoes

10 basil leaves

1 Tablespoon kosher salt

50 grinds of pepper mill

⅓ nutmeg, freshly grated

1. Place a heavy-bottomed pan over medium heat and let it get hot for a couple of minutes.

2. Add the butter and olive oil to the pan, immediately followed by the onion, carrot, and celery. Sauté the *soffritto* until the vegetables are softened and turning very golden in color, 10 to 15 minutes.

3. Add the beef and stir with a wooden spoon until it is browned all over.

4. Add the wine and let it cook until it has evaporated, another 10 to 15 minutes.

5. Briefly pulse the tomatoes in a food processor or blender, or crush them well with your hands. Add them to the meat and mix well.

6. Add the basil, salt, pepper, and nutmeg. Stir to combine. Decrease the heat to medium, and continue to cook until the sauce is well reduced and has no watery liquid left. Once the red of the tomatoes has turned dark brown, the sauce should be at the height of its deliciousness. This takes about an hour.

Make Ahead Prep: You can make the sauce and grill the eggplant 1 to 3 days in advance. Just note that if you are taking the ingredients from the cold fridge, they may need more time in the oven.

" *The whole point is to live life and to use all the colors in the crayon box.*

– *RuPaul*

Sexy Salads

AUTHENTIC CAPRESE

OY VEH, A VEGAN SALAD

TRADITIONAL TRICOLORE

GARBANZO BEAN TRICOLORE

GRILLED ROMAINE WITH LEMON CACIO PEPE

SUMMER ESCAROLE SALAD

TAORMINA SALAD

OLIVE OIL POTATO SALAD

LEMONY QUINOA SALAD

STEAK SALAD WITH GORGONZOLA

CREATIVITY. COLOR. CRUNCH. THESE ARE THE THREE ELEMENTS that can elevate a sad pile of greens into a sensuous salad. A good salad should look beautiful on the plate, with its mixture of colors and textures bringing freshness and variety to every bite. Italians revere a good salad, and the recipes below draw from the Italian tradition, mixing in a little California sunshine to keep things interesting.

Authentic Caprese

TOMATO, MOZZARELLA, AND BASIL SALAD

Everyone and their mother thinks they know how to make a caprese salad, but they're wrong. The irony is that a caprese salad is so simple that it seems impossible to screw it up. First and foremost, I'd like to let the world know that a caprese NEVER has vinegar on it. Balsamic—or any other type—does not belong on this dish, as caprese originates from the island of Capri in the south and balsamic vinegar comes from the north: two different culinary traditions. I didn't make up this rule. It's an Italian culinary statute as old as mozzarella itself. Italian food laws are not to be messed with. They might not be able to run a country properly, but they can cook.

Since a caprese salad has only three ingredients, all uncooked, it's absolutely crucial that they're top-notch. Unfortunately, Americans don't have the same quality ingredients as they have in Italy and often don't know how to choose correctly from what we do have. If you've never been to Naples and eaten a fresh ball of buffalo mozzarella, you don't know what you're missing. (Mozzarella for caprese comes in water. It's not vacuum-packed.) If you manage to find buffalo mozzarella from Italy, grab it. Sadly, there's just no substitute in the States—but with olive oil and salt you can make almost anything delicious. So, choose the best mozzarella available, use plenty of salt, and drizzle it with your best olive oil—the bottle you've been saving for a special occasion.

As for tomatoes, summertime heirloom tomatoes are the best, with vine ripened tomatoes as runner up. Look for the sweetest tomatoes, but not necessarily the ripest ones. Overripe tomatoes are sweet, but too soft for salad—save them for sauces. You want tomatoes that are firm enough to cut neatly. Go ahead and gently squeeze them all in the market until you find the perfect plumpness.

This spiel is over: You're now ready to make a caprese.

Serves 4 to 8

8 medium tomatoes or 4 large heirloom tomatoes, cut into ¼-inch thick slices

1 pound fresh mozzarella (medium-size balls), cut into ¼-inch thick slices

1 teaspoon kosher salt

½ cup extra-virgin olive oil

A small bunch of fresh basil leaves, very thinly sliced (see Page 64)

Ciabatta or country loaf bread (See Note)

1. Layer the tomatoes and mozzarella neatly on a plate so they look like "dominoes" that have fallen down.

2. Sprinkle generously with salt

3. Drizzle generously with olive oil.

4. Sprinkle the basil on top and eat the tomatoes with good bread, performing "la scarpetta," which means wiping your plate with the bread to soak up the juices and oil.

Note: Of course, you don't need to eat bread with a caprese, but it is traditional to do so. To warm the bread and revive it so it tastes like it came fresh from an Italian *forno* (bakery), wrap a loaf (of ciabatta) in foil and put it in the oven at 350°F for about 30 minutes, until the aroma wafts from the oven.

Winter Caprese Variation: When naturally summer sweet tomatoes are still many moons away, just roast the tomatoes to get 'em good! If you are using only cherry tomatoes, you can dress them and stick them under the broiler like we do in *Burrata Crostini with Roasted Cherry Tomatoes* (Page 88). If you are using larger tomatoes or a mixture of sizes, cut the bigger ones in quarters and douse with olive oil and add salt, pepper, and thyme. Place them in the middle of the oven under the broiler for a good 10 minutes or longer, until they are well cooked and soft. Slice mozzarella, add salt, surround the slices with your cooked reds, and top with basil.

Burrata Caprese Variation: A caprese salad with burrata is delicious but messy, so it's best to rearrange the layout. Put each slice of tomato on a platter and top each with a small mound of burrata, and, of course, the salt, olive oil, and basil.

CONSIDER COLOR AND TEXTURE!

Flavor is not the only sensual component of food. Before you eat, you see and smell your food, and while you eat, your mouth feels its texture. So think about how to add colors to the whole plate. I love using radicchio in salad to give a punch of purple. Lemon zest and freshly chopped parsley might be a tasty garnish, but they also add beauty. Likewise, think about what type of bite you want on your plate. You don't want all-mushy or all-crunchy. I love to eat a salad next to mashed potatoes, because I love the contrast in textures. I make sure to toast my bread well, so it stays crisp after I top it with burrata. I add endive and cucumbers to mixed leaf salads for crunch. I top zucchini noodles and *Rosemary Grove Peaches* with whole toasted pine nuts for the same reason. You're crafting a sensual experience, so get in tune with those senses as you eat and cook!

Oy Veh, a Vegan Salad

MIXED GREENS WITH FRESH HERBS AND ROSEMARY-INFUSED BALSAMIC VINEGAR

The last thing a chef wants to hear when she walks into a party she's catering is that someone—the host's brother no less—is vegan. Had I known, I would've made some of the eggplant parmigiana bites and radicchio *arancini* without cheese and made the cobbler with extra-virgin coconut oil instead of butter! I'd spent three days meticulously preparing a six-course tasting menu with wine pairings, knowing there would be a couple of vegetarians, but no one said a word about vegans! Damn vegans!

Of course, vegans are right. Their diet is often clean and healthy and definitely good for the planet. My only defense against their moral superiority is childish ridicule. Hey vegans, fuck you!

Anyway, no one mentioned the brother's veganism, because his own carnivorous family thinks it's a phase that, if ignored, will go away.* Alas, it didn't go away in time for the party, and I was left scavenging an empty fridge for something he could eat. Nobody goes home hungry from my parties!

This recipe is the result of that scavenger hunt. In their cupboard, I found rosemary-infused balsamic vinegar, which can be hard to find, so we'll make our own. I think this might be my favorite salad ever, and I use it as a side dish all the time, with everything from frittatas to fish.

* It did.

2 sprigs rosemary

1 cup balsamic vinegar

1 English cucumber (see Note)

5 to 6 ounces mesclun greens

1 to 2 shallots, sliced thinly

1 cup chopped fresh herbs
(mint, parsley, chives, basil, or cilantro)

2 endive, sliced into thin rounds, optional

½ radicchio, thinly sliced, optional

½ teaspoon kosher salt

⅓ cup extra-virgin olive oil

Freshly ground pepper

Make the Rosemary-Balsamic Vinegar

1. Place the rosemary on a clean kitchen surface and give it a light pounding with a meat mallet or with the bottom of a glass so it will release its oils.

2. Put the vinegar in a little jar or container with the rosemary, shake, and let it sit (up to overnight) while you prepare the rest of the salad or dinner. (At that point remove the rosemary and keep the vinegar in the fridge.)

Make the Salad

1. Peel or partially peel the cucumber. Cut it in half lengthwise and then into ¼-inch thick half-moons.

2. Place the cucumber, greens, shallots, and herbs in a salad bowl.

3. Add the endive and radicchio, if using.

4. Add the salt, two tablespoons of the vinegar, and the oil, one at a time, tossing in between each addition. Adjust the seasoning, adding more salt, vinegar, or oil, if necessary.

5. Finish with a few grinds of pepper.

Note: The mistake a lot of people make with cucumbers in salad: they cut them in pieces that are too large, and then no one ends up eating them. They get left on the plate. You want your cucumbers to be a part of each bite of salad, so cut them smaller. Also trimming off the skin, or part of the skin, tends to make cucumbers more immersed into the flavor of the salad.

Variation: Try adding *Toasted Pine Nuts* (Page 64) when you need some more protein in a meal. Also, the addition of a balsamic reduction or glaze is lovely, though you will want to lower the amount of rosemary-balsamic vinegar used.

Traditional Tricolore

RADICCHIO, ENDIVE, AND ARUGULA SALAD WITH PARMIGIANO

Named after the three colors of the Italian flag, the tricolore salad combines red radicchio with white endive and green arugula for the most patriotic of Italy's salads. The spice of the arugula and the crispy bitterness of the radicchio and endive are tempered by the dressing and by the smooth flavor of the shaved Parmigiano Reggiano, a royal touch on top. I use a non-traditional dash of tamari to add umami to the flavor profile. Patriotic Americans should resist the temptation to replace the green of the Italian flag with a blue ingredient—radicchio, endive, and blueberries would make for a challenging concoction.

This recipe combines equal amounts of arugula, radicchio, and endive, so if you choose to halve it or double it, keep that in mind.

Serves 4 to 6

1 medium radicchio

3 medium Belgian endive

2 large handfuls arugula

½ teaspoon kosher salt

¼ teaspoon tamari or soy sauce

2 scant Tablespoons balsamic vinegar

⅓ cup extra-virgin olive oil

Shaved Parmigiano Reggiano

1. Cut the radicchio in half, remove the core, and cut crosswise into very thin strips.

2. Cut the endive crosswise into medium strips and remove the core.

3. Place the radicchio, endive, and arugula in a salad bowl.

4. Add the salt, tamari, vinegar, and oil one at a time, tossing in between each addition. Adjust the seasoning, adding more salt, vinegar, or oil, if necessary.

5. Finish with the shaved Parmigiano.

Garbanzo Bean Tricolore

WITH RADICCHIO, PARSLEY, AND FETA

Another salad whose colors derive from the Italian flag, this one gets its red from the radicchio, its white from the feta, and its green from the parsley. The feta adds a salty sweetness to the naturally bitter radicchio, the pepper tempers the saltiness of the feta, and the handfuls of chopped parsley cool it down. The lemon lightens everything up and holds the flavors together. With that in mind, you can tweak the flavor balance to get it just right. This is a salad that can live in the fridge for quite a few days and, with its protein and other nutrients, can work as a light meal, buffet salad, or a nosh.

Serves 6 to 10

---

1 head radicchio

2 (15-ounce) cans garbanzo beans, drained

1 cup chopped flat-leaf parsley

7 to 8 ounces feta

½ teaspoon kosher salt

¼ cup fresh lemon juice (2 to 3 lemons)

⅓ cup extra-virgin olive oil

Freshly ground pepper

1. Cut the radicchio in half, remove the core, and cut crosswise into medium strips.

2. Place the radicchio, garbanzo beans, and parsley into a salad bowl.

3. Crumble the feta with your hands into the smallest "bits."

4. Add the salt, lemon juice, and oil one at a time, tossing in between each addition. Adjust the seasoning, adding more salt, lemon, or oil, if necessary.

5. Finish with grinds of pepper until it tastes balanced to you.

6. Let the salad rest at least ten minutes before eating so the flavors can meld.

Taste The Radicchio

As a teenager, food became my enemy. Eating in a boarding school cafeteria, I put on weight and felt terrible about it. Immediately after gorging myself, I was overwhelmed by guilt. This pattern followed me to college, until an epiphany (see *My Story*) led me to take some time off and travel to Europe. That's when I consciously decided to reevaluate my relationship with food.

It began at a table in a country house in France, with friends I'd met travelling. As we ate a colorful salad with cheese and nuts, I picked up a red leaf that I recognized as radicchio and tasted it. *Mmm, this is what radicchio tastes like.* And then the green. It had bite. *This is arugula,* I thought. I savored the cheese, and let it roll all over my tongue and the roof of my mouth. *Mmm, this is what gorgonzola feels like.* I picked up a nut and discovered it was a walnut. I'm not sure I'd ever tasted one on its own. I looked around the table. Everyone was finished eating, and I still had a full plate of food. What a rare occurrence that was. I'd begun to taste food mindfully.

Something miraculous happened when I stopped devouring food as if it was my last meal and began to appreciate it as a gift to the senses. I realized that food had the capacity to nourish not only my body's hunger, but also my soul's deep need to experience beauty through flavor.

This revelation, which cured my teenage compulsive eating, became the basis of my career as a chef and cooking teacher. Before you can cook, you must first learn to eat. I spent the next few months deconstructing plates of food to better understand what individual ingredients tasted like. Fortunately, that's about as good as homework gets.

The lesson: Don't attack your plate right away. Mindfully taste all of the recognizable ingredients. Try the dressing or sauce on its own, and let your tongue wonder what's in it. Let each ingredient introduce itself to you: *Hello radicchio. I see that you are uncooked. You are crunchy and a bit bitter. But when I taste you with feta, your bitterness is tempered by the saltiness of the cheese. I like how the walnut is balancing your flavor. I would like to experience you also with a cooling agent of some sort. Hmmm? Now bring up your library of flavor memory. Parsley or mint could do just that. Yet so could basil, and it would add a hint of sweetness, which would work with the Gorgonzola! Oh radicchio, I am going to make something of you at home, just you wait!*

" *...it was so rich and exotic I was seduced into taking one bite and then another as I tried to chase the flavors back to their source.*

—Ruth Reichl

Grilled Romaine with Lemon *Cacio Pepe*

Cacio Pepe means "cheese and pepper" in central Italian dialect, and it's the basis for one of the most well-known Italian pastas, a simple combination of spaghetti with Pecorino Romano and pepper. I came up with this salad because I just love the crunch of romaine and wanted to add a nice twist by getting a little char on there. Pecorino Romano and black pepper provide most of the flavor, and the lemon juice and zest bring it all to life. It takes seven minutes to heat up the grill, four to grill the romaine, one minute to dress, and 30 seconds to eat!

Though not traditional to Italian coursing, I think this salad makes a great starter course. And, by the way, it makes a fantastic snack. You can pick up the grilled romaine and eat it with your hands. Feel free to lick your fingers afterward!

Serves 2

1 head romaine lettuce

¼ teaspoon kosher salt

Juice of ½ lemon

2 to 3 Tablespoons extra-virgin olive oil

Freshly ground pepper

Zest of ¼ lemon, optional

Grated Parmigiano Reggiano

Grated Pecorino Romano

1. Light a grill pan over medium high heat, and let it get fully hot, about 7 minutes.

2. In the meantime, cut the romaine in half, top to bottom, the long way.

3. When the grill is hot, place the romaine cut side down and cook until that side has strong brown grill marks, about 5 minutes. The romaine will not be cooked through. Remove and place on a serving plate.

4. Sprinkle each piece with salt. You don't need to use all the juice from the half lemon. Squeeze what you want on top, sharing some juice with both pieces.

5. Drizzle each piece with about a tablespoon of olive oil, enough to lightly cover all the pieces.

6. Grind the pepper, 6 grinds each. Use your fingers to sprinkle the lemon zest on both halves, if using. Now go ahead and top with the cheese.

7. If you can be patient, cut with a fork and knife. If not, pick it up with your hands and shove into your mouth! #handheldsalad

Summer Escarole Salad

Similar to radicchio, yet far less bitter, escarole is an excellent nutritious salad green. This particular salad, with its flavor of lemons and anchovies, brings me back to the sexy coast of Southern Italy. Hot sun. Tanned skin. Sea salt lips after a day at the beach. This is what to eat, still in your bathing suit, after a plate of seafood pasta, with a glass of cold white wine.

Serves 6 to 10

½ teaspoon salt

2½ teaspoons anchovy paste or 4-5 anchovies, finely chopped and smashed

Juice of 2 lemons

½ cup extra-virgin olive oil

1 medium red onion, finely chopped

2 large heads of escarole, cut into bite-size pieces

1. Mix the salt, anchovy, lemon juice, and olive oil in a small bowl, making sure the anchovy is well integrated.

2. Add the onion and let sit for at least 10 minutes to meld the flavors.

3. Dip a piece of escarole into the dressing, getting some onion. Taste and adjust the seasoning, adding a little extra salt or lemon, or anchovy, if necessary.

4. Place the escarole in a salad bowl and add half of the dressing. Toss well and taste for seasoning. Add more dressing if needed.

Taormina Salad

WITH FENNEL, ORANGE, AND ONION

On Sicily's northeast shore, hovering between the azure Ionian Sea and towering Mt. Etna, is a beautiful baroque city called Taormina. In the center of the city, overlooking the water, is one of the most stunning, and largest remaining amphitheaters from Ancient Greece, which is still in use today for outdoor concerts. In summer, tourists come in droves to shop at the high-end stores that have filled Taormina's ornate alleyways, which is why I recommend visiting in the fall or spring—though you might not get to enjoy the beaches or jump from the forty-foot cliffs into crystal clear water (yes, your cooking teacher is an adrenaline junkie).

Truth be told, it's actually not easy to get a good meal in Taormina, because most of the restaurants cater to palate-challenged tourists. There's no such thing as a Taormina Salad as far as I know, but there are many variations of a fennel citrus salad in Sicily, which is known for its *agrumi* (citrus fruits). Sometimes it's prepared with olives, sometimes with anchovy, and sometimes with onion. I'm clearly quite fond of this delicately flavored salad and could think of no more beautiful place to lend this salad its name than this lovely gem of a city that, unfortunately, has found itself smack dab in the middle of the beaten path.

Though citrus are winter fruits, this light salad makes for a delicious summer accompaniment to any grilled meat or fish. By letting the salad sit in its own juices before serving, the flavor of the raw onion is tempered, the fennel softens just enough, and the flavors meld together into *perfezione*.

2 to 3 oranges

1 small red onion

3 large fennel bulbs

1 to 1½ teaspoons kosher salt

Juice of 1 lemon

½ cup extra-virgin olive oil

2 handfuls wild arugula

1. Use a sharp knife to slice off the peel and pith (white part) of the oranges. Cut out the natural segments and place them in a salad bowl.

2. Remove the outer layer of the onion, discard, and cut the onion in half vertically. Lay each half face-down, and cut it into very thin half-moons. Add to the bowl.

3. Cut off the top fronds off the fennel bulbs. You can discard the fronds, or use them as a garnish if desired.

4. Cut the fennel bulbs in half. Remove and discard the outer layer. Cut out the core and cut into very thin strips. Add to the salad bowl.

5. Add the salt, lemon juice, and oil one at a time, tossing in between each addition. Adjust the seasoning, adding more salt, lemon, or oil, if necessary.

6. Let sit for a half hour.

7. Add the arugula and toss. Taste and adjust the seasoning.

WHEN DO I SERVE A SALAD?

Traditionally in Italy, *l'insalata* follows the main course. A vibrant leafy salad with a touch of vinegar or lemon after a rich meal is incredibly rejuvenating, especially if you've eaten both pasta and meat. That said, unless I'm creating a special six-course meal for a party or an artsy pop-up dinner, I usually serve salad as a *contorno*, a side dish. I personally love a crunchy, refreshing salad on my dinner plate, alongside other cooked vegetables. I leave it to you where you choose to place the salad in your meal, as long as you don't serve it with the pasta! (See *What Do I Serve Pasta With?* Page 228.)

HOW TO DRESS SALAD LIKE A BADASS... WITHOUT MEASURING!

Just because there's an entire aisle dedicated to salad dressings in the supermarket doesn't mean you need to buy any of them. You won't find store-bought salad dressing in any Italian fridge. In fact, there isn't even an Italian word for dressing. Salads are the freshest, most delicate part of the meal, so the idea of putting a factory-made flavor atop them is simply a foreign concept. A salad's flavor should come from its ingredients.

Alas, the American notion of bland iceberg lettuce enhanced by a bottled dressing epitomizes our concept of food: flavor must be manufactured, added, artificially boosted. You don't have to buy into this! You have the power to create delicious salads with what you have at home, and you don't even have to measure.

I don't make salad dressings. I simply dress the salad. Right in the bowl, Italian-style.

THE ITALIANS HAVE TWO WAYS TO DRESS A SALAD:

» Salt, Vinegar, and Olive Oil

» Salt, Lemon, and Olive Oil

The problem with making a dressing on the side is: one, it gives you one more thing to wash and, two, it's hard to test the flavor because the oil always rises to the top. As Marcella Hazan, Italian cooking teacher and cookbook author extraordinaire, wrote in her *Essentials of Classic Italian Cooking:* "The salad course is dressed at the table, when ready to serve; it is never done ahead of time. The components of the dressing are never to be mixed in advance, they are poured separately onto the salad."

Furthermore, *la maestra* Hazan exclaims, "I have found that people outside Italy never use enough oil. There should be enough to produce a gloss on the surface of all the vegetables [leaves]."

ON THAT NOTE, LET'S GET TO SOME BASICS OF DRESSING A SALAD:

For 2-3 cups/large handfuls of salad:

1. **Keep some greens on the side,** just in case you overdress and need to add more.

2. **Add dressing ingredients one at a time, in this order:** salt, acid, oil. Tossing in between each addition.

    » Use your fingers and add a little salt to the salad, about a ½ teaspoon. Toss.

    » Next, add vinegar or lemon, about 1 tablespoon. (I tend to eyeball measure vinegar in the bottle cap.) Toss.

    » Drizzle about 3 times as much oil as the vinegar or lemon. So for this amount, add about 3 tablespoons. Toss.

3. **Taste and adjust for flavor. Need more acid?** Add vinegar or lemon. **Need a bit more oomph?** Sprinkle in a little more salt. **Need more but you're not sure what?** Add a little more of everything, including oil.

Scared you're going to screw it up? You aren't alone. I have coached hundreds of students through this process. Take the plunge, try it one time. If it fails, who cares. Every cooking mistake brings you closer to getting it right the next time. It's only salad!

Olive Oil Potato Salad

Despite the advances our country has made in technology, trade, and civil rights, our national potato salad remains a dull, gelatinous, mayonnaise-covered disgrace, signifying far deeper social unrest. The recipe below is my one-woman effort to lead our country into a new era, where mayonnaise is replaced by olive oil, where the salad is tossed while still warm, letting the ingredients melt into the potatoes, and where flavor is inspired by the ancient civilizations that came before us. Greece and Rome laid the foundations for our democracy; it's now time to let them redefine our potato salad!

Kosher salt

4 medium russet potatoes, about 3 pounds

½ red onion

½ cup extra-virgin olive oil

3 Tablespoons capers packed in salt, rinsed and finely chopped

½ cup chopped flat-leaf parsley

Freshly ground pepper

1. Bring a large pot of water to boil over high heat.

2. Once boiling, add a handful of salt. Add the potatoes whole. Cover, and let them boil for about 30 minutes or until they are just done. (Timing will depend on the size of your potatoes.) When you stick a knife into one, it should feel soft in the center.

3. Gently drain the potatoes in a colander, and let them cool for 20 to 30 minutes.

4. Cut the onion in half, and slice one of these halves into thin half-moons.

5. Cut the potatoes into one-inch cubes. (Some will break apart and give you smaller pieces and yummy warm potato crumbles. That's good!)

6. Put the potatoes in a serving bowl. While still warm, drizzle generously with the olive oil. Throw in the onion, capers, and parsley.

7. Gently toss, being careful. Since the potatoes will still be warm, they will break easily. (A little breakage is good.)

8. Top with freshly ground pepper.

9. Taste and adjust the seasoning. If it's dry, add more oil. If it's bland, add salt or more capers. Let it sit for at least 20 minutes to let the flavors merge.

Lemony Quinoa Salad

WITH GARDEN HERBS AND PINE NUTS

A few years ago, when I taught a cooking class of easy, healthy recipes for students at the International House of Brown University, the head of the Italian Studies Department, Massimo Riva, refused to taste the quinoa. I understood his hesitation.

Quinoa isn't a traditional Italian grain, hailing as it does from the Andes, and its light, fluffy, gluten-free texture is a departure for the Italian palate. But in the last ten years, quinoa has become a staple for us here in California, delicious on its own, wonderful on a buffet, or delightful as an accompaniment to fish or lamb. I insisted that Professor Riva try it. When he ate my quinoa salad, he changed his mind about quinoa.

The reason Italians love my quinoa is that I use a lot of olive oil, fresh herbs, lemon, and toasted pine nuts. Quinoa soaks up the flavors of whatever it's dressed with, making it suitable for an Italian interpretation. Make sure you dress it while it's hot, and, if possible, serve it while it's still warm. By doing that, you avoid that typical grainy, dry quinoa salad where every quinoa grain seems to be on its own journey. We're not looking for mush, but we *are* looking for a forkful that convinces your mouth that all the ingredients were born to be eaten together.

1½ cups dry quinoa

1½ teaspoons kosher salt

Zest of 1 small lemon

Juice of 2 small lemons, about 3 Tablespoons

⅓ cup extra-virgin olive oil, plus more for drizzling

¾ cup *Toasted Pine Nuts* (Page 64)

1½ cups chopped fresh herbs
(mint, cilantro, and/or basil)

½ pint cherry tomatoes, quartered, optional

1. Cook the quinoa and 3 cups of water in a rice cooker or according to package instructions.

2. Once the quinoa is done, let it rest uncovered for 3 to 5 minutes.

3. Transfer the quinoa to a large serving bowl, giving it a little more space to breathe.

4. Add the salt, zest, and juice of the lemon to the quinoa. Add the olive oil and stir.

5. Taste it. Want more citrus? Add more lemon. Want a tad more flavor? Add more salt.

6. Add the pine nuts, herbs, and tomatoes, if using. Mix to combine.

7. Adjust the seasoning again as you like. Drizzle with olive oil and, if possible, serve while still warm.

Note on leftovers: I love quinoa leftovers. However, you might find that the next day your quinoa needs a little extra umph. I give it a little extra olive oil, salt, and lemon. This does the trick.

Steak Salad with Gorgonzola

Steak salad is the most paradoxical of dishes, the salad you order when you're feeling defiant. It's the openly gay boxer, the gun-toting liberal, the nun-with-a-neck-tattoo of salads. Everything about this salad screams wrong! But when you want a mouthful of meat with your greens, there's nothing that tastes so right.

My steak salad strikes a delicate balance between the herb-rubbed steak, the sweet balsamic reduction, the creamy, pungent gorgonzola, and the crispy greens, to create a distinctly satisfying meal. The rosemary rub gives this salad an Italian flavor, but I've also used an Indian *chat masala* rub on the beef, inviting all manner of bad karma. Hey, everything about this dish is non-kosher!

1 Tablespoon plus 1 teaspoon kosher salt

1 Tablespoon ground thyme and/or rosemary

2 pounds flank steak

6 handfuls spring salad mix

1 radicchio, thinly sliced

3 Belgian endives, thinly sliced

A small handful thinly sliced basil, about ¼ cup

1 teaspoon Tamari or quality soy sauce

2 to 4 Tablespoons red wine vinegar

½ to ¾ cup extra-virgin olive oil

6 ounces Gorgonzola dolce, broken into nuggets

Rosemary-Balsamic Reduction (Page 61)
or store-bought balsamic glaze, warmed

Prepare the Meat

Rub 1 tablespoon of salt and the ground herbs all over the steak, and let tenderize and flavorize for at least one hour. If you are using the steak within a couple of hours, leave it on the counter. If letting it sit longer, store it in the fridge and take it out an hour before cooking to bring the steak to room temperature.

Cook the steak

Heat an indoor grill pan for 10 minutes over medium heat. Cook the meat for 5 minutes per side for medium rare. Let it rest for 5 minutes before slicing thinly.

Prepare the Salad

1. Add the spring salad mix, radicchio, endive, and basil to a salad bowl.

2. Add 1 teaspoon salt, followed one at a time by the tamari, vinegar, and olive oil, tossing in between each addition. You'll wanted this lightly dressed because it will be topped with the reduction.

3. Top the salad with the sliced steak, sprinkle with the Gorgonzola, and drizzle with the *Rosemary-Balsamic Reduction*.

Note: This recipe can easily be halved or quartered, but if you have smaller pieces of flank steak, your cooking times will be shorter.

Make Ahead Prep: You may prepare the meat a day in advance. Be sure to bring it to room temperature before cooking.

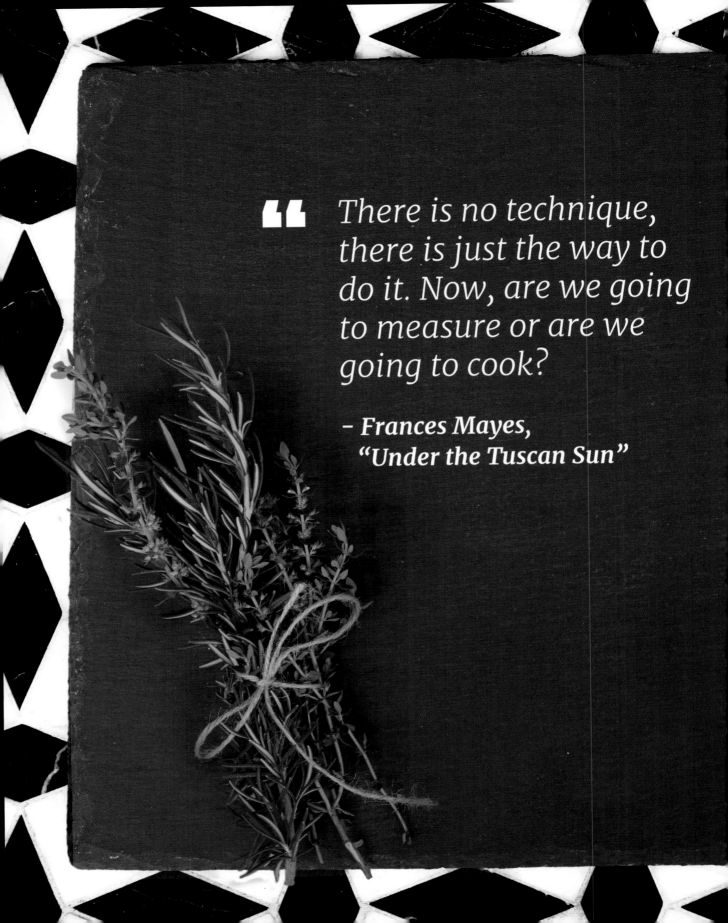

" There is no technique, there is just the way to do it. Now, are we going to measure or are we going to cook?

– Frances Mayes, "Under the Tuscan Sun"

It's All in the Vegetables

ROASTED CAULIFLOWER WITH LEMON

SALT AND PEPPER ROASTED ASPARAGUS

ROASTED PORTOBELLO MUSHROOMS WITH THYME

GREEN BEANS WITH BLISTERED CHERRY TOMATOES

TUSCAN GARDEN GROVE BRUSSELS SPROUTS

TUSCAN MIXED VEGETABLES

LITTLE ITALIAN POTATO STICKS

CRISPY SMASHED FINGERLING POTATOES AL LIMONE

CELERY ROOT PUREE

RUSTIC OLIVE OIL MASHED POTATOES

GRILLED ZUCCHINI WITH LEMON AND MINT

GRILLED ENDIVE WITH ARUGULA PESTO

BRAISED TUSCAN KALE

Tuscan Mixed Vegetables, page 308

WHEN I WAS A CHILD, VEGETABLES WERE LESS OF A FOOD THAN a challenge. My parents insisted on preparing vegetables in the healthiest way possible, which meant steaming them until they were absolutely void of texture or flavor. The only vegetable we baked was a potato, and forget about sautéing. Steamed carrots and broccoli might be healthy, but they don't provide many nutrients if you never eat them. Until I left home, I didn't understand that vegetables could be the most delicious thing on the table. But they can if they're cooked right, and in the recipes that follow, they are!

Lick Your Fingers

I've always eaten with my hands and licked my fingers as I cooked, but when I started teaching professionally, I absolutely did not lick my fingers in class. I associated finger-licking with bad manners, lack of social graces, and Kentucky Fried Chicken.

Ironically, my mom—who'd always chastised me for eating with my hands—showed me the error of my ways. She explained that no less a culinary icon than *Julia Child* advocated finger-licking. Armed with that knowledge, I changed my approach, incorporating finger-licking *into the curriculum* of my cooking classes!

Roasting vegetables is perfect for this demonstration. My students drizzle olive oil onto the chopped vegetables, sprinkle salt with their hands, and then grind fresh pepper. "Is this enough?" they ask every step of the way. "Probably not," is my usual answer.

I insist they use their hands to mix everything together. Predictably, about half of them immediately rush to the sink to wash off. *No, no. Stay right where you are.* I make an example of them: *Lick your fingers.*

Pause.

How does it taste? If the answer is "good," we're done. If they aren't sure, my response is usually to add more kosher salt.

You're responsible for your food, and the only way to know it's good is to taste. The purest way of tasting food is directly from your skin. Be thankful that you're not a restaurant chef, but rather a home cook who can pleasantly dip a finger directly into the pan to decide what your food needs. If you want others to have a visceral reaction to your food, then you have to get primal with it. Lick your fingers.

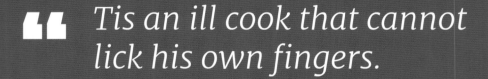

> ❝ *Tis an ill cook that cannot lick his own fingers.*
>
> **—William Shakespeare**

Roasted Cauliflower with Lemon

Roasted vegetables are the home chef's secret weapon. Easy, delicious, and filling, they're uniquely satisfying right out of the oven and make great leftovers to use in frittatas, soups, and salads. The recipe below has probably gotten more mileage than any other recipe I've made. I taught it in my first ever cooking class. Family friend Lori Tessel, who came to a class once seven years ago, still makes it twice a week for her family and on Passover.

Most chefs put a lot of "stuff" in their roasted cauliflower. I like to keep it simple. Cauliflower already has a unique flavor and, when roasted, the slightly sweet, browned caramelization comes forth so beautifully that I can't imagine adding heaps of garlic, cumin, chili pepper, or whatever else in God's name people tend to use to overpower, and hence ruin, this delicious vegetable. Let the cauliflower take center stage. It requires no more than olive oil, salt, and pepper. The fresh lemon juice at the end will lighten the dish and send your taste buds into fervent applause.

WHAT IS PARCHMENT PAPER FOR?

For those of you experienced cooks who can't believe I'm actually answering this question in a cookbook, I gotta tell you that there was a time in my life when, if I saw a recipe that required parchment paper, I would gulp and turn the page, because I had no idea what parchment paper was. So yeah I'm going to write about it!

Parchment paper is basically a layer between the baking sheet and the food. It makes clean-up a helluva lot easier. It also helps to even out the heat, which is why when you put it beneath cookie dough, you'll stop getting burnt bottoms and raw middles. It's healthier than using tin foil, because it doesn't leach metals. However it can't be used under the broiler, because it will burn.

1 large head of cauliflower

¼ cup extra-virgin olive oil

2 teaspoons kosher salt

Freshly ground pepper

1 lemon, halved

1. Preheat oven to 450°F.

2. Cut the cauliflower head in half, and use your knife to remove the thick stem from the florets. Break apart the florets into various-sized pieces. You will find the lack of uniformity in size will lead to juicy and to well-browned pieces alike, both of which you will savor equally. Itty bitty pieces will brown more easily and might even get crunchy, so be sure to break apart the florets well.

3. Place the cauliflower on a parchment-lined baking sheet. Pour on the oil, sprinkle the salt, and grind the pepper. Use your fingers to mix it all together evenly. Lick your fingers. If they taste quite salty and peppery, you have done well. Some of the seasoning will burn off in the oven, so adjust pepper and salt accordingly. Separate the florets so they don't touch.

4. Place in the oven for about 20 minutes.

5. Squeeze the lemon juice on top, catching the seeds in your hands, and serve hot!

Note: You can always make more cauliflower than you need and withhold the final squeeze of lemon and use extras to make *Quick Cauliflower Soup* (Page 154).

Salt and Pepper Roasted Asparagus

These are so quick and so easy. I use a particularly heavy hand with salt and pepper to give them a potato-chip-like taste. Good luck getting these to the table. They're just so delicious to eat with your fingers right from the pan.

Serves 4

1 bunch asparagus, about a pound

¼ cup extra-virgin olive oil

1 teaspoon kosher salt

30 grinds of the pepper mill

1. Turn on the broiler, and place the rack two inches from the heat element.

2. Take one asparagus and break off the bottom. Where it naturally breaks is where you need to cut it off. Use that as a measure to cut off the bottom of the rest of the asparagus (usually the bottom quarter), which will be too tough to use.

3. Place the asparagus on a foil-lined baking sheet.

4. Generously drizzle with the olive oil, sprinkle with salt, and grind the pepper on top.

5. Use your fingers to mix, making sure each piece is well coated with the oil and spices. Lick your fingers. You should taste a burst of salt and pepper. Now separate the asparagus so they don't touch. This will help them get nice and browned.

6. Place the sheet in the oven, and cook until the asparagus begins to brown on top but is still crunchy on the inside, 3 to 5 minutes.

THE FUNDAMENTALS OF ROASTING DELICIOUS VEGETABLES

Vegetables taste fantastic when roasted well. And it's a very simple process to master. Here are some tips to getting flavorful, caramelized, juicy vegetables:

» **Smaller is better.** Don't cut your vegetables too big. With smaller pieces, you proportionally increase the surface area that will be covered in olive oil, receiving the heat of the oven. More surface means more flavor.

» **Cut your vegetables into uneven pieces.** This will ensure that some get brown and crisped, some maintain denser texture, and some stay soft and juicy. The combination in your mouth is heaven.

» **Don't put wet vegetables on your baking sheet.** This prevents browning and caramelization. So, either dry your vegetables well or buy organic and don't wash them at all, like I do. Anything that could harm you will get killed in the oven anyway, so don't sweat it.

» **Use enough olive oil so that each vegetable is lightly coated in it.** This ensures browning and caramelization.

» **Add enough kosher salt and freshly ground pepper so that when you swipe a finger across the baking sheet and lick it, you get a wow sensation in your mouth.** Roasting will dull the flavors, so you really want to add enough before cooking.

» **Don't overcrowd your veggies. If they're touching one another, they'll steam off each other and reduce the caramelization process.** Get big baking pans and don't be afraid to use two of them at the same time on convection. (Sometimes you will be doubling a recipe and you will need to overcrowd veggies. If so, cook for longer and/or on a higher temperature so you get nice caramelization.)

» **Jack that oven up!** The higher the roasting temperature, the more of that delicious caramelization you get. Of course, you also risk burning your vegetables before they're fully cooked, so play around until you get the temperatures right for each type of vegetable. 400°F should be the minimum.

Roasted Portobello Mushrooms with Thyme

Serves 4 to 6

6 portobello mushrooms, stems removed

¼ cup extra-virgin olive oil

2 teaspoons kosher salt

40 grinds of fresh pepper

10 to 12 sprigs fresh thyme

1. Preheat the oven to 400°F.

2. Line a baking sheet with parchment paper.

3. Cut the mushrooms into ½-inch slices.

4. Lay the mushrooms on the baking sheet. Drizzle with the olive oil and sprinkle with the salt. Add some fresh ground pepper.

5. Holding the thyme sprigs at one end, use your other hand to gently slide down the stem, pulling off the leaves. Mix the seasoning with the mushrooms, and lay them back down flat. Lick your fingers and adjust seasoning as necessary.

6. Bake for 15 minutes.

7. Serve hot or at room temperature.

Green Beans with Blistered Cherry Tomatoes

When it comes to vegetables, kids can be picky eaters, which is why the mothers who take my cooking classes love this recipe. When the onions caramelize and the sweet tomato juices burst all over the beans, this dish tastes like pizza, and I encourage moms to call it "Pizza Green Beans." But these beans are also very popular with adults. In fact, I serve them every year at my birthday party.

Make sure you cook this nice and long to bring out all the best flavors of the fresh ingredients.

2 pounds green beans, ends trimmed

1 large red onion, halved and cut into ½-inch slices

1 pint cherry tomatoes

6 sprigs fresh rosemary, optional

½ cup extra-virgin olive oil

2 teaspoons kosher salt

40 grinds of the pepper mill

1. Preheat the oven to 425°F.

2. Line a baking sheet with parchment paper. Throw on the green beans, onion, tomatoes, and rosemary, if using.

3. Drizzle on the olive oil and add the salt and pepper.

4. Use your fingers to mix all of the veggies with the flavorings. Lick your fingers. Taste good? You are done. Need something? Add salt? Feel dry? Add more oil.

5. Place on the center rack of the oven for about 40 minutes. Toss them about halfway through and lay them back out flat-ish. You want the tomato skins to burst and the green beans to take on a golden, or even brown, color. Go even longer if you like a little char. (As I've discovered by mistake on a few occasions, they taste good a little burnt.)

6. Toss together to coat the beans with tomato goodness and serve.

Variation: If you want to give this recipe a little protein, add some *Toasted Pine Nuts* (Page 64) before serving.

Tuscan Garden Grove Brussels Sprouts

Every year for Thanksgiving, I teach a very full and merrily hectic class called "Everything But the Turkey." It's the same menu every year. Naturally, I have a Brussels sprouts recipe for the holiday, but it turns out to be a favorite of students all year round—as long as they can find fresh Brussels sprouts. Don't skimp on olive oil or salt (do I even have to say that at this point in our relationship?!) and be sure to cook it extra long, until not just tender, but succulent, with crispy, browned outer leaves.

Serves 4

1½ pounds Brussels sprouts

3 vine-ripened tomatoes, cut into ½-inch pieces

2 to 3 large shallots, cut into ½-inch pieces

4 garlic cloves, halved

2 sprigs fresh rosemary, cut into 1-inch pieces

¼ cup extra-virgin olive oil

1 teaspoon dried thyme

1 teaspoon kosher salt

A generous amount of freshly ground pepper

1. Preheat the oven to 400°F.

2. Trim off the root ends of the Brussels sprouts and pull off any yucky looking yellowish leaves. Cut in half lengthwise.

3. Place the Brussels sprouts, tomatoes, shallots, garlic, and rosemary in a medium casserole dish or on a parchment-lined baking sheet.

4. Drizzle with the olive oil. Sprinkle with the thyme and salt. Grind fresh pepper.

5. Use your fingers to mix and lick fingers to test seasoning. Adjust if needed.

6. Make sure the rosemary and garlic are evenly dispersed.

7. Bake for 45 to 60 minutes.

TO CONVECT OR NOT TO CONVECT?

Some ovens have convection settings, which means that a fan at the back of the oven swirls the heat around, so food cooks evenly on multiple oven racks at the same time. Bakers use convection ovens, for example, to make many trays of cookies at a time to the same degree of doneness. The swirl of heat also makes the oven hotter. This can be good and bad. It's great when you want to speed up the roasting of vegetables or crisping of potatoes. However, with the convection setting on, you increase your risk of overcooking food until it's charred, or worse, dry. (You might like some char—I do!) I've put my *Tuscan Mixed Vegetables* to roast in convection settings while catering in order to get dinner ready faster, and then got so busy in the kitchen that I burnt said vegetables, particularly the green beans, and had to throw out half of them. Shit happens. But have I used the convection setting since? Hell yeah! When using convection, I recommend lowering the temperature by 25 degrees in order to avoid disaster. Does this conversation stress you out? Then skip convection. You don't need it!

Tuscan Mixed Vegetables

My sister Tamara is one of the directors of UCLA's Barbra Streisand Women's Cardiovascular Center, and when I lead cooking classes for donors, *Tuscan Mixed Vegetables* are the number one request of the doctors. The culmination of all the other roasted vegetable recipes you just learned, these taste like candy. The secret is lots of olive oil and leaving them in the oven long enough so they can caramelize.

I've even come home from a night of heavy drinking and eaten these straight from the fridge with my hands—who eats vegetables when they're drunk? They're that good.

ADDING THE TASTE OF TUSCANY TO YOUR VEGETABLES

IF YOU SIMPLY ADD...

1. Chopped or sliced red (or yellow) onions

2. Chopped well-ripened tomatoes **AND**

3. Whole sprigs of rosemary

...to any vegetables pieces, and season them with olive oil, salt, and pepper, you can make any roasted veggies "Tuscan." The onion provides sweet juiciness, the tomatoes add a sweet and tart saucey coating, and the rosemary adds the essence of the Italian countryside.

1 butternut squash or large yam, cut into 1-inch cubes

1 red onion, cut into 1-inch pieces

2 fennel bulbs, cut into 1-inch pieces

1 small head of cauliflower, broken into florets of varying sizes

2 vine-ripened tomatoes, cut into 1-inch pieces (See Note)

8 ounces cremini mushrooms

½ cup extra-virgin olive oil

8 (2-inch) pieces of fresh rosemary

2 teaspoons kosher salt

40 grinds of the pepper mill

1. Preheat the oven to 400°F.

2. Place squash or yam, onion, fennel, cauliflower, tomatoes, and mushrooms on a parchment-lined baking sheet so that they're in a single layer. They can be overlapping a bit and touching. It's ok. Drizzle with olive oil. Sprinkle with salt and add the pepper.

3. Place the rosemary on the pan so it's evenly dispersed.

4. Use your fingers to mix it all together so the vegetables have an olive oil/salt/pepper coating. Lick your fingers. Taste good? Adjust the seasoning until it really pops in your mouth! A little too much salt and pepper is better than not enough! Some will burn off in the oven.

5. Bake on the lowest rack of the oven for about 1 hour and 10 minutes. (If you are using 2 baking sheets, switch them halfway through so each gets time on the bottom and closest to the heat source.) At about the 40-minute and the 60-minute marks, stir the vegetables and lay them back down until cooked.

Note: One student added the tomatoes whole by mistake, and then tossed the roasted tomato in with the veggies after they were cooked. She then went back to my original method of chopping tomatoes. But she insists her "mistake" tastes better. It's less chopping, so feel free to give it a try and thank Julia Nickerson!

Veggie Variations: Substitute some vegetables for others depending on the season or your personal preference. However, it will be the onion and the tomato that create the juice, so don't get rid of those! Some other veggies you can use: carrots, celery, sweet potatoes, potatoes, zucchini, beets, parsnips, peppers, or eggplant.

Little Italian Potato Sticks

WITH ROSEMARY AND THYME

One night, returning from an art opening, I had a chance to talk to a couple of Italian friends and tell them what I was preparing for my first ever "Hot Summer Tuscan Nights Cooking Class for Couples." I was, of course, looking for their approval. My friend Barbara is from Tuscany, so I was particularly eager for her praise. I passionately described the potato recipe below and asked for advice on naming it. "They're basically french fries," I muttered. Barbara's strikingly gorgeous face suddenly soured. "Noooo, not French! Don't call them FRENCH fries," she retorted.

The Italians and the French have a centuries-old rivalry that sometimes makes me laugh. They argue about their soccer teams, their wine, their cheese, and their lovemaking. As you can tell from this cookbook, I tend to side with the Italians.

The irony is, these E.U. allies have a lot in common, particularly when it comes to food, art, and romance. The French just take all the credit. French toast, French kissing, and the French press are actually Italian! (The Romans started dipping their bread in egg and milk in the 4th century, tongue kissing was originally called "Florentine kissing," and the so-called "French" press was invented by an Italian guy named Attilio Calimani.)

Whichever of the two cultures you prefer, the fact is: THE ITALIANS COOK BETTER. And so these un-fried, un-French potatoes have been lovingly named after the peninsula that has always loved me back.

Italia, *ti amo.*

2 russet potatoes (See Note)

2 Tablespoons extra-virgin olive oil

2 teaspoons dried thyme

1 teaspoon dried rosemary

2 teaspoons kosher salt

15 grinds of the pepper mill

1. Preheat the oven to 425°F. (400°F for the convection setting.)

2. Place each potato on a cutting board. Slice potatoes lengthwise into ¼-inch "oval sheets." Stack the sheets on top of one another and cut to make them ¼-inch or ½-inch wide matchsticks. It's OK if they aren't perfect. The smaller ones will get crispier and the larger ones will be juicier. It's a good mix. Ultimately, you want some to look like matchstick potatoes, while others should look like skinny imperfect French fries.

3. Place the potato sticks on a parchment-lined baking sheet.

4. Add enough olive oil to liberally cover all the sticks. Add the thyme, rosemary, salt, and pepper.

5. Use your fingers to mix it all together. Lick your fingers. The taste should be bordering almost on too salty, peppery, and herby, as flavor tends to burn off in the oven. If the flavor has no kick on your finger, add more salt and the rest.

6. Bake for 25 to 40 minutes, checking periodically to see if they need to be flipped or shaken up. Baking time will depend on the size of the potato sticks and your oven. Also, if you double or triple the recipe, you will need more baking time. You want them to be golden, browned, and crisp!

Note: This recipe is based on medium-sized organic russet potatoes. If yours are larger, just be more generous with the olive oil and spices. Better too much oil than not enough.

Variation: Follow the same process but add salt and freshly ground pepper generously, omitting the herbs. This is equally good and pairs well with a chicken or meat that has been made with lots of herbs.

Crispy Smashed Fingerling Potatoes *al Limone*

When I make these, I can barely bring the dish to the table without eating quite a few on the way. That said, when I tell people about the recipe, everyone has the same question: "Lemon with potatoes?!"

Yes! It's an unexpected flavor, but that's what makes the dish so enticing. Plus, lemon is a natural *digestivo*. It helps to break down fats. So when paired with olive oil crisped potatoes, it lightens everything up.

That said, if you're serving this with a lemony main, like *Pesce alla Mamma di Edo* (Page 338), skip the lemon. They're delicious with just salt and pepper.

Serves 4 to 6

2 pounds small mixed fingerling or peewee potatoes (See Note)

Scant ½ cup extra-virgin olive oil

1 teaspoon kosher salt

40 grinds of pepper

Zest and juice of 1 lemon

1. Preheat the oven to 450°F.

2. Place the potatoes in a medium pot of water to cover and bring to a boil until you can easily pierce them with a fork, about 20 minutes. Drain and let cool.

3. Line a baking sheet with parchment paper.

4. Using paper towels, your countertop, and the palm of your hand, smash each potato into a flattened "pancake." Place the smashed potatoes on the baking sheet, making sure they don't touch each other.

5. Drizzle on the olive oil, sprinkle with the salt, and grind the pepper. Use your fingers to make sure every potato is coated well with the oil and spices.

6. Cook for 30 minutes. Carefully flip the potatoes, and cook for another 10 minutes.

7. Plate the potatoes in one layer. Drizzle with the lemon juice and scatter the zest on top.

Note: Small fingerling potatoes are sometimes known as peewee potatoes. I prefer these. If you can't find them, use regular fingerlings. If they are large, cut them in half after boiling them, so you get smaller smashed pieces.

Celery Root Puree

This is one of those dishes that makes people think I'm a fancy, culinary-school-trained chef. That's because people usually encounter the distinct flavor of celery root in fine restaurants. Fortunately for us, this celery root puree requires no training, no intricate rule following, and no *haute cuisine* ingredients.

The celery root itself looks like an ugly, bumpy hairball, which is probably why few incorporate it into their home cooking repertoire. But trust me, when it's available in the fall and winter months, celery root is delicious and easy to use.

The reason this puree works so well is that the three main ingredients—celery root, potato, and onion—hang out and get to know each other in a hot tub of homemade *No-Chop Chicken Broth*. By the time they're pureed together, with a little olive oil, butter, and salt, and baked again in the oven, these root veggies achieve the highest level of harmony. What you taste is not restaurant food. What you taste is the heart of homemade. And trust me, it *is* easy.

"So what you're telling me is I have to make a whole pot of soup every time I want celery root puree?" Think of it this way: every time you make a pot of homemade chicken broth—which you'll do more often now that you know how easy and impressive it is—throw in a celery root, a potato or two, an onion, and voilà. Think of it as a blissful by-product of broth, a treat to look forward to that no one will expect. However, you could also simply boil the celery root, potato, and onion in water or store-bought broth.

1 large or 2 small celery roots, peeled

1 or 2 russet potatoes

1 onion

No-Chop Chicken Broth (Page 150) or
No-Chop Veggie Broth (Page 153) or water

¼ cup extra-virgin olive oil

2½ Tablespoons butter,
or olive oil for a non-dairy option

1½ teaspoons kosher salt

20 to 30 grinds of the pepper mill

1. Preheat the oven to 350°F.

2. Place the celery root, potatoes, and onion in a medium pot with enough broth or water to cover. Bring to a boil and cook until tender, about 40 minutes. Let cool. Drain liquid.

3. Remove the skin from the onion. Cut the onion, celery root, and potatoes into pieces and add to a food processor with the butter (or oil), salt, and pepper. You may need to do this in batches. Puree until very smooth.

4. Spread the mixture out in a medium baking dish and cover with aluminum foil.

5. Bake until very hot, about 30 minutes.

6. Serve immediately.

Make Ahead Prep: You can do steps 1 through 4 several days in advance and then bake when ready to serve.

No-Potato Variation: For a lighter version, just omit the potatoes and add more celery root. Your puree won't be as thick, but it'll be lighter.

Rustic Olive Oil Mashed Potatoes

These potatoes have passed the taste tests of my most sophisticated friends as well as my toddler nieces. This is food that will have the whole *mishpacha* wanting seconds.

Of course, like in most of these recipes, the key is the quality of the ingredients. In this case, it all comes down to the broth. If you're not a homemade broth maker, use *Cheater's Chicken Broth*. It's so easy even a *schlemazel* could make it.

These mashed potatoes are textured, not whipped, and keep their skins. Eat them with juicy mains like *Angie's Chicken* (page 362), *Chicken alla Cacciatora,* or *The Best Brisket Ever.*

2 pounds russet potatoes, about 4 small or 2 large

4 bay leaves

4 1-inch pieces of fresh rosemary

⅓ cup extra-virgin olive oil

1½ to 2½ cups *No-Chop Chicken Broth* (Page 150) or *No-Chop Veggie Broth* (Page 153), warmed

1 to 2 teaspoons kosher salt

20 to 30 grinds freshly ground pepper, optional

1. Preheat the oven to 400°F.

2. Slice the potatoes in half, keeping the skin on. Place 1 to 2 bay leaves and 1 to 2 pieces of rosemary in between the two halves, and wrap them back together in a double layers of parchment paper and then in aluminum foil. (This way it's not wrapped in metals.)

3. Bake the potatoes for about an hour or more. They should be soft and easily "squeezable" with oven mitts on. The exact timing will depend on the size of your potatoes.

4. Remove the potatoes and let them sit in their wrapping until they cool a little and continue to soften, about 20 minutes.

5. Unwrap the potatoes, remove and discard the herbs, and cut them into the smallest pieces possible.

6. Place the potatoes in a large bowl. Add the olive oil, 1½ cups of the warm broth, salt, and pepper, if using. Use a potato masher or potato ricer to mash the potatoes and get out as many chunks as possible, adding more broth to help you smooth them out. You will still have some small chunks which I find add a delightful texture. Taste, and add salt or pepper, if needed. Add more broth if you prefer a lighter, thinner consistency.

7. Place the mixture into a medium casserole dish, cover with aluminum foil, and bake until very hot, about 30 minutes.

Note: If you happen to be making broth, cook the potatoes in it! See "As Long As You're Making Broth" (Page 150).

Make Ahead Prep: If you choose, you can do steps 1 through 6 earlier in day or several days in advance. When preparing the dish ahead, err on the side of adding too much broth, as the dish will dry out a bit in fridge. Transfer the mixture to a medium casserole dish, cover, and refrigerate. If you bake it directly from the fridge, give it extra time in the oven.

Grilled Zucchini with Lemon and Mint

When I teach my grilled zucchini recipe, students often ask, "Shouldn't I put salt or olive oil on the zucchini before I grill it?"

Absolutely not. Salt pulls water out of any vegetable, which means you'll steam them instead of getting dark and delicious grill marks. Oiling vegetables before grilling them is also a bad idea. The olive oil burns on the grill and leaves a rancid flavor on the vegetable. Clearly not everyone agrees, as this is a common practice in restaurants. But I hope you'll start paying attention to these details in your own cooking.

Here, we are adding the olive oil after the zucchini have been cooked, so we can savor the raw extra-virgin flavor of it. Be liberal with the lemon. It gives a bright, sunny hello to your mouth. Salt, yeah, you know the drill. The mint should be abundant, as it will be the star of this dish.

Serves 4

4 zucchini, quartered lengthwise into strips

2 Tablespoons extra-virgin olive oil

1 lemon

½ to 1 teaspoon kosher salt

20 grinds of pepper mill

A handful of chopped mint leaves, about ½ cup

1. Heat a grill pan over medium high heat for about 7 minutes. (Alternatively, use your outdoor grill! It will taste even better, but not all of us are that ambitious!)

2. Grill the zucchini until dark grill marks appear on both sides, about 3 to 5 minutes per side. (Don't worry if they are not as soft on the inside as you would like, they'll continue to cook off the grill.)

3. Lay the zucchini flat. (You may overlap to serve, but each piece must first be flavored.)

4. Drizzle with the olive oil. Juice the lemon over it, catching the seeds in the palm of your hands.

5. Sprinkle with salt, about a generous ½ teaspoon. Grind the pepper mill over the platter, about 20 grinds.

6. Sprinkle with the mint.

7. Taste and make sure you like it. Adjust accordingly.

Grilled Endive with Arugula Pesto

This recipe is kind of like a pesto pizza with a grilled vegetable crust (use your imagination a bit!). If you prefer not to fork and knife these, just pick them up with your hands and deliver to an open mouth.

Serves 4 to 6

4 Belgian endive

Arugula Pesto (Page 60)

1. Place a grill pan over medium high heat and let it get hot for 7 minutes.

2. Slice each endive in half, vertically. (You will need the core at the bottom to keep the endive intact.)

3. Once the pan is very hot, place the endive cut-side down on the grill. (That's right, you are not using oil to grease the pan, as it distorts the flavor.) Grill until you have nice dark grill marks and the endive is cooked but still crunchy, 5 to 7 minutes.

4. Top with the *Arugula Pesto*.

Variations: Make the pesto with pine nuts as a variation for this dish. You can also simply top the endive with olive oil, lemon, salt, and pepper.

Braised Tuscan Kale

In case you've forgotten, kale wasn't created for hippies alone! It was placed on earth by God in the rolling, fertile lands of Tuscany so that Italians could eat it while sipping goblets of red wine, feasting on cuts of wild game, laughing, and ferociously arguing with the people they love most.

Kale gets a bad rap because hippies and health food freaks eat it raw or turn it into chips, when, in fact, it's a sturdy vegetable whose true beauty is only released by cooking it on a low flame for a long time. It becomes soft, supple, almost sweet, and yet still brings forth the slight bitterness of its dark green color. It oozes of comfort and tastes of timelessness.

Thanks to the current trendiness of kale, the darker, flat *cavolo nero* (also known as dinosaur kale and lacinato) is now readily available. Don't even look at the curly variety. Leave that one for the hippies!

3 Tablespoons extra-virgin olive oil

1 red onion, thinly sliced

2 vine-ripened tomatoes, cut into ½-inch chunks

2 bunches lacinato or dinosaur kale, lower tough stems removed, cut into 1-inch strips (See Note)

1 to 2 teaspoons kosher salt

¾ cup *No-Chop Chicken Broth* (Page 150) or *No-Chop Veggie Broth* (Page 153)

1. Place a heavy-bottomed pan or a braiser, which has a lid, over medium heat for about 7 minutes.

2. Add the the olive oil followed immediately by the onion. Cook until lightly caramelized, about 7 minutes.

3. Add the tomatoes, and stir around the onion mixture to cook them down. After 3 to 4 minutes, add the kale and salt, and use your tongs to toss the pieces well with the tomatoes and onions.

4. Add the broth, cover, and decrease the heat to medium low.

5. Cook until the kale is darkened in color and very soft, about an hour.

Note: Many recipes will call for removing the center stems of the kale because they can be tough. This isn't necessary when slow-cooking. Just be sure to cut off the thicker stems at the bottom of the bunch.

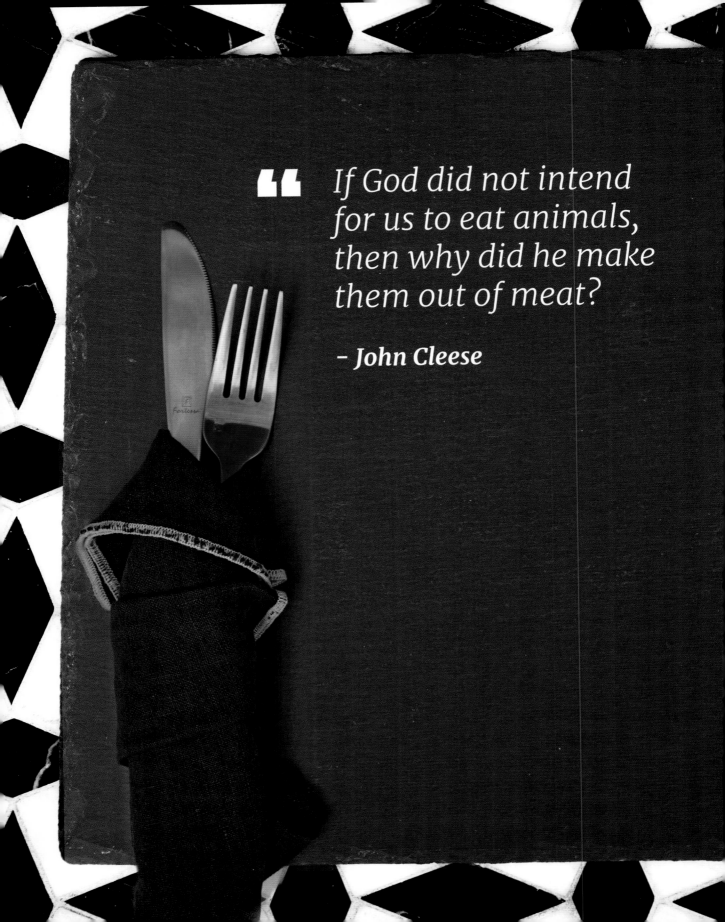

> *If God did not intend for us to eat animals, then why did he make them out of meat?*
>
> – John Cleese

Mind-Blowing Mains

ALLA GRIGLA — **ON THE GRILL**

12-MINUTE CHICKEN WITH HERBES DE PROVENCE

CHICKEN SORRENTINO

PESCE ALLA MAMMA DI EDO

GRILLED STEAK

AL FORNO — **INTO THE OVEN**

THYME ROASTED SALMON

PISTACHIO-CRUSTED SALMON

ONE-PAN WHITE FISH

HERB-CRUSTED RACK OF LAMB

RISTORANTE ROASTED WHOLE BRANZINO

ANGIE'S CHICKEN

ROAST LEG OF LAMB

CARNE MACINATA (MAH-CHEE-NAH-TA) **GROUND MEATS**

ELANA'S FAMOUS TURKEY MEATBALLS

CHICKEN CRACK

BELLO LENTO — **NICE AND SLOW**

CHICKEN ALLA CACCIATORA

MARIA'S CHICKEN

SKI CHALET CHICKEN

SEPPIE COI PISELLI

THE BEST BRISKET EVER

MY STUDENTS ARE ALWAYS ASKING ME FOR MORE CHICKEN recipes, more fish recipes, and more meat. That's because menu planning usually starts with the main course. Once you've chosen the big, dominant flavor, you can balance it with salads, soups, sides, and desserts that complement, rather than clash with, the main dish. In response to their requests, I created a series of classes: "Monday Night Chicken," "Monday Night Fish," and "Monday Night Carnivore." From the many recipes I taught in those classes, I've chosen the ones here for two simple reasons: they're really good, and they're really easy. This chapter will introduce you to a handful of techniques for cooking them, which will allow you to apply your knowledge to a variety of proteins. As with all Italian cooking, the ingredients are key: fresh, organic, local meat and fish will taste far better than the factory-farmed variety. Take your time and enjoy the process!

LIFE LESSON THROUGH FOOD

Don't Give The Thigh To The Dog!

I was raised on dry, rubbery chicken breasts, and well into my adult life I suffered under the delusion that white meat, with all its flavorless protein, was the pinnacle of chicken consumption. I had to travel to Rome to see the truth.

It happened like this: I was living with my then-boyfriend Federico, cooking him lunch and dinner—and there's no better culinary education than cooking for a real live Italian man. One day, I roasted a chicken, and as I was waiting for Federico to come to the table, I trimmed some of the thigh and leg and tossed it to his dog.

Federico nearly lost his temper, a rarity for this uncharacteristically mellow Italian man. His hands flew into the air as he struggled to give meaning to words he couldn't articulate. "You gave the thigh to the dog?! You don't give the thigh to the dog. *La coscia* (the thigh) *è la parte piu buona. La coscia, la coscia,* I can't believe it, *la coscia,*" he kept repeating. He went on about this for a week.

Jesus Christ. What did I know? I grew up in a Jewish neighborhood, brainwashed by the American Ashkenazi Dry-and-Rubbery-White-Meat Chicken Society. We went on expensive vacations just to eat dry white meat chicken in a change of scenery. I didn't know what I was missing.

That night, Federico ate the remaining thigh, but the next time I roasted chicken, I made sure to try a thigh myself. From that moment on, I've been a hard-core convert.

Because dark meat is juicier, it's nearly impossible to overcook, which makes it foolproof for home cooks. It absorbs the flavor of whatever spices or liquids you cook it in, increasing the love-taste quotient. Using dark meat chicken will up your game even if you're all thumbs in the kitchen.

❝ *We all like chicken.*

—Malcolm X

Me with Back, who's full name was Back to the Scene of the Crime, pronounced of course with an Italian accent.

Alla Griglia

ON THE GRILL

12-Minute Chicken with Herbes de Provence

This is the meal that launched the spiel. Years ago, a family friend paid me to teach her to cook. Her husband was battling aggressive melanoma, and she wanted to learn to prepare healthy, delicious food for him. At that point, he refused to eat anything healthy that she cooked, and the only kind of chicken he would eat was fried. She felt desperate.

In my first cooking class ever, I taught her to make chicken with herbes de Provence, which couldn't be easier, and her husband loved it. She called, elated: "He ate my chicken, Elana! And he loved it! I need another cooking class now!"

So I taught another class, and another, and another, and before I knew it, I was transforming my community in Los Angeles into badass cooks.

The secret to this chicken—besides grilling *thighs*—is the sprinkled salt on each piece and the extra kick of fennel we give our herbes de Provence. It's a perfect combination, and it's worked from Day One.

Serves 4 to 6

2 Tablespoons herbes de Provence

2 Tablespoons fennel seeds

8 boneless, skinless chicken thighs, room temperature

1½ teaspoons kosher salt

8 fresh rosemary sprigs,
cut into 1 or 2-inch pieces, optional

1. Place a grill pan over medium high heat and let it get hot for a couple of minutes.

2. Mix the herbes de Provence and fennel in a small bowl.

3. Place the chicken thighs on the grill pan, and sprinkle each with half of the herbes de Provence mixture and salt. Place a piece of the rosemary branch to rest on top of each piece, if using.

4. After 6 minutes, remove the rosemary and flip the chicken. Sprinkle the remaining herbes de Provence mixture and salt on the other side, and replace the rosemary. Cook for another 6 to 8 minutes, until done.

5. Serve hot or at room temperature.

Chicken Sorrentino

WITH CHOPPED TOMATOES AND CAPERS

If you've been paying attention, you know that I feel very strongly about dark meat chicken. It will make a beginner cook seem like a badass. That said, some people still insist on white meat, for its lower calories and fat or because they have no taste buds. So I challenged myself to create a white meat chicken recipe that would be juicy and delicious and *better* because it's white meat. This is that recipe.

The trick is to pound your chicken thin, soak it in lemon and olive oil, and grill it quickly, so it doesn't have time to dry out. I top it with a tomato-caper topping, but if capers aren't your thing, feel free to use the tomato-basil topping from my *Tomato Bruschetta*.

For the chicken:

4 boneless, skinless chicken breasts

2 Tablespoons extra-virgin olive oil

2 to 3 fresh lemons

1 teaspoon kosher salt, divided

For the tomato-caper topping:

1 pint cherry tomatoes, or 2 to 3 vine-ripened or 8 roma tomatoes

2 to 3 Tablespoons salt-packed capers, rinsed

½ cup finely chopped flat-leaf parsley

1 Tablespoon thinly sliced basil, about 5 to 6 leaves

3 Tablespoons extra-virgin olive oil

½ teaspoon kosher salt

20 to 30 grinds of the pepper mill

Prepare the chicken:

1. Place the chicken on a clean work surface. Hold a long sharp knife on the long side of the chicken and slice into the breast with a sawing motion, until you get most of the way through. Do not cut all the way across . Fold it open like a book. If it's not perfect, don't worry.

2. Place one breast between two pieces of plastic wrap or wax paper. Use a meat mallet, a rolling pin, or my personal favorite, a flat-bottomed mug, to pound it out so that's it's ¼-inch thick—very thin! Repeat with the other breasts.

3. Place the pounded breasts in a bowl with a healthy drizzling of the olive oil, the juice of one lemon, and ½ teaspoon of the salt. Make sure the breasts are well covered by the oil and lemon juice, and let sit for a half hour.

Prepare the tomato-caper topping:

1. Cut the tomatoes into ½-inch cubes or smaller and place in a medium bowl.

2. Finely chop the capers. Add the capers, parsley, and the basil to the bowl.

3. Drizzle generously with the olive oil, add a sprinkling of salt and freshly ground pepper until it tastes fantastic.

Finish the dish:

1. Place a grill pan over medium high heat and let it get hot for a good ten minutes. You want it very hot!

2. Remove the chicken from its marinade, and put it directly on the pan for about 2 minutes per side, depending on the thickness. (It's better to take it off while it's a little pink inside than to overdo it. By the time you get the chicken to your plate, it will be cooked.)

3. Squeeze the remaining lemons with a sprinkle of salt over the chicken, and serve with the tomato-caper topping. Feel free to pour the juices from the tomatoes on there too.

Pesce alla Mamma di Edo

GRILLED BRANZINO WITH LEMON AND OLIVES

Two minutes prep. Six minutes cook time. A meal worthy of your finest guests.

This recipe was inspired by Edo, the kind of Italian man that American girls can't help but fall for. With long dark curls that bounce in joy as he walks and gray-blue eyes that sparkle with depth and intelligence, Edo has a smile that runs across his face like an Italian sports car. Even the way he dresses, in loose jeans, driving loafers, and a soft cashmere sweater, draws you toward him. Yet when shirtless, he boasts tattoos of gruesome monsters, as well as a naked girl with a slit throat. So there's that. He's like a golden retriever on bad acid: a huge heart laced with danger, drawing in unsuspecting women with the mysterious waggings of his tail.

The only child of divorced parents in once-royal, now-industrial Turin, in Northern Italy, Edo grew up quite alone. Edo's mother, unlike a typical *mamma italiana*, worked full-time, leaving Edo's rearing to a series of hired hands. In the summers, when everybody went to the seaside on vacation, Edo went with Irma and Lino, an elderly couple, to a rented apartment on the Riviera, where his mother met him on the weekends. Though happy to be free to run around the beachside town, Edo missed his mom. So she sent Irma to the shore with a list of her favorite recipes to make for her son. *La mamma di Edo* made her love and presence known through food.

This is one of her recipes.

The secret to this fish: You grill it, and then place it on a platter with abundant lemon juice, and some olive oil, salt and oregano. The fish soaks the juices right in, so there is no way this fish could ever be dry, even if you overcook it. Another magical touch to turn beginners into badasses.

Serves 2 to 4

For the topping:

20 pitted Kalamata olives, coarsely chopped

¼ cup coarsely chopped flat-leaf parsley

3 to 4 Tablespoons extra-virgin olive oil

40 grinds of pepper mill

For the fish:

2 juicy lemons

2 Tablespoons extra-virgin olive oil

½ teaspoon kosher salt

½ teaspoon dried oregano

2 whole branzinos, filleted (See Note)

Note: Each fish has two fillets. In a dinner that has other courses, one fillet per person is enough. That said, I always make extra, in case someone wants seconds. Since this fish is also great served at room temperature, I sometimes use it on a buffet with salads or *Grilled Eggplant Burrata Involtini* (Page 133). In that case, I cut each fillet in half before grilling to make smaller servings.

Make Ahead Prep: This fish will not dry out while it sits in the lemon juice, so it's ok to prepare it a couple of hours ahead and serve at room temperature.

Fish Variation: Edo originally made this recipe with a fully cooked tuna steak. For years I taught the recipe with swordfish fillets. In Hawaii, I've made it with opah and Mahi Mahi. The point is you can try this with all kinds of grilled fish, though cooking times will vary. Just think of Edo and his mom when you do!

Topping Variation: You can also use the tomato-caper topping from *Chicken Sorrentino* (Page 336).

Prepare the topping:

1. Place the olives and parsley in a small bowl and drizzle with the olive oil until the ingredients are well coated. Grind in the pepper, which will temper the saltiness of the olives. Mix well and set aside.

Prepare the fish:

1. Light your grill or grill pan and let it get very, very hot.

2. Squeeze the lemons on the platter you intend to use to serve the fish. Add the olive oil, salt, and oregano. Swirl it around and lick your finger to taste. Adjust the seasoning. You want it lemony, but with enough salt and olive oil to temper the lemons.

3. Dry your fish really, really well with paper towels. Drying the skin will prevent it from sticking to the pan. This is important. Cook the fish for about 4 to 5 minutes skin-side down, until you get some nice grill marks and a golden skin. Your skin might stick until it is nice and cooked, so just chill out. (If you find that your skin is sticking completely for some reason, just drizzle a little oil on the side of it while it cooks. That will help loosen it up.)

4. Flip it over and cook for about 2 minutes on the other side, until you see golden marks on the flesh.

5. Place fish flesh-side down on the prepared lemon platter and let it sit for 5 minutes, to soak in the juices. Before serving, flip the fish over and spoon some of the lemony juices over it. Top with a nice spoonful or two of the olive mixture. (Alternatively you can serve it skin side up, which is quite pretty.)

6. Serve warm or at room temperature.

ABOVE: Edo and his mom.
RIGHT: Edo, decked out.

THE SIMPLE TWO RULES YOU NEED TO KNOW
SO YOUR MEATS GRILL TO PERFECTION

» **Always bring your meat or chicken to room temperature before grilling it,** removing it from the fridge at least 30 minutes before grilling, or longer for thick pieces. (This goes for roasting, too.) Otherwise the inside won't cook as quickly as the outside, resulting in meat that's burnt on the outside and raw in the middle. How many times has that happened to you?!

» **Get your grill HOT before you put anything on it.** Otherwise, you'll mess up your cooking times and temperatures and risk drying out your meats.

TENDERIZING RED MEAT AND THE BIG MISTAKE I MADE
WHILE CATERING A DINNER PARTY

Years ago, thanks to food blogger Jaden Hair of *SteamyKitchen.com*, I learned a quick and easy way to make sure that steak always comes out tender: salt it. Salting your meat—steaks, roasts, and racks of lamb—means letting it sit in salt for about an hour before cooking it. Little beads of water will appear on your meat. This is part of the tenderization process and ensures a juicy piece of meat, granted, of course, you don't overcook it. (Breathe. It's okay. We've all overcooked meat in our time.)

Attenzione: not just any salt will do! Once, when I was catering a dinner party, I found that the hostess didn't have kosher salt in the house. Instead of running to the market only blocks away, I went ahead and covered the meat with table salt from her pantry. Needless to say, the steak turned out so tough that I refunded her money—and to add salt to a wound (pun intended) this woman's daughter is the owner of many popular restaurants in LA. How embarrassing is that?! The only explanation for the tough meat is the shitty salt she had in the kitchen, and my lazy belief that all salt was interchangeable. I now bring a box of kosher salt to every home I cook in. Got it? Only tenderize with kosher or coarse sea salt.

Grilled Steak

WITH ARUGULA, PARMIGIANO, AND BALSAMIC REDUCTION

Every Valentine's Day, I teach a couples' cooking class. Since I want to get everyone outside to the flower-laden and candle-flooded courtyard at a decent hour, we don't have time for elaborate dishes. After making burrata crostini and getting the potato sticks in the oven, I want the main course done fast, and I want it to speak sensuality. Americans aren't accustomed to greenery atop their meat, but this style of steak is typical Roman trattoria fare. To me, the red meat paired with spicy bites of raw arugula and nutty Parmigiano Reggiano, screams "Ravage me! (even though we've been married fifteen years and need a vacation, and I can't stand the sweater you're wearing tonight)."

I prefer a flank steak to the wimpier cuts that are used traditionally in this recipe, and I think you will too. Leftovers are highly recommended for sandwiches.

GIVE IT A REST!

If you're impulsive and impatient, like me, this will be innately difficult for you. When you take your steak off the grill or your lamb or chicken out of the oven, just let it sit. Allow it to fill your kitchen with tantalizing aromas like a siren's song, but don't eat it quite yet, no matter how hungry you feel. Hard, right? Red meat, and roasted chicken too, need time to do their thing. Don't cut it or serve it immediately, or you'll lose a lot of the juices that make it tender and flavorful.

Attenzione: meat finishes cooking even after you take it away from the heat source. If you want your steak light pink on the inside, take it off when it's medium pink and let it rest a good five minutes. For a rack of lamb, a touch more. For a whole chicken, let it rest a minimum of 10 minutes. For a roast, up to 20. These are minimums! A tiny taste on the side to see if it's cooked to your liking (or because you can't control yourself) is permitted by me. Other chefs don't allow this, but I'm giving you a pass. Practice makes perfect.

Serves 4 to 6

1½ to 2 pounds flank steak, ideally in one large piece

Kosher salt

Freshly ground pepper

1 lemon

Rosemary-Balsamic Reduction (Page 61) or store-bought balsamic glaze

Baby arugula, about 3 handfuls

Parmigiano Reggiano, shaved

1. Lay the flank steak on a plate and let it come to room temperature.

2. Cover the steak with a thin layer of salt on each side. Let it sit for 45 minutes.

3. Place a grill pan over medium high heat and let it get hot, 7 minutes.

4. Rinse off the steak and pat it dry with paper towels.

5. Generously grind pepper on both sides.

6. Grill the steak for about 5 minutes on each side for medium rare. (It will continue to cook after you take it off, so err on the side of a little too pink.)

7. Transfer the steak to a cutting board and let it rest for 5 to 7 minutes. Squeeze the lemon over it.

8. Slice the steak across the grain into thin pieces, about ½-inch thick.

9. Place the slices on individual plates or on a serving platter. Drizzle lightly with balsamic.

10. Top with arugula, garnish with shaved cheese, and finish with another drizzle of the balsamic

11. Eat immediately and expect silence.

Dairy-Free Variation: Replace cheese with *Toasted Pine Nuts* (Page 64).

Al Forno

INTO THE OVEN

Thyme Roasted Salmon

Do you avoid cooking fish at home because you think it's too scary? I know your type. I used to be like you.

You only eat seafood at restaurants, convincing yourself that you could never deal with all those scales, skin and bones—not to mention fish's delicate flavors—at home. After all, how could you compete with a restaurant full of professional cooks?

For starters, you choose the freshest fish available. (Restaurants can't always be kept to this standard.) Second of all, you aren't a line cook working for a measly hourly wage. Passion is in your pocket!

This easy, delicious recipe can get you started. It's an instant addition to all of my students' repertoires. I have always made it without skin, because it cooks quicker in the oven that way. As long as you don't overcook it, it's even good at room temperature. That said, my editor Seth was dismayed to read that I was cooking salmon without the skin. "That's my favorite part," he said.

Well, I love crispy salmon skin too, so I came up with a variation of this recipe. We just place the fish under the broiler with the skin up, so it crisps while the salmon finishes underneath it, in its juices. I'm a genius, again!

2 pounds fresh Atlantic salmon fillets, skinned and cut into 6 equal pieces, about 1 to 1½-inches wide

Juice of 2 lemons

2 Tablespoons tamari or quality soy sauce

⅓ cup extra-virgin olive oil

1½ teaspoons kosher or Celtic salt

2 Tablespoons dried thyme

Freshly ground pepper, optional

1. Turn on the broiler. Place an oven rack on the second from the top rung. Let it get hot for at least 7 minutes.

2. Place the salmon on a foil-covered baking sheet. Squeeze fresh lemon juice all over the fillets, not worrying whether seeds come out. It's ok, they won't hurt anyone.

3. Drizzle the tamari and olive oil liberally on each piece. (Yes, some will fall off the sides, that's why we are drizzling liberally.)

4. Sprinkle the salt and thyme over each piece, making sure the salmon is mostly coated with the thyme. Grind the pepper, if using.

5. Place the salmon under the broiler for 7 to 8 minutes. (Exact cooking times are contingent on the width and thickness of the fillets. You want salmon just cooked, or even a touch raw. It will have finished cooking by the time you get it on the plate.)

6. Serve with pan juices, if there are any.

Crispy Skin Variation: Move your oven rack to the second rung from the bottom. Let the broiler heat up for at least 7 minutes. Dress the salmon as above, then flip it over so the skin is face up. Give a little extra drizzle of oil on the skin. Place it in the oven for about 8 minutes. Timing will greatly depend on the thickness of your salmon, so just take a peek on the side of one piece and remove from the oven when it's just a hair from being fully cooked.

Pistachio-Crusted Salmon

WITH PECORINO AND LEMON ZEST

Effortlessly impressive and packed with protein and omegas, this one will leave your taste buds, your body, and your guests thanking you. Anyone can make it, provided, of course, you know how to go to the market and buy salmon, pistachios, and pecorino. (And you know how to turn on your oven, which by this point in the book, you should have covered.)

Want to make this for lots of people? No problem—it's a great ladies' luncheon dish. Just "bread" the salmon ahead of time and keep it in the fridge until you're ready for it. Cook as instructed.

Want to make it just for yourself? Go ahead and make the pistachio mixture, and freeze most of it. Use a small portion for just one piece of fish. Go back to your freezer when you want more.

¾ cup roasted, salted pistachios

¼ cup grated Pecorino Romano

60 grinds of the pepper mill

Zest of 1 lemon

2 pounds Atlantic salmon, without skin, cut into 6 equal vertical slices

Juice of 1 lemon

1. Preheat the oven to 450°F and line a baking sheet with parchment paper.

2. Place the pistachios in a food processor or spice grinder and pulse until they are ground up. You want them in a small, gritty grind, but not a powder. It's ok if there is unevenness, meaning some bits are a little bigger. This will add texture.

3. Place the pistachios in a small bowl along with the Pecorino Romano, pepper, and lemon zest. Mix with your fingers and take a moment to love and thank the food you are cooking.

4. Coat each piece of salmon with the pistachio mix and gently press down until all sides are coated with this yumminess. Lay the salmon on the baking sheet, making sure the fillets don't touch.

5. Bake for 10 minutes.

6. Serve immediately with fresh lemon wedges, or squeeze the lemon on it yourself.

Mangia, Mangia Che Ti Fa Bene!

It's impossible to get through more than a few meals in Italy without someone saying *"mangia, mangia che ti fa bene,"* to you, meaning, "Eat, eat, it's good for you for to eat."

And it's not just grandmothers—in Italy, men and women *flirt* using this expression. (Italian men like their women like they like their lamb: with some meat on the bones.)

Given the diet-obsessed LA world I grew up in, it was incredibly healing for me, at 20 years old, to enter into a culture where men encouraged women to eat with passion.

It *is* important to take care of our bodies and to feed them healthy food. But it's *also* important to allow ourselves to indulge. Our spirits need it.

Italians understand this. And that's why they're such a gorgeous and playful people.

Have you ever ordered the lightest thing on the menu and then gone to the movies to eat a pound of popcorn and a box of Milk Duds because your appetite wasn't satisfied? So satisfy your appetite! Find the balance between indulgence and self-care. Find the calm point between shoving food in your face and fearfully picking at your plate. Live along the fine line between passion and consciousness. Cooking gives us the opportunity to get our hands involved in orchestrating this harmony.

Please don't just choose the deliciously light fish and vegetable dishes I provide you with here because you feel you don't deserve the sensually hardier meaty, bready, and cheesy ones. You deserve it all! Give yourself permission to access your inner Italian and truly enjoy all kinds of foods. (It's when we don't give ourselves permission to indulge that we overindulge in junk.)

Some recipes in this book are richer than others. But all of them are made with whole, unprocessed and hopefully organic ingredients. When cooked with love, they will feed your spirit. So *mangia, mangia, che ti fa bene!*

 I'd much rather eat pasta and drink wine than be a size zero.

—Sophia Loren

One-Pan White Fish
WITH SHALLOTS AND WHITE WINE

Beginners, listen up: this is how it's going to roll. Basically, you're going to sauté shallots and garlic first, then place the white fish in the pan, and spoon the shallots and garlic on top of the fish. You will add a little wine (and salt and pepper), and place the whole thing in the oven. You can do this!!

Serves 2 to 3

2 Tablespoons extra-virgin olive oil

2 large shallots, finely chopped

1 garlic clove, finely chopped

1 pound fresh white fish fillet, ideally in one piece

Kosher salt, about a ½ teaspoon

Freshly ground pepper

¼ cup white wine

Zest of ½ lemon

Juice of one lemon

Finely chopped flat-leaf parsley

1. Preheat the oven to 450°F.

2. Place an oven-safe or cast-iron pan over medium high heat and let it get hot for a couple of minutes.

3. Add the olive oil to coat the bottom of the pan. Add the shallots, and let them sauté for a couple of minutes until soft. Cook longer if you want them sweeter. Add the garlic, and sauté for an extra minute or so.

4. Scooch the shallots and garlic to the side, and place the fish skin-side down in the pan. Sprinkle with salt and pepper.

5. As best you can, place the shallots and garlic on top of the fish and drizzle with the wine.

6. Transfer the pan to the oven, and bake until you can break off a piece of fish easily with a fork and the flesh is just opaque, about 12 minutes.

7. Top with lemon zest, lemon juice, and parsley. Needs more flavor? Add more salt!

Variation: Feel free to try this recipe with different fish. I tested it with a fresh rainbow trout fillet, skin on. It cooked in 5 to 7 minutes.

Herb-Crusted Rack of Lamb

Rack of lamb is another one of those recipes that looks so impressive that people assume only a true chef can cook it. In fact, I was one of those people.

But all you need to do is brown the lamb in a pan with olive oil, and then stick it in the oven for 12 minutes. It couldn't be easier. The crust is herbs, rather than breadcrumbs, so you save the carb calories for dessert. When I'm catering, I love to cut this rack into chops, and send servers out with them on wooden boards. It has so much flavor it doesn't need a sauce.

2 Tablespoons ground coriander

1 Tablespoon dried thyme

1 teaspoon dried sage

⅛ teaspoon cumin

1 Tablespoon kosher salt

1 rack of lamb (1.3 to 1.5 pounds)

1 to 2 Tablespoons extra-virgin olive oil

1. Mix the coriander, thyme, sage, cumin, and salt in a small bowl.

2. Rub the herb mixture all over the lamb (front, back, sides, the fleshy parts of the bones, etc.)

3. Let it sit for at least an hour.

4. Preheat the oven to 400°F and line a baking sheet with parchment paper.

5. Place a heavy-bottomed pan over medium high heat and let get hot for a couple of minutes.

6. Add the olive oil to cover the bottom of the pan. Add the lamb and brown on all sides until it's nice and golden brown. Remember the top! You have to flip the lamb upside down to do this! Tongs are very helpful here.

7. Place the lamb on the baking sheet, and let it rest for at least 10 minutes.

8. Bake the lamb in the oven for about 12 minutes. Remove from the oven, tent with foil, and let rest it for at least 7 minutes.

9. Hold the lamb up by the bones, and use a sharp knife to slice it into chops. You may need to wiggle the knife around a bit to find that perfect place where you can slice the bones apart.

Make Ahead Prep: You can season the lamb up to a day in advance. You can also brown it several hours before finishing. But if you put it in your fridge, be sure it sits at room temperature for at least an hour before it goes in the oven.

Ristorante Roasted Whole Branzino

WITH GARLIC, LEMON, AND ROSEMARY

This is one of those dishes that you order at a fancy Italian restaurant, plunking down around $40 for a whole fish and watching a white-clad waiter filet it tableside with surgical precision. Well, guess what? You can make it at home! The finest Italian restaurants can't serve a fish any more delicious than the recipe below. And you don't need to be a career waiter to filet it properly. Neanderthals ate fish, and most of them barely graduated high school. This is how humans are intended to eat fish, and once you've tried it, you'll get the hang of it in no time.

This recipe is an adaption of Coleman Andrew's *Roast Whole Seabass* from his book *The Country Cooking of Italy.*

P.S. You don't need to filet the whole fish before you eat it. Just use your fork to gently pull some of the top flesh off and start eating. When you've finished the top, use your fingers and maybe the help of a fork or knife to cleanly lift off the bones. Now eat the bottom!

1 whole branzino (about 1 pound), cleaned and butterflied

½ teaspoon kosher salt

½ lemon, cut into 2 to 3 slices

1 sprig fresh rosemary

3 garlic cloves, divided

2 Tablespoons extra-virgin olive oil

1. Preheat the oven to 425°F, and line a baking sheet with parchment paper.

2. Rinse and dry the fish well. Make three slits through the fish's skin on one side with a sharp knife. This will allow the flavors to seep in from the top.

3. Salt it generously inside and out. Lay the fish down with the slits up. Place the sliced lemon, rosemary, and 2 garlic cloves inside the cavity of the fish.

4. Chop the remaining garlic, and heat the olive oil in a small pan over medium heat. Add the garlic and sauté until golden, just a few minutes. Don't let it burn! Pour the oil and the garlic over the fish.

5. Place the fish in the oven for about 18 minutes. (You'll know it's done when the flesh easily pulls away with a fork.)

6. EAT! (Squeeze the roasted lemon slices on the fish if you like.)

IS IT SAFE TO KEEP PUTTING MY HANDS INTO THE SALT JAR?

Well, it's never killed me. Salt is naturally antibacterial. That's why it's a great preservative. In fact, "salt" and "salary" have the same etymological root, because mercenary soldiers in Ancient Rome were paid in salt. Before the days of refrigeration, people risked lives for salt, not because it flavored food, but because it preserved it. Salt was necessary for survival. That's how powerful it is. So just chill out and stick your fingers in there.

Angie's Chicken

WITH JUICY ONIONS AND HERBS

It wouldn't be honest to write a book that shares my personal cook's journey without paying homage to Angie. Before there was Maria from Tuscany, there was Angie from Granada.

Angie was my family's housekeeper for 27 years and a fabulous cook and mentor. As you've read, my mother, a feminist whose beliefs precluded cooking, and my father, a Midwesterner raised on canned peaches, fed me and my sisters a diet of frozen food, taco nights, and jars of spaghetti sauce for my first 13 years. That's when, in the name of having healthy teenage daughters, my parents hired Angie.

Angie's from Granada, a tiny island in the Caribbean that, throughout its history, has suffered devastating hurricanes, poverty, and colonialism. In Granada, cooking isn't a luxury like it is here. It's a necessity. Fortunately for Angie, she has the touch. She knows how to cook for over a hundred people, because, as she's explained, there's no such thing as a Caribbean party with fewer than a hundred people. Years ago, my grandmother taught her how to make matzo ball soup and other Jewish recipes, and every year on Passover, this badass from the Caribbean cooked us a feast for forty.

If Angie had been raised with the same opportunities I had, this brilliant multi-tasker would likely have spent her career managing a huge business operation. Instead, she was a blessing to our family, and particularly to me, as she generously let me into the kitchen and patiently helped as I took my first steps toward learning to cook.

Angie has lots of chicken recipes, but this one is by far the favorite of my nieces and nephew. It's flavorful in a gentle way that humans of all ages can't help but love. Angie insists that kosher chicken is the juiciest, and that's all she buys, even for the stews and curries she makes for her Caribbean parties. The chicken is cooked on a thick bed of onions and herbs. Inside the oven, it all transforms into a juicy goodness you can't resist.

Thank you Angie!

6 large sprigs of rosemary plus 1½ Tablespoons chopped fresh rosemary

2 large yellow onions, coarsely chopped

12 sprigs of thyme plus 1½ Tablespoons chopped fresh thyme

4 to 5 stems of sage

5 garlic cloves, cut in half vertically

4 pounds bone-in chicken parts

½ cup extra-virgin olive oil

Kosher salt (1 Tablespoon or ½ to 1 teaspoon if using kosher chicken)

4 to 5 grinds of the pepper mill

1 teaspoon paprika

1. Preheat the oven to 350°F.

2. Break up the sprigs of rosemary into 1 to 2-inch pieces.

3. Line a medium roasting pan with the onions. Follow by making a "bed" for the chicken with the rosemary sprigs, thyme sprigs, sage, and garlic.

4. Angie's Major Rule! Whether you choose to rinse the chicken or not, make sure you dry it very well with paper towels.

5. Rub the dried chicken with about half of the olive oil, the salt, the chopped rosemary, chopped thyme, pepper, and paprika. Place on top of the bed of onions and herbs in the pan, preferably without the chicken pieces touching one another. Drizzle the rest of the olive oil onto the onions.

6. Roast uncovered for 1 hour. Take the chicken out of the oven, and baste it with its juices using a baster or a spoon. Place the chicken back in the oven for another 45 minutes. I know, it roasts a long time!

7. Top with the juices and onions and enjoy!

Angie and me.

Roast Leg of Lamb

WITH TANGERINE AND THYME

Okay, here we go. This is the hardest recipe in this chapter, but you can do it.

The first time I made leg of lamb, I learned a great trick from the head butcher at Gelson's in Century City. He offered to cut out the bone from the center of the leg of lamb, then stick it back in and tie it together with twine. This way, the bone flavors the meat as it cooks, and you can easily remove the bone to slice all the way through the meat when it's done. I know there's a low-hanging bone joke here, but this is a dignified cookbook and I won't resort to that kind of juvenile humor. Plus I don't like low-hanging bones. Bazinga!

Five things that make this lamb so unbelievably good:

1. It's cooked on the bone, which means more flavor and juiciness.

2. The bone "magically" disappears, making it easy to slice.

3. Since the bone has been cut out, you can rub the zesty herb mixture inside and out before cooking. At the end, when you're slicing, each piece will be fully circled by the yummy flavors.

4. By rubbing the lamb with salt and the rest of the zesty herbs a day before you cook it, the lamb's sure to be super tender and flavorful. Though cooks debate endlessly whether pre-salting meats adds or detracts from juiciness and flavor, most agree that pre-salting lamb adds extra yumminess.

5. We get the fat without the fat. Fat helps to insulate meats as they roast, holding in juices and adding to flavor. However, the problem with cooking a leg of lamb with the fat is: First, most people don't like to be served a fatty piece of meat. Second, the fat is covering surface area that our yummy herb rub can't reach. So ask your butcher to cut off the fat (or you can easily do this yourself), but don't throw it out. We'll cover the lamb with the rub, reaching the area that would have been underneath the fat. Then, we will lay the fat on top, and roast the lamb so the fat can insulate the meat and add its prized flavor. We'll then discard it before serving.

Serves 10

Special Equipment:

Kitchen twine

Meat thermometer

Roasting pan with a rack

1 bunch fresh thyme

1 bunch fresh rosemary

1 bunch fresh sage

Zest of and juice 8 satsuma tangerines
or 2 large oranges

2 Tablespoons kosher salt

40 grinds of a pepper mill

½ cup extra-virgin olive oil

1 (6-pound) leg of lamb (See Note)

2 Tablespoons *Rosemary-Balsamic Reduction*
(Page 61) or store-bought balsamic glaze

6 garlic cloves, cut into slivers

The Day Before:

1. Remove the thyme and rosemary leaves from the sprig. The thinnest twigs are ok to leave in. Remove the sage leaves from the stems. Chop until you have a combined ½ cup of the three herbs.

2. Make a rub by combining the chopped herbs, tangerine zest, kosher salt, pepper, and olive oil in a small bowl. Set the tangerines or oranges aside.

3. Open up the lamb, and remove the bone temporarily. Rub the herb and zest mix all over the lamb, inside and out. Put the bone back in, then close up the lamb. Wrap with plastic wrap and place in the fridge overnight.

Day of, Step 1:

1. Take the lamb out the fridge about two hours before you intend to cook it, and let it come to room temperature.

2. Turn on the broiler, and position a rack in the center of the oven. Let the oven get hot for at least 10 minutes.

3. Open up the lamb, temporarily remove the bone, and rub the balsamic glaze inside and out. It will encourage just a touch of charred bits, which I love.

4. Put half of the garlic pieces inside the lamb. Replace the bone, and use your kitchen twine to wrap around the lamb. You will need about 6 pieces of twine at 2 to 3-inch intervals so they hold the lamb tightly together. Reserve the removed layer of fat (See Note).

5. Use a sharp knife to stab small slits in the surface of the lamb, and insert the remaining garlic.

6. Place the lamb on a rack in a roasting pan. Add 1 to 2 cups of water to the bottom of the pan so it covers the surface.

7. Broil the lamb for 8 to 9 minutes, until very browned and, perhaps, even a touch charred in places. Carefully flip it over, and broil for another 8 minutes. Take the lamb out of the oven.

Day of, Step 2:

1. Cover the top of the lamb with the reserved fat.

2. Turn off the broiler and set the oven temperature to 325˚F.

3. Return the lamb to the oven, and cook for nearly an hour. Calculate cooking time at about 9 to 12 minutes per pound. It is better to err on the side of undercooking. You want to aim for medium rare, which is perfect for lamb. Because the lamb will have thinner and thicker parts, some of it will be more well done than others. As a result, those people who like more well-cooked pieces will have meat to select from.

4. Check the thickest parts of the lamb with your meat thermometer. When the temperature is 130° to 135˚F, remove the lamb from the oven.

5. Tent the lamb with foil, and let it rest for at least 10 minutes.

Day of, Step 3:

1. Turn off your oven and turn on your broiler.

2. Remove the lamb from the roasting pan, and set it on a platter to capture the juices.

3. Place the roasting pan on your stove over medium high heat. (If yours can't go on the stove, transfer the juices to a sauce pan for now.) Add the juice of the tangerines or oranges and ½ cup of water. Scrape up the brown bits from the bottom of the pan. This should take a few minutes.

4. Open up the lamb, remove the bone, and give it to the dog. You may need to cut a little to expose the full surface of the meat. You will likely see that some parts are totally raw. If so, place the lamb back in the roasting pan, inside part up, and broil it for a minute or so. Don't over-broil! Remove from the oven, and turn off the broiler.

5. Slice the lamb, place it on serving platter, and serve with hot juices on top or on the side.

6. Mazel tov. You just made a leg of lamb!

Note: Ask your butcher for a bone-in leg of lamb that weighs about 6 pounds. Ask for it to be boned (this means having the bone taken out). But ask that the detached bone be put back in the lamb. Then ask for the top layer of fat to be removed and put back on the lamb. (The fat doesn't have to be all in one piece.) If your butcher looks at you funny, don't worry. These are awesome tricks. Finally ask for some extra kitchen twine.

Make Ahead Prep: You can do the "day of" steps 1 and 2 earlier in the day, about four hours in advance. That said, if you roast the lamb early, it won't be hot when you serve it. But that's ok. Just make sure the pan juices are steaming!

Chicken Crack, page 372

Carne Macinata
(mah-chee-nah-ta)
GROUND MEATS

Elana's Famous Turkey Meatballs

IN TOMATO SAUCE

Italians think turkey meatballs are ridiculous. "Basta!" they say, "Meatballs are supposed to be made of meat!"

I get it. Americans substitute turkey for beef to be healthy, but then we go ahead and eat three times the Italian portion size, so we're still fatter than them. "Just eat the meat!" they demand.

Here's my excuse: I made these turkey meatballs after I took a blood-type allergy test that barred beef and chicken, but permitted turkey. So for three months, I made everything out of turkey. There were some failed experiments. You'll notice you don't see my turkey gelato in this book. But the turkey meatballs were a hit.

I make my turkey meatballs with the same care, fresh herbs, tomato sauce, and wine as I would make any succulent Italian meat dish. I don't add any bread or bread crumbs because one, they're not needed, and two, wheat flour is no good for allergies, mine or anyone else's. As a result, my turkey meatballs may not hold their shape as perfect balls—the bottoms flatten out in the oven as they cook—but nobody ever notices, and imperfect shapes mean better flavor.

I'm back to eating meat, but one thing I will not eat are turkey meatballs that taste like they were made in a health food store. These are definitely not those!

For the meatballs:

1 onion, quartered

1 garlic clove, quartered

1 bunch flat-leaf parsley, thick stems removed

2 pounds dark meat ground turkey (you may substitute up to 1 pound with white meat)

1 teaspoon kosher salt

20 to 30 grinds of the pepper mill

¼ of a whole nutmeg, grated

2 eggs

Extra-virgin olive oil

For the sauce:

1 carrot, cut into 1-inch rounds

1 celery stalk, cut into 1-inch pieces

¼ cup extra-virgin olive oil

2 garlic cloves

½ large onion, finely chopped

½ to 1 cup red wine

One (28-ounce) can whole peeled tomatoes, crushed

1½ to 2 teaspoons kosher salt

1 handful fresh basil, with stems

Prepare the meatballs:

1. Preheat the oven to 500°F, and line a baking sheet with aluminum foil or parchment paper.

2. Add the onion, garlic, and parsley to a food processor, and pulse until it's almost a pulp.

3. Combine the onion mixture with the turkey, salt, pepper, nutmeg, and eggs in a mixing bowl.

4. Shape the turkey mixture into 1½ to 2-inch meatballs and place them on the baking sheet. Drizzle liberally with olive oil.

5. Bake for 12 to 15 minutes or until the tops have begun to brown and the shape holds. It's ok if they are still a bit raw inside at this point. (Don't freak out at all the white gunk that seeps out of the meatball. It is the juice from the onion. We will use it in the sauce!)

Prepare the sauce:

1. Add the carrot and celery to a food processor and pulse until it's in tiny, tiny pieces, but not mushed. Alternatively, chop by hand.

2. Place a heavy-bottomed pan over medium heat and let it get hot for a couple of minutes. Add the olive oil to the pan.

3. Add the carrot, celery, garlic, and onions. This is called a soffritto in Italian. Cook for about 8 minutes or longer.

4. Carefully add the meatballs to the pan, scooching the soffritto aside.

5. Pour in the wine, the tomatoes, and a good sprinkling of salt.

6. Add the basil leaves, pushing them into the sauce so they are covered.

7. Cover, lower the heat, and simmer for about 45 minutes.

8. If the sauce is watery, uncover the pan and increase the heat to medium high. Let the liquid evaporate until the sauce is more condensed.

9. Serve and enjoy!

Variations for Kids:

The wine will cook off, but for flavor reasons you might want to substitute chicken broth.
You can add a couple of handfuls of chopped baby spinach or grated zucchini into the meat mixture.

Chicken Crack

SICILIAN JEWISH MEATBALLS WITH CARAMELIZED ONION AND FENNEL JAM

This dish pays homage to the lost Jewish heritage of Sicily. In the Middle Ages, the vibrant merchant posts of southern Italy and Sicily were part of the Spanish Empire, and hundreds of thousands of Jewish merchants lived there, trading, studying Torah, and complaining about the humidity. These Jews traded with Arab and North African neighbors, adopting elements of their cuisine.

But in 1492, while Columbus was sailing the ocean blue, Spain instituted its infamous Inquisition, forcing all Jews in its empire to convert or to leave. Nowadays, there are few Jews in Sicily, but there is a sense among many Sicilians that they're Jew-*ish*. I've spent a lot of time in Sicily and have met too many look-alikes of my Jewish friends to chalk it up to coincidence. Several Sicilians have told me that they know they're ancestrally Jewish, even if they have no proof. Time to order some genetic testing kits, *ragazzi!*

Regardless, the Jews of Sicily, via their Arab trading partners, have left their mark on Italian food. The combination of raisins and capers, the salty jewel of Sicilian gastronomy, is emblematic of its Jewish roots. And, although, to my knowledge, nobody in Sicily actually makes meatballs out of chicken, in my American Ashkenazi mind, using chicken makes them that much more Jewish.

These meatballs can make wonderful appetizers as well. I like to serve them with a caramelized onion jam. They're delicious right out the pan, at room temperature, or as cold leftovers. But be warned: you may find it very difficult to stop eating this highly addictive *Chicken Crack.*

Be sure to use salt-packed Sicilian capers and only dark meat chicken!

THE BASICS OF BALLS

» **You want your balls juicy.** That's the bottom line. To achieve this, mix the meat with very finely chopped, grated or pulped onion. (See *When Can I Put Onions in the Food Processor?* Page 227.)

» **Banish the breadcrumbs.** Another way to keep them juicy is to leave out the breadcrumbs that many recipes include. In addition to drying them out, breadcrubms are just empty calories we don't need. The meat will be held together by the egg. I tend to use the least amount of egg possible, since I like lighter balls. (Read into that what you will. You're not my therapist!) I'd rather be able to eat more light meatballs than fewer heavy ones, without feeling too full afterwards. With your hands, form the meat into imperfect rounds for a rustic look.

Attenzione: if you choose to make meatballs with white meat chicken or turkey, and your balls aren't juicy, this is your "I told you so." If you're like 30 percent of my cooking students and have a mental block against dark meat, and you've already read *Don't Give The Thigh To The Dog* (Page 328) and discussed your neurosis with a licensed therapist, then go ahead and use up to 50 percent white meat in your meatballs. Similarly, red meat that is overly lean won't result in juicy balls. Aim for 85 percent lean red meat. Ask your butcher.

Makes 40 (1 -inch) meatballs

For the jam:

2 Tablespoons fennel seeds

½ cup extra-virgin olive oil or duck fat

2 large yellow onions,
cut in half and thinly sliced

1 Tablespoon plus 2 teaspoons
Rosemary-Balsamic Reduction Page (61)
or store-bought balsamic glaze

For the meatballs:

2 pounds ground dark meat chicken

1 yellow onion, quartered

1 bunch flat-leaf parsley, thick stems removed

⅔ cup dark raisins, soaked in warm water

3 Tablespoons salt-packed capers, rinsed

1 teaspoon kosher salt, plus more for garnishing

¼ cup extra-virgin olive oil

40 to 60 grinds of your pepper mill

Microgreens, optional

Pomegranate seeds, optional

Prepare the jam:

1. Grind the fennel seeds finely in a mortar and pestle. Alternatively, place in a Ziploc bag and pound them with the back of a wooden spoon until ground.

2. Heat a saucepan over medium high heat for about 5 minutes.

3. Add the olive oil, followed by the onions and the fennel, stir, and cook until they are dark golden brown, about 25 minutes. Add the balsamic and cook for a final few minutes until bubbly.

4. Add all the ingredients to the food processor and bring to a puree.

Prepare the meatballs:

1. Allow the chicken to come to room temperature, and place it in a large mixing bowl.

2. Add the quartered onion to a food processor and pulse into very finely chopped pieces. Be careful not to turn the onion into a puree. Add to the chicken.

3. Drain raisins. Add the parsley, raisins, and capers to the food processor and pulse until very finely chopped. Add to the chicken.

4. Throw in the salt and mix up the chicken so it's completely amalgamated. Let rest a good 30 minutes.

5. Form 1-inch meatballs, I like a rustic look, so my meatballs are not perfectly rounded. I think they taste better!

6. Heat a heavy-bottomed pan over medium heat for a few minutes.

7. Add about two tablespoons of olive oil, enough to cover pan. Carefully drop in the first batch of meatballs, making sure they don't touch each other.

8. Cook each side 3 to 5 minutes until they are cooked on the inside and well browned on the outside. Remove the meatballs from the pan, and set them on a paper towel to drain. Grind pepper generously over the meatballs, and give an extra sprinkle of salt.

9. Add more oil to the hot pan and repeat with the next batch.

10. Plate the meatballs and top with a touch of onion jam. Garnish with the microgreens and pomegranate seeds, if using.

Note: Any leftover fennel onion jam is ideal for a cheese board or a leftover steak sandwich. Store in the fridge indefinitely.

Make Ahead Prep: You can make the meat mixture in advance and either refrigerate or freeze it in an airtight container or Ziplock baggies. Just bring it to room temp before cooking. You can also cook the meatballs in advance. They are wonderful at room temperature. Or to reheat, place them in a covered "pouch" made out of aluminum foil and bake for 5 minutes at 350°F.

Bello Lento

NICE AND SLOW

PRINCIPLES OF SLOW COOKING

Braising literally means searing and then slowly cooking in liquid. It's great when you aren't in a rush to get food on the table and don't want to babysit your cooking.

There are seven steps to braising any type of meat:

1. **Choose meat that lends itself to braising,** avoiding lean, tender cuts that you'd use for a steak. Aim for the tougher, fattier cuts like beef chuck, brisket, stew meat, lamb shoulder, or dark meat chicken on the bone.

2. **Brown the meat.** *Attenzione:* don't worry about over-browning. The brown bits on the bottom of the pan will add flavor to the juices you add later. They are "gold" for slow cooking. Remove the meat while you:

3. **Add onions,** making sure they sauté in the fat from browning. Yum! If you want, add carrots and celery to the *soffritto*, or leeks, garlic, green onion, and/or ginger, if you're making Asian food, etc. When the *soffritto* is done, return the meat to the pot.

4. **Add your cooking liquid.** Depending on what liquid you use, you'll get a different final flavor outcome. Having some acid in your liquid helps to break down the fibers of the meat, and hence tenderize it. Alcohol does a good job of this, which is why many foods are braised in **white** or **red wine**. **Tomatoes** also add good acidity. Another common cooking liquid is **broth**.

5. **Throw in some herbs.** Fresh, hardy herbs are ideal for slow cooking. The juices in your braise will pull out all of their goodness. I always toss the herbs in with the stems. I particularly love the woodsy stems of **rosemary** and **thyme**. They add the flavor of the countryside. If it grows in Italy, it goes in your Italian food: **bay leaves, thyme, marjoram, sage, oregano, rosemary, basil,** and **parsley**.

6. **Cook the meat slowly in the oven or on the stove.** Cover your Dutch oven or oven-safe pan tightly, and either place it over a low flame on the stove or in the oven, set to a low temperature. The longer you cook this way, the more tender and delicious it will be. As long as you have enough liquid and have the temperature low enough—no more than 350°F in the oven, lower than a medium flame on the stove—don't worry about overcooking.

   Here are some general cooking temperatures and times to give you an idea:

   > » **Dark meat chicken on the bone:** 300°F for 2½ hours or 350°F for 1 to 1½ hours
   >
   > » **White meat chicken:** Half the time of dark meat chicken, on average
   >
   > » **Brisket (6-8 lbs):** 200°F for 9 hours, 300°F for 5 to 6 hours, or 350°F for 4 hours
   >
   > » **Stew meat:** 200°F for 7 to 8 hours, 300°F for 3 hours, 350°F for 1½ to 2 hours

7. **Honor the cooling process.** It's tempting to pull food out of the oven and eat it immediately, but braised meat continues to tenderize as it cools, so leave it alone for a bit. Chicken doesn't need much time at all to cool before eating, but red meat does. If you're dealing with a huge brisket, give it at least an hour, or better yet, let it cool to room temperature all day, put it in the fridge at night, and then reheat. Braised meat tastes even better the next day!

Chicken alla Cacciatora

WITH TOMATO, WINE, ROSEMARY, AND OLIVES

In Italian, *il cacciatore* is the hunter. *Alla Cacciatora*, literally "in the style of the (feminine) hunter," means the chicken is cooked in the style of the hunter's *wife*. This recipe implies a domestic division of labor: while the hunter kills the food, he doesn't eat unless his wife cooks it up.

Putting that aside, what you're really doing with this recipe is hunting for flavor. There are lots of hunters in Italy, and thus lots of hunters' wives; hence, no two recipes are alike. Some use mushrooms, others add chopped celery and carrots. I like the addition of olives, but feel free to omit them.

This recipe is hard to screw up, so even if you have little cooking experience, try on your hunter's hat and be the hunter's wife!

SLOW COOKING VS. BRAISING?

Braising is essentially the same thing as slow cooking. Both cook meats and/or vegetables in liquid on a low temperature, until fork tender. Braising starts with browning the meat and the onion, which is essential to the flavor wow you're looking for.

¼ cup extra-virgin olive oil

½ teaspoon kosher salt, plus more for browning

3 pounds bone-in chicken thighs, about 6 or 7

1 large onion, coarsely chopped

2 garlic cloves

1 sprig fresh rosemary, cut into 1-inch pieces

2 to 3 sprigs fresh thyme, optional

1 (28-ounce) can whole peeled tomatoes, crushed

1 cup red wine

½ cup green or mixed olives

1. Brown the chicken: heat a braiser, a Dutch oven, or another heavy-bottomed pan (use one fitted with a lid, which you will need later) over medium high heat and let it get hot for 7 minutes. Dry and salt the chicken. Add the olive oil to cover the bottom of the pan, and add the chicken skin-side down, ideally without the pieces touching. Brown the skin until dark golden, about 15 minutes. Remove the chicken and set aside.

2. Add the onion, garlic, rosemary, and thyme, if using. Decrease the heat to medium and let cook for 5 minutes.

3. Return the chicken to the pan, skin-side up.

4. Add the tomatoes, wine, and olives. Sprinkle with 1½ teaspoons salt. Let rise to a little "boil." Decrease the heat to low, and cover.

5. Let the chicken cook until the meat can easily be pulled from the bones, about 75 minutes.

6. If the sauce needs thickening, remove the chicken and raise the heat to medium or medium high, and continue to cook with the pot uncovered. Serve the chicken covered in sauce.

HOW TO BROWN CHICKEN SO IT DOESN'T STICK TO THE PAN

If you don't brown your chicken before you slow cook it, the skin will look like it did when you were a child and your grandmother served it boiled: gross. Browning adds flavor along with color. Here's the trick:

1. **Heat a pan over medium high heat for about 7 minutes.** You want it hot before you put anything in it!

2. **In the meantime, whether or not you choose to rinse your chicken (I don't rinse it!), dry the chicken** VERY well with paper towels.

3. **Salt your chicken skin**—a light, even dusting on all of the skin. About 1½ teaspoons for 3 pounds of chicken.

4. **Add olive oil to cover the bottom of the pan, and add the chicken skin-side down,** ideally with the pieces not touching. If needed, work in batches. Cook for about 15 minutes, until dark golden. If you try to turn it over too early, it'll stick. SO GIVE IT TIME!

WHAT IF MY CHICKEN IS KOSHER?

Dishes that call for kosher chicken require substantially less salt because kosher chicken has already been brined. When going kosher, consider that although the chicken itself doesn't need to be salted for flavor, its sauce and/or topping does. I would advise cutting the suggested salt measurements by at least a third. Add a sprinkle of finishing salt if it lacks *umph*.

(Remember, if you're browning it in a pan, you still need to salt the skin so it won't stick.)

Maria's Chicken, page 384

Maria's Chicken

WITH ROSEMARY AND VINEGAR

A few years ago, I returned to Florence to work on this book. My Italian cooking guru, Maria, had left the country home at Geggianello and was living in the city. She was happy to live closer to her children, who own *La Rosa Canina*, a prominent floral design studio that does all the big weddings in Tuscany—they're even featured in Martha Stewart's magazine. We decided to have lunch in their studio workshop, and Maria brought this chicken from home. It really stuck with me.

When I got back to the States, I consulted her favorite cookbook.

Cookbook?! Don't all Italian mammas learn how to cook from their grandmothers, absorbing recipes through osmosis? No. In fact, she regularly consults a cookbook at home: Paolo Petroni's *Il Libro Della Vera Cucina Fiorentina (The Book of Authentic Florentine Cooking)*. It took me a month to get the cookbook on Amazon. It's in Italian, and the recipes don't include any measurements. But I worked on the recipe that Maria had used until I found a version that I could teach. We'll still call it *Maria's Chicken*.

Serves 4

3 Tablespoon extra-virgin olive oil

3 pounds bone-in chicken thighs, about 6 or 7

1 teaspoon kosher salt, plus more for browning

1 large yellow onion, chopped

1 cup white or red wine

3 Tablespoons finely chopped rosemary

2 garlic cloves, finely chopped

2 Tablespoons white wine vinegar

½ cup pitted niçoise olives, roughly chopped

Me with Maria and her daughter, Tania.

1. Brown the chicken: heat a braiser, a Dutch oven, or another heavy-bottomed pan (use one fitted with a lid, which you will use later) over medium high heat and let it get hot for 7 minutes. Dry and salt the chicken. Add the olive oil to cover the bottom of the pan, and add the chicken skin-side down, ideally without the pieces touching. Brown the skin until dark golden, about 15 minutes. Remove the chicken and set aside.

2. Add the onion to the pan and cook until translucent, about 5 minutes. If the pan gets too hot, lower the heat. Scrape up any bits clinging to bottom of pan. Add the chicken back to the pan.

3. Add the wine and a teaspoon of salt, cover, and decrease the heat to medium low.

4. If you are using white meat, remove the breasts after about 30 minutes. Keep cooking the dark meat for another 30 to 40 minutes or so, until it starts to fall off the bone.

5. Add the rosemary, garlic, vinegar, and olives. Stir. Cook uncovered for another 8 minutes on medium high heat. Turn off the heat, and let the sauce rest uncovered. This lets the juices thicken.

Ski Chalet Chicken

WITH MUSHROOMS, HERBS, AND A RED WINE REDUCTION

The first time I went to Italy, I road-tripped in with some Italians I'd met while backpacking around Europe. We crossed over from the French Alps into the beautiful Valle d'Aosta in the far north of Italy, a snowy region known for skiing, castles, and rustic mountain cuisine. Their friends had a house there, and we decided to bunk up and enjoy the area. Our first day, we went on a beautiful hike in the foothills and picked local mushrooms on the way back for a delicious lasagna that our hosts cooked.

The next day, my new friends were looking at me strangely. They eventually explained that in the middle of the night I had rolled over in bed and beaten the girl who was sleeping beside me. Normally I'm good for hogging the sheets, but no violence. Two of the other guests had gotten sick and thrown up. The lesson: be very careful with wild mushrooms.

In any case, that's my most memorable experience in Northern Italy, since I've spent most of my time in Tuscany, Rome, and the south. When I taught a slow-cooking class, I wanted to make a chicken dish that would honor that region and the poor girl I nearly pummeled to death in the night.

Serves 4

1 bottle red wine

1 bunch thyme

1 bunch marjoram

1 bunch rosemary

1 bunch sage

2 bay leaves

1 ounce dried mushrooms (such as porcini, shiitake, oyster, or cremini)

1 Tablespoon kosher salt, plus more for browning

3 pounds bone-in thighs and drumsticks

2 to 3 Tablespoons extra-virgin olive oil

2 medium onions, sliced

4 portobello mushrooms, stems removed and cut into ½-inch slices

60 grinds of the pepper mill

1. Pour the wine into a medium saucepan and place over medium high heat. Add a third of the herbs, including the bay leaves. Reduce the wine to about one cup. Set aside.

2. Break up the dried mushrooms into smaller pieces and place them in a small bowl. Add a cup of warm water, and let the mushrooms soak for at least 30 minutes.

3. Brown the chicken: heat a braiser, a Dutch oven, or another heavy-bottomed pan (use one fitted with a lid, which you will use later) over medium high heat and let it get hot for 7 minutes. Dry and salt the chicken. Add the olive oil to cover the bottom of the pan, and add the chicken skin-side down, ideally without the pieces touching. Brown the skin until dark golden, about 15 minutes. Remove the chicken and set aside.

4. Add the onions and cook in the remaining fat (don't let the onions burn). Stir every so often, then decrease the heat to medium low for another 15 minutes. You want these onions to be sweet and partially caramelized.

5. Add the chicken back to the pan, skin-side up.

6. Add the wine with the remaining fresh herbs. Add the dried mushrooms and their liquid, the portobello mushrooms, and 1 tablespoon of salt and pepper. Bring to a boil, cover, and decrease the heat to medium low.

7. If you are using white meat, remove the breasts after about 30 minutes. Keep cooking the dark meat for another 30 to 40 minutes or so, until the meat starts to fall off the bone. (Alternatively, you can cook the chicken in oven at 350°F for about an hour and a half).

8. Serve the chicken with mushrooms, onions, and pan juices. Either pick out the herb twigs or serve it rustic style as I do, perhaps with *Rustic Olive Oil Mashed Potatoes* (Page 316) or *Celery Root Puree* (Page 313).

Make Ahead Prep: You can reduce the wine, revive the mushrooms, brown the chicken, and caramelize the onions well in advance, either the same day or the day before.

Seppie coi Piselli

ROMAN TRATTORIA-STYLE CALAMARI AND PEAS

In Italy, there are four main types of dining establishments: *il ristorante, l'osteria, la trattoria,* and *la pizzeria.* The *ristorante* is the highest level of eating establishment, with prices that reflect its chef-inspired specialties. The *osteria* is a tavern—large, likely with tall ceilings and a long list of options on the menu, though the food will be more rustic and lower priced than *ristorante* fare. The *trattoria* is a neighborhood mom-and-pop shop. This is where you go when you want to spend less money and feel like you're eating in a home away from home. I didn't go to millions of *trattorie* all over Rome. I went to the three I knew and liked in Trastevere, and I got to know the families that owned them. (Finally, there is the *pizzeria,* and I assume you know what's served there.)

When you go to a typical Roman *trattoria,* assuming you aren't a tourist, nobody hands you a menu. The waiter might come to your table and ask you what you want without even telling you your options. If not, he (they are rarely, if ever, she) will rattle off a list of dishes at incredible speed, without a beat between one dish and the next. He expects you to know what's offered.

Trattorias don't reinvent the wheel. They serve traditional, regional dishes. In Rome, for pasta, you can expect *Amatriciana, Carbonara, Alla Gricia, Cacio Pepe* and sometimes an *Arrabbiata.* For secondi, lamb chops, a steak, tripe, chicken with peppers, beef *involtini* in tomato sauce, braised oxtail, and my personal favorite, *Seppie coi Piselli.* (In Roman dialect, words often get truncated, so *seppie con i piselli* becomes *coi.*) This is always what I order at *Da Lucia,* one of my favorite trattorias in Trastevere on the picturesque *Vicolo del Mattonato* (brick-paved alleyway), where laundry is strung from the apartments overhead because fashion-obsessed Italians don't trust their clothing to a machine.

2 pounds calamari, tubes and tentacles

1 yellow onion, chopped

¼ cup extra-virgin olive oil

2 garlic cloves, chopped

½ cup dry white wine

1 pound frozen peas

1½ teaspoons kosher salt

40 grinds of pepper mill

¼ cup chopped flat-leaf parsley, plus more for garnish

1. Use scissors to cut the tubes of the calamari into ½-inch rings.

2. Cook the onions with the olive oil in a saucepan (use one with a fitted lid, which you will use later) until nice and golden, 7 to 8 minutes.

3. Add the garlic to the onions and cook another 2 minutes.

4. Add the calamari to the pot and stir. Let the seafood pick up all the oniony goodness.

5. Add the wine and let it evaporate for a few minutes.

6. Juices will begin to pour from the calamari. This is ok. Add the peas, the salt, the pepper, and the parsley, decrease the heat to medium low, and cover. Let the mixture cook for an hour.

7. Remove the lid and keep cooking on medium low until the juices have thickened, about an hour.

8. Top with freshly chopped parsley.

Make Ahead Prep: This can be made the day before and reheated.

Squid Ink Variation: Roman trattorias don't usually serve *Seppie coi Piselli* with squid ink. That's a tradition of Venice, which is on the Adriatic Sea. But I love squid ink. It adds umami, richness, and a good dose of iron that I can feel in my bloodstream as soon as I eat it. For those of you who love and crave squid ink, this is a great opportunity to use it. Limit the amount to 1 teaspoon, add it when you uncover the calamari, and stir well. Continue as instructed. Note that the squid ink will thicken with time and will get richer in flavor. So, though you may think you need more, be gentle until you are familiar with the way it behaves.

WHY I NEVER USE A SLOW COOKER!

» Food cooked in a slow cooker won't taste as good as food cooked in a ceramic-coated Dutch oven. Except for the rare slow cookers that have a clay pot inside, the inserts are made of artificial, often toxic, non-stick materials, and the flavor of your food won't benefit from being cooked for hours in that.

» If I did use a ceramic slow cooker, I would still have to brown the meat first, so this means more dirty dishes. More cleaning? No way! Braising starts with browning meats and sautéing onions as part of a *soffritto*, so if you just throw your ingredients into a slow cooker and skip this step, you won't technically be braising. (You'll also be forgoing the essential process that will bring your dish that "O, mamma mia" flavor!)

» I don't like the idea of my food being being cooked in a pot that is surrounded by electric wires and is directly connected to an outlet. I prefer it to cook in a hearth, like an oven, or to create a hearth feeling over a gas stove. My Dutch oven allows me to brown meats on the stove, and finish them off in the same pot in the oven, which is great if you need to leave the house or take a nap.

The Best Brisket Ever

TASTES LIKE ITALY, FEELS LIKE SHABBAT

Yes, the best.

I don't compliment myself easily. In fact, I have typical neurotic Jewish insecurity, compounded by a family of overachievers. I'm terrified that everything I do will end in disaster and bring shame to my parents and the Jewish people at large. I've tried everything to overcome this neurosis: therapy, energy healers, yoga, acupuncture, alcoholism, Zoloft... nothing works. Nothing but brisket.

Let me explain. A few years ago, before I created *Meal and a Spiel*, I was stricken with a wave of depression. Cooking had always brought me joy, so I decided to make a brisket. I made it with Jewish heart and Italian flavors, cooking it in much the same way a central Italian might braise a different cut of beef: in wine, tomatoes, and aromatics—meaning rosemary, thyme, and bay leaf.

Just as I was taking it out of the oven, one of my Italian friends called. He was in the neighborhood with a group of friends and wanted to swing by to pick up a scarf he'd left. When they walked in, they saw and smelled an eight-pound brisket resting on my counter. "Spezzatino!" my friend shouted, Italian for a similar cubed beef recipe. "Who is this for?" they asked. "You," I told them. They almost went through the roof with excitement, calling other friends to come over and bring wine. Before I knew it, we had a full-on dinner party that my Italian friends still talk about to this day, and the wave of depression passed right on by.

The lesson: If you brisket, they will come.

Brisket is a wonderfully forgiving dish. You can add a little too much of this or too little of that, but as long as you understand the basics, all the flavors will meld perfectly with time in the oven. The problem with some briskets is that they're either too sweet, too dry, or too fatty. Sweet briskets can be tasty, but I don't want dessert for dinner, and the sugars can exacerbate the inevitable hangover of a dinner party.

And don't let anyone tell you that you have to choose between dry and fatty: briskets don't need to be either. Just cook the meat with the fat still on it and with the fat side up, so that the fat will insulate the beef and keep in the juices. Don't worry, once the brisket is done, you'll scrape off the fat.

¼ cup extra-virgin olive oil

1 (6 to 8 pound) brisket

2 onions, chopped

2 to 3 celery stalks with leaves, chopped

2 to 3 carrots, chopped

2 to 3 garlic cloves

2 to 3 sprigs fresh rosemary

2 bay leaves

2 to 3 sprigs fresh thyme

5 to 6 fresh basil leaves

1 (28-ounce) can whole
peeled tomatoes, crushed

½ bottle red or white wine

2 to 3 teaspoons kosher salt

WHAT IF I DON'T HAVE A DUTCH OVEN?

A good Dutch oven will last a lifetime, so it's worth the investment. However, if you're in the process of saving up, or are having 40 people over for Passover and don't have enough room in your Dutch oven to make enough chicken or brisket for the whole tribe, you can still slow cook without one. Here's how:

1. **Brown the meat** in any pan and remove it.

2. **Sauté** the onions and the rest of the *soffritto* in that same pan.

3. **Put the browned meat and onions in a casserole dish,** or multiple casserole dishes, and add herbs and liquid.

4. **Cover it very, very well with aluminum foil** (I cover it in parchment paper first then wrap it all around three times with the heavy duty stuff) and place in the oven to cook.

One or two days ahead:

1. Preheat oven to 325°F.

2. Heat a large pot or Dutch oven over medium heat, and let it get hot for a couple of minutes.

3. Add enough olive oil to cover the bottom of the pot. Add the brisket, fat side up, and brown about 10 minutes on all sides. (In order to fit the whole brisket in the pot, you might need to cut it into two pieces, or just squeeze it in there with meat flaps up the side as I do. The brisket will shrink as it cooks.)

4. Remove the brisket and set aside. If there is too much melted fat in the pot for your taste, remove a little before continuing.

5. Add the onions and cook until translucent, about 5 minutes.

6. Put the brisket back in the pot, fat side up.

7. Top with the celery, carrots, garlic, rosemary, bay leaves, thyme, and basil.

8. Add the tomatoes with their juices and the wine.

9. Sprinkle generously with salt.

10. Cover well and stick in the oven for 4 to 5 hours. You can cook it for even longer, but at a lower temperature. (See: Principles of Slow Cooking, Page 378)

11. Go take a walk and a nap.

12. When your brisket cuts itself with a fork, it is done.

13. Remove the pot from the oven and let it cool until you can handle it easily, about an hour. Take the brisket out of the pot and let it and the juices cool completely.

14. Return the brisket to the pot and refrigerate.

One day ahead or the day of:

1. Place the brisket on a large cutting board. Use a knife and/or your fingers to remove all the fat from the brisket. Cut the brisket against the grain into ¼-inch slices.

2. If the brisket juices appear thick enough, you can place the brisket slices back in the pot. If you think the brisket juice should be thicker, boil it down uncovered on the stove. You can also take out a portion of the juices and veggies and blend it to add some creaminess.

3. Once the brisket juices are just right, you can place the sliced brisket back in the pot or in a large casserole dish. Cover the meat with the sauce.

4. Cover and refrigerate until ready to use.

The day of:

1. When you are ready to serve, you can heat up the brisket in one of two ways.

2. If using a casserole dish, cover it VERY well in heavy-duty foil or wrap it in two layers of regular foil, and bake at 350°F for almost an hour until the brisket is well heated through.

3. If you've kept everything in the original pot, reheat it on the stove using medium low heat or place it in the oven at 350°F for one hour. Once it's heated through, place the meat on a serving platter, top with the remaining juice, and serve.

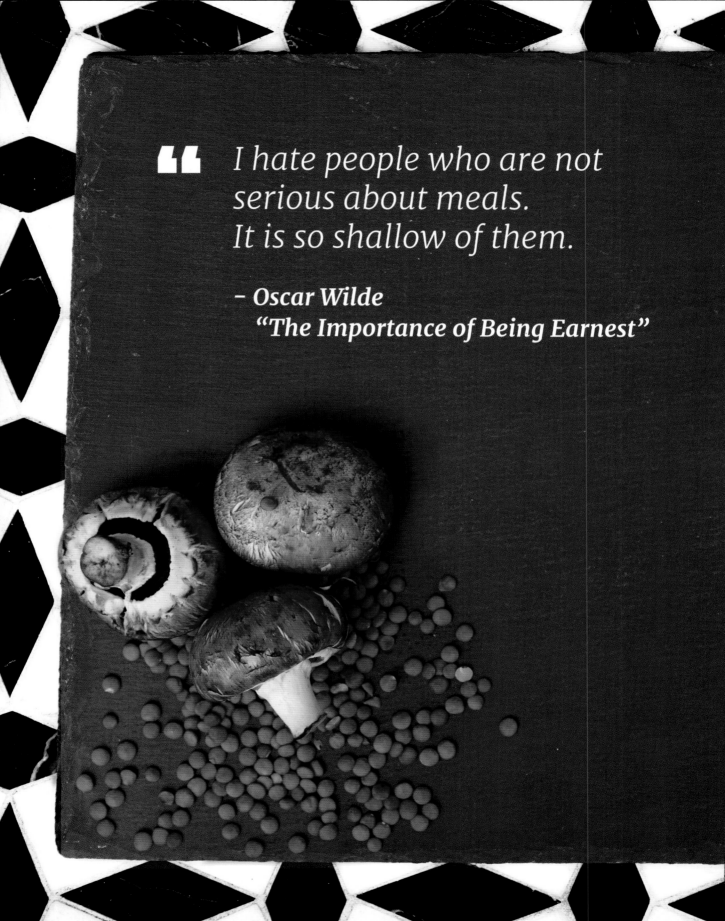

> ❝ *I hate people who are not serious about meals. It is so shallow of them.*
>
> – **Oscar Wilde**
>   ***"The Importance of Being Earnest"***

Not Just Another Meatless Monday

ROBERTO'S BAKED-NOT-FRIED EGGPLANT PARMIGIANA

ZUCCHINI RISOTTO WITH LEMON AND BASIL

RADICCHIO RISOTTO

WOODSY MUSHROOM FRITTATA

SPRINGTIME FRITTATA

NO-STIR POLENTA WITH LENTIL RAGÙ

Zucchini Risotto, page 404

MEATLESS MONDAY STARTED AT JOHNS HOPKINS UNIVERSITY AS a movement to promote public health and has since become a major social media hashtag, encouraging vegetarianism for the sake of our bodies and our planet. Personally, I don't need a political movement to enjoy eating delicious vegetarian and vegan meals often, as long as they're prepared right. While it's easy to throw together salads and veggie sides, my students are often at a loss for meatless mains. Here are some we've enjoyed in our community, which won't leave you feeling like your meal is missing something.

Roberto's Baked-Not-Fried Eggplant Parmigiana

This dish is named for the man who gave me my first professional cooking job, Roberto Benabib, writer and producer of the popular Showtime series *Weeds*. He and his wife, Samantha, a college friend of mine, were new parents who hired me to deliver homemade food twice a week following the birth of their daughter, Carolina. Considering the nature of Roberto's show, I imagined I might be preparing stoner food—you know, nachos, corndogs, cookie dough. Alas, for the record, Roberto and Samantha are not stoners.

I needed to prepare foods that reheat well and taste just as good the second time on the stove or oven: saucy, slow-cooked foods like stewed chicken thighs, brisket and lamb meatballs. Unfortunately, at our initial consultation, they rejected all those dishes.

Roberto and Samantha wanted lean, healthy proteins. Nothing fried. Nothing too heavy. I set to work in my kitchen, testing out turkey meatballs that never touched a hot oiled skillet, salmon crisped in the oven and then cooked in a puttanesca sauce, and ultimately *this* baked-not-fried eggplant parmigiana.

Now let me be very clear: Prior to this invention, I'd never liked eggplant parmigiana. I found it too heavy. Of course, Italians always told me I'd never eaten a *proper* one. The fact is, I don't like fried foods with sauce and cheese. That's why I came up with this recipe: The eggplant slices are lightly breaded and baked instead of fried, then served with a sweet and tangy tomato-basil sauce with Parmigiano Reggiano and mozzarella added *only on the top layer*, so it's not weighed down with melted cheese.

For Roberto and Samantha, it worked, with fireworks on top. This became Roberto's favorite dish, and we made sure there was one waiting for him every week.

Serves 4 to 6

2 eggplants (about 1 pound each)

3 eggs

3 cups panko bread crumbs

1 cup grated Parmigiano Reggiano

1 large "ball" fresh mozzarella cheese (about 4 ounces)

Simple Tomato and Basil Sauce (Page 58), room temperature

1. Preheat the oven to 400°F, and line 2 baking sheets with parchment paper.

2. Cut the eggplant into ⅓ to ½-inch slices. This is my easy way: cut off the green top of the eggplant and the bottom round. Cut the eggplant in half horizontally so you can have each half stand easily upright on your cutting board. Now, seeing the eggplant as a "square," go ahead and cut off the skin on two opposite sides so you will have an eggplant that has skin on two sides and not on the other two. Starting on a naked side, with the eggplant standing upright, cut it into slices. Each will have skin on the sides. Continue with the rest.

3. Lightly beat the eggs in a shallow bowl. Put the panko in another shallow bowl.

4. One by one, dip each slice of eggplant in the eggs to cover. Then dip in the panko to cover. Place on the baking sheet.

5. Bake the eggplant until soft, about 12 minutes. Some pieces will be mushier or less cooked than others. This is ok. Let the slices cool.

6. Lightly cover the bottom of a medium baking dish with the tomato sauce and sprinkle the Parmigiano to lightly cover. (An 8 x 8-inch square dish, or any configuration that adds up to around 64 square inches, is the right size for the portions listed above. But if you have a larger dish, just double the recipe.) Layer the tomato and Parmigiano with eggplant, followed by another light layer of sauce, followed by another sprinkling of the Parmigiano. (I use a silicone pastry brush to paint the tomato sauce into every crevice.)

7. Continue until you have three layers of eggplant, making sure you finish with tomato sauce and Parmigiano.

8. Cut the mozzarella cheese in slices and place them on top of the eggplant, equally spaced.

9. Bake uncovered until bubbly, 35 to 40 minutes. If you would like to serve it neatly and you have some self-control, let it sit for a good 10 minutes before cutting.

Note: You can easily double this recipe and use a large (9 x 13-inch) baking dish.

Make Ahead Prep: Make the tomato sauce and prepare the eggplant several days in advance. If you want to make the whole thing in advance, go ahead and bake the dish as instructed, let it cool, cover it with foil, and keep it in the fridge. Reheat at 350°F, uncovering halfway to let the mozzarella bubble.

Zucchini Risotto with Lemon and Basil

This risotto was first conceived as part of my comfort food class, for which I'd promised my students four or five of the world's coziest dishes. I knew we'd begin by making a huge pot of chicken stock, since its aroma, steaming on the stove, fills the kitchen with flavor memories that reach back generations. The broth, veggies, and meat would all contribute to dishes that scream *"home!"* (Exactly whose home is debatable, but I always go for a rustic Tuscan country home, as opposed to the Beverly Hills one filled with Lean Cuisine where I grew up.)

Beyond that, I was totally stuck. What kind of risotto is both easy enough for neophytes and can live up to the all the cozy, comfort food hype I had guaranteed? Risotto requires constant attention, both hands working to hold the pan, ladle the stock, and stir the creamy goodness into the rice.

I called my Italian friend Andrea, whom I often call for culinary inspiration. He'd thrown a risotto party several weeks before, serving 16 people three types of risotto at once, with the help of only one friend in the kitchen, which to me seems unfathomable. As I asked him about the three risottos he made, all of which he claimed were simple, one of them piqued my interest: zucchini risotto.

Creamy and mildly sweet from the cooked zucchini itself, the risotto Andrea described had a delicate balance of flavor, the perfect offspring for the grandma chicken stock from which it would be borne.

Over time, I've adjusted the recipe to more vibrantly recall the notes of summer, the season of the zucchini. For me, the lemon evokes sunlight shining through a row of cypress trees. The basil tastes like fairy dust from *A Midsummer Night's Dream.* That said, if you can get zucchini and basil all year round, the fresh gratings of Parmigiano will ensure that this risotto will warm your heart in any season.

8 cups *No-Chop Chicken Broth* (Page 150)
or *No-Chop Veggie Broth* (Page 153) (See Note)

4 Tablespoons butter, divided

2 Tablespoons extra-virgin olive oil

1 yellow onion, finely chopped

2 large zucchini, cut into ⅛-inch cubes
or chopped finely in food processor

1½ cups Arborio or carnaroli rice

1 cup dry white wine

¾ cup grated Parmigiano Reggiano,
plus more for serving

Zest from ½ lemon

9 basil leaves, thinly sliced

Freshly grated black pepper

1. Bring the broth to a gentle simmer in a large saucepan. Make sure it's seasoned with salt.

2. Melt 2 tablespoons of the butter and the olive oil in a heavy-bottomed pan over medium heat (I always use my Le Creuset cast iron braiser).

3. Add the onion and sauté until it becomes translucent and begins to take on a golden color.

4. Add three-quarters of the zucchini, stir, and let it cook for a few minutes.

5. Add the rice and stir. Once the rice becomes translucent, 2 to 3 minutes, add 2 big glugs of wine, about 1 cup. Let it evaporate.

6. Add 2 ladles of stock, about 1½ cups at a time. STIR THE RISOTTO (with a wooden spoon) CONSTANTLY FROM THIS POINT ON!

7. Once the liquid is completely absorbed, add another ladle or so of broth, enough so that the rice is well covered. Add the remaining zucchini on your third 'ladle-ing" of broth. Continue like this, stirring constantly, adding broth only when the previous ladle of broth has fully evaporated and the rice softens but is still *al dente,* about 20 minutes.

8. Off the heat, add the remaining butter, the cheese, another ladle of broth, the lemon zest, and the basil, sparing some basil for the garnish. Stir them in, and let the risotto sit for a minute or two. The consistency should be like porridge, and if you tilt the pan up, it will flow like a wave.

9. Serve on individual plates, topping generously with more grated cheese, about 4 grinds of pepper per serving, and extra basil for beauty.

Note: This recipe does not call for salt because the saltiness should come from the broth. Taste your broth and make sure it has enough salt so that it's lip-smacking good. This amount of broth (8 cups) will need about 2½ teaspoons of kosher salt. If your broth isn't salty enough, your risotto will suffer. Remember that the addition of cheese will also add saltiness.

Radicchio Risotto

It's hard for me to accept that some people just can't stomach radicchio since I love it so much that I stock my fridge with it at all times. I believe that its bitterness, along with its magnificent magenta tone, is its unique beauty.

For those of you who aren't radicchio fans, I wonder if you have ever tried it cooked? In creamy risotto? With butter? And homemade chicken broth? And Parmigiano Reggiano?

I first ate radicchio risotto at the hands of family friend Jeff Thickman, a private chef to the Florentine nobility. (Yes, there's still nobility in Italy, though many of them have run out of money due to a congenital aversion to work.) Anyway, it's unheard-of for an American—from Wyoming no less!—to become a prestigious chef in any Italian city. But Jeff's a remarkable character. While getting a PhD in musicology from Columbia, his professor told him he should play piano with the passion he had for baking cakes. And that was it. In that moment, Jeff understood his true calling and became a chef.

I met Jeff in a WWII-era hospital in Florence, while I was waiting for an appendectomy. My mother knew him through the ever-exciting game of Jewish geography and asked him to visit me while she booked a flight. Tired, bloated, and with horribly greasy, unwashed hair, I welcomed him onto the ward, and we became fast friends. Once I recovered, he invited me to his best friend Elisabetta's house, which happened to be a medieval tower on a private beach on the Tuscan coastline. I mean, this shit happens in Italy.

Jeff made us the most delicious risotto. I'm not sure I even really had an appreciation for risotto before that. His secret: use lots of radicchio, cut it very finely, and let it cook down for as long as you have the patience. Use only homemade broth if you want the full effect, and don't ever stop stirring your rice!

Cooked with red wine, this risotto takes on a deep purple color. Try it—this could be your chance to fall in love with radicchio.

8 cups *No-Chop Chicken Broth* (Page 150)
or *No-Chop Veggie Broth* (Page 153) (See Note)

4 Tablespoons butter, divided

2 Tablespoons extra-virgin olive oil

1 large yellow onion, finely chopped

2 medium heads of radicchio, cored and cut into 1-inch strips

1½ cups Arborio or carnaroli rice

1 cup red or white wine

½ cup grated Parmigiano Reggiano, plus more for serving

¼ cup grated Pecorino Romano, plus more for serving

Freshly grated black pepper

1. Bring the broth to a gentle simmer in large saucepan. Make sure it's seasoned with salt.

2. Melt 2 tablespoons of the butter and the olive oil in a heavy-bottomed pan over medium heat (I always use my Le Creuset cast iron braiser).

3. Add the onion and sauté until translucent.

4. Add the radicchio and stir for a few minutes, until it's covered in the oil and slightly wilted. Cover, decrease the heat to medium low, and cook for 30 minutes, checking every so often to give it a stir.

5. Uncover, increase the heat to medium/ medium high, and let any water remaining from the radicchio evaporate.

6. Add the rice and stir. Once the rice becomes translucent, 2 to 3 minutes, add 2 big glugs of wine, about 1 cup. Let it evaporate.

7. Once the wine is absorbed and evaporated, add 2 ladles of broth, about 1½ cups at a time. STIR THE RISOTTO (with a wooden spoon) CONSTANTLY FROM THIS POINT ON!

8. Once the liquid is completely absorbed, add another ladle or so of broth, until the rice is well covered. Continue like this, stirring constantly, adding broth only when the previous ladle of broth has fully evaporated and the rice softens but is still *al dente*, about 20 minutes.

9. Off the heat, add the remaining butter, both cheeses, and an extra ladle of broth. Stir and let it sit for a minute or two. The consistency of the risotto should be like porridge, and if you tilt the pan up, it will flow like a wave.

10. To serve, place immediately on individual plates, topping with freshly grated Parmigiano Reggiano, Pecorino Romano, and fresh ground pepper.

11. Consider making *Radicchio Arancini* (Page 142) with the leftovers!

Make Ahead Prep: You can cook the onion and the radicchio ahead of time, and then restart the process by adding the rice in step 6.

Note: This recipe does not call for salt because the saltiness should come from the broth. Taste your broth and make sure it has enough kosher salt so that it's lip-smacking good. This amount of broth (8 cups) will need about 2½ teaspoons kosher salt. If your broth isn't salty enough, your risotto will suffer. Remember that the addition of cheese will also add saltiness.

THE RIGHT ROAD TO RISOTTO

Risotto, like most soups and pasta dishes, is part art, part science. The art is in your homemade broth and in the way you stir the risotto, mindfully as it cooks. The science is a step-by-step process, as follows:

1. **Sauté the onions** in a heavy, wide-bottomed pan, using a combination of both olive oil and butter. Yep, this is a *soffritto*, so give those onions time to get nice and sweet, and make sure they're diced about the same size as a cooked grain of rice. You don't want big pieces of onion in there.

2. **Add the key ingredient.** Sometimes your key ingredient, like the radicchio or zucchini in this chapter, needs to be cooked in the pan before you begin cooking the rice. Add it now. Please note, though, that sometimes the key ingredient is added later, usually when you're halfway through step 5.

3. **Toast the rice** by adding it to the onions and stirring until the rice starts to glisten. Give it 2 to 3 minutes over medium heat. ***Attenzione:*** use the proper rice for risotto, such as carnaroli or Arborio.

4. **Add wine** and let it evaporate almost completely. Be sure to give a stir so rice doesn't stick. (Red wine works well with richer recipes and adds a beautiful burgundy color to your risotto, while white wine is great for lighter dishes, and won't color the rice.)

5. **Add two ladles of broth at a time, stirring constantly** until all of the broth is absorbed before adding more. Continue this process until the risotto is just a hair away from being *al dente*. You do not stop stirring. Ever. If you have guests over, get them to stir while you pour someone a prosecco. Everyone loves to stir a risotto, round and round. You may now also add **salt**, unless your broth is already salted enough.

6. ***Mantecare il risotto****. This final step, which essentially means "add butter," is necessary to achieve the creamy consistency that makes you want to shout *"mammmmma."* Once the risotto is just a moment away from being al dente, take it off the heat and add another ladleful of broth, a couple of tablespoons of butter and cheese (usually Parmigiano)* and stir them in. Let rest for a couple of minutes. It should move like a wave—*all' onda*— from one end of your pan to the other. Serve immediately with more cheese if the recipe calls for it.

*For seafood or vegan risottos, *"mantecare il risotto"* with olive oil instead of butter. Omit the cheese and top with chopped parsley.

Woodsy Mushroom Frittata

In Italy, eggs aren't considered a breakfast food. Most Italians wake up to espresso and a pastry and save their frittatas for dinner.

There are two types of frittatas: the kind that are cooked in a pan on the stove and the kind that are baked in a casserole in the oven. Oven-baked frittatas, like this one, are ideal for company, for a variety of reasons. One, there is little to no chance you will burn it. Two, you can feed more people with a large casserole than with most pans. Three, you can make a few frittatas and stick them in the oven at the same time, or double the recipe and bake for a little longer. And finally, you can make these frittatas in advance, store them in the fridge, cut them neatly while cold, and bring them to room temperature before serving.

Leftovers make wonderful snacks, appetizers with wine (when cut into bite-size pieces), and excellent sandwich fillers on crusty bread.

The trick to this frittata, as to any good meal, is its simplicity. Contrary to most American egg concoctions, this frittata focuses on only one ingredient, the mushroom. We don't distract from its unique flavor with peppers and onions and broccoli and tomatoes.

We do, however, enhance it with a good Gruyère, aged from 18 months to two years, still soft enough to melt. Ask your cheesemonger for a taste. Remember, we're not looking for a cheese to steal the show, but rather one to play in harmony with the woodsy mushrooms and thyme. When you taste the right Gruyère, you'll know.

⅓ cup extra-virgin olive oil, plus more for the baking dish

2 garlic cloves

A pinch red pepper flakes

2 pounds cremini mushrooms, stems removed and sliced

½ bunch thyme

1 teaspoon kosher salt, divided

½ teaspoon tamari or quality soy sauce

45 grinds of the pepper mill

12 eggs

⅔ cup half-and-half or whole milk

5 ounces Gruyère, thinly sliced

1. Preheat the oven to 350°F and lightly oil a medium baking dish.

2. Place a heavy-bottomed pan over medium heat and let it get hot for a couple of minutes.

3. Add the olive oil, garlic, and red pepper flakes. Sauté until the garlic is golden, about 3 minutes. (Be careful not to burn the garlic. If you do, start over.)

4. Add the mushrooms, throw in the sprigs of thyme, and stir.

5. Add salt, soy sauce, and pepper.

6. Increase the heat to medium high and let cook, stirring only occasionally until the mushrooms are tender and the liquid has evaporated, about 15 minutes.

7. Lightly beat the eggs with the half-and-half in a large mixing bowl.

8. Remove the thyme branches and garlic, and transfer the mushrooms to the baking dish. Pour the eggs on top. Use a fork or a spoon to even it all out, and top with the sliced cheese.

9. Place the baking dish in the oven, and cook for 30 to 45 minutes, depending on the size of the dish. It is ready when the eggs are firm to the touch or a toothpick comes out clean.

10. Let the frittata cool slightly before cutting.

Note on reheating: Though good cold, the frittata can be loosely covered with foil and reheated in the oven at 350°F.

Springtime Frittata

WITH ROASTED ASPARAGUS, GOAT CHEESE, AND FRESH HERBS

I learned about combining lots of herbs in eggs in Israel, where the green egg omelette blows my mind. The fresh herbs make the eggs much lighter, and more digestible, and pair perfectly with the creamy goat cheese, which I personally love in eggs. (Notice how often you see chevre rolled in herbs at the grocery store.)

This recipe has been a huge hit at brunch events I've catered. It's my mother's favorite.

HOW TO MAKE AN OVEN-BAKED FRITTATA FROM ANYTHING

Basically, all you need are eggs, milk, and some cooked vegetables—like leftovers from any recipes in *Chapter 9: It's All in the Vegetables.* I'd recommend cheese as well. Grease a casserole with olive oil and throw in the veggies. Whisk together eggs and milk and pour over the vegetables. (***Attenzione:*** use whole milk (not skim or 2%) or, better yet, half-and-half for a creamier outcome.) Top with cheese, if you like. Bake at 350°F, until it fluffs up and there's no liquid on top. Times vary depending on the size and shape of your dish.

If you prefer a **dairy-free option,** then forget the milk. You will have flatter, less creamy eggs, but the frittata will still be delicious—and more authentically Italian, to tell you the truth. Cut into bite-sized pieces, this is a classic happy hour appetizer in Italian bars.

Serves 6

⅓ cup extra-virgin olive oil, plus more for the baking dish

1 to 2 pounds asparagus (See Note)

1 teaspoon kosher salt

20 grinds of the pepper mill

⅔ cup loosely packed flat-leaf parsley leaves, chopped

⅔ cup loosely packed basil leaves, thinly sliced

½ to 1 bunch chives, chopped

½ cup loosely packed mint leaves, chopped

12 eggs

⅔ cup half-and-half or whole milk

6 to 8 ounces goat cheese

1. Turn on the broiler and place an oven rack on the top rung. Lightly oil a medium baking dish.

2. Remove and discard the bottom third of the asparagus. Cut the remaining asparagus into bite-size pieces, and place them on a foil-lined baking sheet.

3. Generously drizzle with olive oil. Add salt and pepper. Mix with your hands, making sure each piece is well coated with the oil, salt, and pepper. Lick your fingers. It should taste like a burst of salt and pepper. (Don't worry, some of the flavor will burn off in the oven, and the rest will help to season the eggs.)

4. Place the baking sheet under the broiler until the asparagus begins to brown on top but remains crunchy on the inside, 3 to 4 minutes. Remove and preheat the oven to 350 F.

5. Beat the eggs with the half-and-half and the remaining salt in a large mixing bowl.

6. Transfer the asparagus to the baking dish. Add the parsley, basil, chives, and mint, and mix well. Pour the eggs on top.

7. Slice the goat cheese into ¼-inch rounds and place in rows on top of the egg mixture.

8. Bake for 30 to 45 minutes, depending on the depth of your casserole dish.

Note: Use 1 to 2 pounds of asparagus based on your personal preference. Any leftovers can be used for the *No-Chop Veggie Broth* (Page 153).

Variation: If you'd like a little tomato for more of a "pizza feel," broil the tomatoes as instructed in *Burrata Crostini with Roasted Cherry Tomatoes* (Page 88) and add them to the frittata along with the goat cheese.

No-Stir Polenta with Lentil Ragù

WITH WINE REDUCTION AND TRUFFLE CHEESE

The word on the streets, *le strade*, is that polenta must be stirred constantly while it cooks, similar to risotto. In fact, there are even automatic polenta stirrers made in Italy to alleviate the monotony of the task. For $165, plus $60 shipping, you can get a bronze automatic polenta maker delivered to your doorstep. It will stir corn grits for you while you hop on your Vespa and grab the paper at your local *edicola*.

Now, I'm not someone to tell you that you don't need a Vespa, but I'm happy to inform you that you can make polenta without stirring constantly. You just need to stir it every ten minutes to get a lump-free, creamy polenta, and even for the luxurious folks out there (read: lazy), that's doable.

I'm very proud to present you with a vegetarian ragù that won't make you miss meat. It's hearty and deeply satisfying. But what takes it over the top, in my humble opinion, is the sweet and tangy red wine reduction that gets stirred in at the end. Off to the side on your stove, you let red wine simmer with onion, thyme, and a stick of cinnamon, which ultimately warms the feeling of the whole dish, like meat might. You'll finish it off with a grated truffle sheep's milk cheese, because I know my cooking students and they really like cheese and truffles. What about you?

P.S. The first time making this, in order to get the timing right and to just be relaxed while cooking, I recommend getting your ragù done first before starting on the polenta, and reheating it when you're ready for it.

For the wine reduction sauce:

1 Tablespoon unsalted butter

½ cup finely chopped red onion

1 carrot, cut into 1-inch pieces

1 celery stalk, cut into 1-inch pieces

1 cup red wine

1 teaspoon raw honey

1 stick cinnamon

3 to 4 sprigs fresh thyme

For the lentil ragù:

¼ cup extra-virgin olive oil

1 large onion, halved and thinly sliced

1 pound portobello mushrooms, stems removed and cut into ½-inch slices (or 1 pound cremini mushrooms, stems removed and halved)

1 bunch chard, bottom stems removed and cut into ½-inch strips

1 cup cooked French green lentils (See Note)

1½ teaspoon kosher salt

10 to 20 grinds of the pepper mill

Wine reduction sauce

For the polenta

1 teaspoon kosher salt

1 scant cup polenta or coarsely ground yellow cornmeal

2 Tablespoons unsalted butter

¾ cup grated Parmigiano Reggiano

4 ounces Moliterno al Tartuffo
(or another truffle cheese)

Prepare the wine reduction sauce:

1. Place a small saucepan over medium heat. Add the butter and onions. Sauté until the onions are soft and golden, about 10 minutes.

2. Add the carrot and celery, and sauté for another 5 minutes.

3. Add the wine, ½ cup of water, and whisk in the honey. Add the the cinnamon and thyme.

4. Let it reduce until you have about ¼ cup of wine. Let cool.

5. Remove the carrot, celery, cinnamon, and thyme.

Prepare the lentil ragù:

1. Place a heavy-bottomed pan over medium high heat for a couple of minutes.

2. Add the olive oil followed by the onion, and cook without much stirring until you see dark brown spots form on the edges, 7 to 10 minutes.

3. Decrease the heat to medium and continue cooking until the onion is nice and caramelized, another 7 to 10 minutes.

4. Add the mushrooms, give a stir, and sauté for a few minutes.

5. Add the chard, give a stir, and sauté until it wilts.

6. Add the cooked lentils along with any remaining cooking water, not exceeding ½ cup.

7. Add the salt and pepper, and cook until the mushrooms and chard are tender.

8. Add the wine-reduction sauce and stir to combine.

Prepare the polenta:

1. Bring 4 cups of water to boil with a teaspoon of salt in a medium saucepan fitted with a lid.

2. Add the polenta slowly, whisking the whole time as you do in order to prevent lumps. Once all the polenta has been added, reduce the heat to low and whisk for two minutes. Cover. Set a timer for 10 minutes.

3. After the 10 minutes has passed, uncover the polenta, and whisk for one minute. Reset your timer for 10 minutes. Continue the process, being conscious to scrape the sides and corners of the pan. Switch to a wooden spoon when the polenta has thickened. After the polenta has cooked for about 45 minutes, remove from the heat.

4. Stir in the butter and Parmigiano. Taste for salt. Cover and let rest for 5 minutes.

5. Serve topped with the lentil ragù and shaved truffle cheese.

Note: To make the one cup of needed lentils, I cook my lentils in a rice cooker using ½ cup of water for ¼ cup lentils. (The truth is, I make extra and dress them like a salad with avocado and fresh herbs.) Alternatively, you can cook them on a stovetop, using ¾-cup water for ¼-cup dry lentils. Bring to a boil, cover, reduce heat, and simmer until they are tender, about 25 minutes.

Meaty Variation: This polenta would be delicious with any of the slow cooked chicken or meats in the "Mind-Blowing Mains" chapter. Of course, you would never top those mains with truffle cheese, as the strong flavor isn't compatible. You can also choose to omit the Parmigiano if you prefer a lighter meal.

> **All you need is love.**
> **But a little chocolate now**
> **and then doesn't hurt.**
>
> – **Charles Shulz**
> **"Peanuts"**

Dolci

CAFFÈ CORRETTO

LAVENDER LATTE

STRAWBERRY MACEDONIA

HAZELNUT AND SEA SALT CHOCOLATE BARK

ANDREA'S PEACHES IN MOSCATO

CARAMELIZED APPLES FOR DUMMIES

GUILT-FREE BLUEBERRY COBBLER

FLOURLESS CHOCOLATE BLENDER CAKES

GREEK YOGURT PANNA COTTA

CLOUD NINE CUSTARD

CANTUCCI TOSCANI

SFRATTI

Flourless Chocolate Blender Cakes, page 440

YOU SHOULD ALWAYS SAVE ROOM FOR DESSERT, BUT DON'T
make it an annihilation. You don't want to overstuff yourself or your guests and end up in a sugar-induced food coma as soon as the meal is over. Instead, think of dessert as the final chapter, one intended to complete the soul-nourishing journey of the meal. Already served crostini and pasta? Then don't serve a carby dessert! Try *Strawberry Macedonia* or *Greek Yogurt Panna Cotta*. Have you had a lighter dinner? Throw in some *Cantucci Toscani*. Already delivered dairy more than once in the meal? Choose a dessert that isn't dairy based! Had a huge meal? Give them a *Caffe Corretto* and a taste of *Hazelnut and Sea Salt Chocolate Bark*. You're aiming for balance—sweet, delicious, satisfying balance.

Caffè Corretto

I once catered a New Year's party for four generations of the Rosenblatt family—from great-grandparents on down to toddlers, all in matching Menorah pajamas. They requested a menu that was really too rich for one night: crostini, arancini, pasta, chicken meatballs, Barolo-braised short ribs, celery root puree, and more.

I'm usually strict about balancing my menus so I don't overstuff my clients, but this time I caved. The Rosenblatts have been dear supporters and students of *Meal and a Spiel* for years, and they talked me into serving a "greatest hits" of the classes they'd taken. But I knew before the meal even started that it would be too much. So I picked up a bottle of grappa on the way, and after dinner, I made each adult a *Caffè Corretto*.

Caffè Corretto literally means "corrected coffee." How does one "correct" coffee? By adding alcohol, duh. Grappa is a seriously strong potion made from fermenting and distilling grape skins, stems, and seeds—basically everything that's not used to make wine. (Italians don't waste anything that could boost a buzz.)

In Rome, a *Caffè Corretto* is also called *il caffè e l'amazza caffè:* the coffee and the "kill the coffee." When paired with grappa, the caffeine won't keep you up all night, so it's perfect as a balanced after-dinner digestivo, particularly when you've eaten too much.

One by one, a sigh of relief overcame the face of each Rosenblatt. Digestion! A dainty, delicious demitasse cup corrected the dizzying indulgence in seconds.

What makes this Italian speedball taste so darn good? Well, you gotta add a spoonful of sugar!

Serves 1

1 cup hot espresso

1 to 2 teaspoons grappa

1 teaspoon brown or turbinado sugar

Add the grappa and sugar to your hot espresso, stir, and drink up!

Hazelnut and Sea Salt Chocolate Bark

The combination of chocolate and hazelnut is called *gianduja* in Italy and dates back to Napoleon, who prevented goods from Great Britain from entering European harbors under French control—including Italy's. So a chocolate maker in Turin, named Caffarel, extended the little chocolate he had by mixing it with hazelnuts. In the 1960s, the Piemontese confectioner Ferrero popularized the recipe worldwide, calling it Nutella. Ever heard of it?! The recipe below is like addictive Nutella for adults, with crunch. And better for you.

The addition of sea salt makes this recipe unique. Desserts need salt. It's simple science: sodium flips a switch in the tastebuds that alerts normally dormant receptors to the presence of sweetness. So go ahead and sprinkle-sprinkle the little bars, how I wonder where you are... Oh, I ate you already.

Serves 6 . . . or 1 Chocoholic

⅔ cup hazelnuts

7 ounces dark chocolate, chopped

2 teaspoons flaky sea salt

1. Preheat the oven to 350°F, and line two baking sheets with parchment paper.

2. Place the hazelnuts on one of the baking sheets, and bake for 15 minutes.

3. Transfer the hot nuts to a dish towel, and cover for one minute. Roll the towel back and forth so the brown skins come off. It's ok if some stay on.

4. Roughly chop the nuts so some are cut in half while other pieces are much smaller. Set aside.

5. Pour a few inches of water into a small saucepan. Fit a heatproof bowl over the saucepan, making sure it doesn't touch the water. Heat the water to a simmer.

6. Add the chocolate to the bowl, and stir gently to melt.

7. Using a silicone spatula, pour the melted chocolate onto the prepared baking sheet. It will not cover the entire sheet. You want your bark to be of medium thickness. Sprinkle the hazelnuts and salt evenly onto the chocolate.

8. Put the baking sheet in the freezer for 20 minutes or in the refrigerator for about 40 minutes. Once hardened, break into pieces and eat!

9. Store in the freezer.

Lavender Latte

You know those beautiful movies set in the English countryside, where proper English ladies drink tea served to them by servants amid a field of flowers, and the young damsel falls in love at the end with a gallant gentleman whose family is the richest in the region? Well, this is that movie in a cup. Creamy and soothing, this drink will transport you to a romantic dreamland without making you squeeze yourself into a corset. It's a perfect treat on a rainy afternoon, or any night before bed. The lavender will deliver you to a peaceful slumber. I use the natural sweetener stevia for this, but feel free to use raw honey if you're in a particularly indulgent mood.

Serves 1

1¼ cups cups unsweetened almond milk
(or milk of your choice)

1 teaspoon dried lavender flowers (See Note)

1 teaspoon raw honey
(or sweetener of your choice)

1. Pour the milk and lavender in a small saucepan and almost bring to a boil. (The trick to heating milk is not to set it on the stove and forget it. It will bubble over and make a mess!)

2. Turn off the heat and let it sit for five minutes or more.

3. Reheat the milk to the desired temperature, and strain through a fine mesh sieve into a cup.

4. Add sweetener, and kick your feet up somewhere cozy.

Note: Dried lavender flowers are available at specialty cooking shops (such as Williams Sonoma), spice shops, and health food stores.

Strawberry Macedonia

WITH LEMON AND MINT

It's rare to finish a meal in Italy without a little something sweet, but that something is often a light touch, meant to kiss the palate and awaken the diner. Thus, fruit is common, particularly after a lunchtime feast or a regular weeknight meal.

Macedonia is basically a fancy name for a fruit salad. But as fruit salads go, it doesn't get much better than this. The trick: leaving the salad to saturate in its juices and flavors for a couple of hours in the fridge. That process is called maceration, thus: *macedonia!* Take it out and voilà.

Fruit with lemon and sugar was deeply ingrained in me during my years in Italy. I use powdered sugar—and only a touch—because the first time I made it that was all I had in the house. I found that because powdered sugar dissolves completely, it leaves no grainy residue and can sweeten without overpowering the delicious tang of the strawberries and lemon or overshadowing the cool wink of mint.

You can serve it as is or with freshly whipped cream.

Serves 4 to 6

2 pounds strawberries, stems cut off

Juice of 1 lemon

2 Tablespoons powdered sugar, or more if desired

1½ Tablespoons finely chopped mint

1. Place the strawberries in a serving bowl and drizzle with the lemon juice.

2. Add the powdered sugar a little bit at a time, making sure it is fully integrated and not clumpy before adding more. You don't want these to be too sweet, so taste to adjust the flavor with more or less sugar or lemon.

3. Sprinkle generously with the chopped mint, stir gently, cover with plastic wrap, and put in the refrigerator for at least an hour.

Andrea's Peaches in Moscato

Andrea Pallaoro and I crossed paths when I was 28 and he was 21. I was back in LA, having just returned from Florence with a Master of Arts in Jewish Italian History through Film, and I was desperate to return to Rome, to a passionate love affair with a Greco-Roman rogue that would ultimately chew me up and spit me out. Andrea was a creative genius from a small town in Northern Italy, fulfilling a lifelong dream of attending film school in Los Angeles.

Enticed by a shared sense of curiosity, we both volunteered to edit a short documentary about Italian Jewish Partisans with Zepporah (she of the *Sonoma Squash Soup* and *Cloud Nine Custard*). Inspired by tales of resistance fighters escaping concentration camps and battling alongside the Allies in the Alps, Andrea told me his visions for the films he would one day create. Gigantic wings of angels in a desert landscape. A camera that moves across the screen slowly, like a molecule of blood moves through a vein, a pace that authentically connects us to the truth of the human experience. I was in awe of his confidence and certainty. This is exactly the type of person, I realized years later, I love to cook with.

And cook together we do! Seduced by the idea of curating immersive sensory experiences for others, we've developed and executed a series of pop-up dinners in candlelit art galleries and lush garden oases across Los Angeles. In truth, we regularly overextend ourselves with impossible ambitions that turn into masochistic labor.

The event that featured these peaches took place only days before Andrea's first feature film, *Medeas*, needed to be delivered for its screening at the Venice Film Festival. Though he hadn't slept, we cooked together in the 4' by 4' kitchen of an art gallery with no oven or wiggle room, preparing a six course, sit-down Italian seaside dinner for 25 paying guests. We were in the trenches together, stacking plates on the floor to create space from one course to the next. The only way to deal with the insane pressure and stress was with bursts of uncontrollable laughter, the true glue of a friendship.

In our dinners, Andrea is always in charge of desserts. His inevitably involve peaches, the sweet jewels of summer. "I want to do a dessert that my family has at our summer home," he says, speaking extremely dramatically, in a thick Italian accent with over-pronounced consonants

FACING PAGE: Top - At the opening of Andrea's movie at the Venice Film Festival. Bottom - Set up for a popup dinner in Santa Monica.

and elongated vowels. "I want it to be sublime, *soob-limmmeh*, I don't even want to cook the peaches. I want people to experience the purity of the fruit. Naked, raw, subtle, and seductive to the palate."

Since then, Andrea has come up with multiple peach desserts in moscato, a white dessert wine, some of them cooked. Every time I ask which is his favorite, he changes his mind and passionately describes the latest way he's made a peach and moscato dessert. Thus, in the variations section below the recipe, you will find a few ways to play with peaches, Pallaoro-style.

1 peach, peeled

¼ cup Moscato wine

A pinch of lemon zest

½ amaretti cookie, crushed

1. Andrea would have you use a sharp paring knife to remove the peel from the peach. It will be better this way, but I can't be bothered. Do as you like.

2. Cut each peach in half, and then into ¼-inch slices.

3. Place the peaches in a container or a bowl, and cover with the wine.

4. Cover the container, and place it in the refrigerator for 1 to 4 hours.

5. Use a ladle or a large spoon to scoop out the peaches with their liquid. Place into individual serving bowls.

6. Top with a pinch of lemon zest and a sprinkling of the crushed amaretti.

7. Serve immediately.

Poached Peaches Variation: Prepare the peaches as you would in steps 1 and 2, but make each slice a little thicker. Place the peaches in a pan, add moscato to just cover the peaches, add a couple of bay leaves, and let simmer uncovered on low until the peaches are cooked. Top with vanilla ice cream or mascarpone and some orange zest and/or toasted, crushed pistachios, if you like.

Seared Peaches Variation: Prepare the peaches as you would in steps 1 and 2, but make each slice about a ½-inch thick. Put a pan over medium heat for a few minutes, and add a knob of butter large enough that it stretches across the pan when melted. Add the peaches, and let the slices brown on each side. Add a good glug of moscato and let it cook for couple of minutes. Top with vanilla ice cream or mascarpone and some orange zest and/or toasted, crushed pistachios, if you like.

Guilt-Free Blueberry Cobbler

As a Jew, I know a little something about guilt. However, the Italian in me absolutely cannot stand to bring that guilt to the table. It's *so* not sexy.

As a result, years ago I started creating desserts that I could feast on to my heart's content without worrying about calories or sugar. This cobbler has become my go-to. It's famous amongst my students and friends. We love it because it only takes minutes to assemble, isn't too sweet or filling, and makes a delicious, healthy end to a dinner party or potluck.

Put it in the oven during appetizers or the first course, and by the time you're done with dinner, dessert is ready! Going to a dinner and know that the dessert will be terrible for you? Bring this cobbler uncooked to your friends' homes, as I do, and stick it in their oven when you get there. Everyone will be thrilled.

As far as *guilt-free,* I'm referring to:

1. There is no sugar added to the fruit. The topping is also not sugary. The sweetness comes from the cooked fruit. Check out other cobbler recipes and you will see CUPS of sugar.

2. There is no white flour. I use protein-rich almond meal and fiber-rich oats.

3. Yes, there is butter, but since a little butter is actually good for us and since I rarely ever cook with it, I have no guilt using it here.

This cobbler is a decent size, intended to fill the baking dish you have at home. If you like, you can halve the recipe and prepare individual servings in ramekins, which I love to do at parties. Leftovers make for a fabulous breakfast right out of the fridge.

3 pounds blueberries, about 8 cups

¾ cup (gluten-free) oats

¾ cup almond meal

¾ cup (gluten-free) oat flour

1 stick butter, room temperature

⅓ cup raw honey or agave

Dairy free ice cream, optional

1. Preheat the oven to 350°F.

2. Scatter the fruit in the bottom of an 8 x 11-inch or 9 x 9-inch baking dish.

3. Place the oats, almond meal, oat flour, butter, and honey in a mixing bowl. Get your hands in there to squeeze and mix until amalgamated. Alternatively, you can put all the ingredients in the food processor and pulse until it comes together.

4. Take the mix bit by bit, flatten into misshaped pieces, and place on top of the fruit. You are not looking to create a perfectly even top crust. It's good if there are "holes" where the juices of the fruit will bubble through, letting you know when it's done.

5. Place the baking dish in the oven, and bake until it's light brown on the top and the fruit looks as if it has gotten syrupy and bubbly, 40 to 45 minutes.

6. Remove from the oven, let the cobbler rest for 10 minutes so the juices can thicken, and serve with ice cream.

Paleo-Vegan Variation: Make the topping with 2¼ cups paleo flour (I like Bob's Red Mill), ⅓ cup unrefined coconut oil, and ⅓ cup agave, raw honey or sugar-free honey. Add more coconut oil if you find it's needed to bind the mixture. Continue with the rest of the recipe as instructed.

Caramelized Apples for Dummies

If you know how to slice an apple in half and turn on the stove and oven, you can make caramelized apples! Without ice cream, the leftovers make a healthy snack or breakfast, but once you go fully *à la mode* with a hot one, get ready to feast your eyes on some undies, because you're about to wow the pants off someone. Go ahead and take all the credit. Snap your fingers like a flamenco star, tell them you just whipped it up in no time and that this type of effortless razzle-dazzle is just who you are. You won't be lying.

Serves 4 to 8

1 Tablespoon unsalted butter

4 apples, halved and cored

1 large or two small oranges

1 Tablespoon raw honey

2 cinnamon sticks

2 bay leaves

Ice cream or mascarpone cheese, optional

Pomegrante seeds for garnish, optional

Mint leaves for garnish, optional

1. Preheat the oven to 400°F.

2. Place an oven-safe or cast iron enamel pan over medium heat, and let it get hot for five minutes.

3. Melt the butter in the pan and lay each half-apple flesh-side down. Let this side brown liberally until a dark golden, 7 to 10 minutes.

4. Use a paring knife to cut 3 to 4 large pieces of rind from the orange, and squeeze the juice into a small mixing bowl. Gently whisk the honey in with the juice until it's almost incorporated, and pour on top of the apples.

5. Add the cinnamon, bay leaves, and orange rinds to the pan, and transfer to the oven for 15 to 30 minutes (I have found that the time will vary greatly depending on the apples). You want them nice and soft to the touch.

6. Top with pomegranate seeds and mint leaves, if desired. Serve with any extra pan juices, and top with your favorite ice cream or a dollop of mascarpone cheese.

Flourless Chocolate Blender Cakes

WITH OLIVE OIL AND COCONUT MILK

This is essentially a soufflé for people who aren't perfectionists.

Basically, if you whip melted chocolate up with eggs, and bake it, it'll puff up. However, if you aren't a super-obsessive French pastry chef who measures everything by weight and flawlessly whips egg whites in surgically clean bowls, the puff will fall. That's why most of us don't even attempt soufflés.

My question is: who cares if it falls?! The flavor will be just as good, and you'll get a richer texture inside. I'm okay with that if you are—especially if we can do it all in a blender!

This dessert is all about the chocolate and my other favorite ingredient: olive oil. These two were made to be married, and it's a sophisticated partnership. I leave it to you how much extra olive oil to drizzle, but if you want to accentuate the darkness of the dark chocolate, go ahead and pour on the *oro liquido.*

In addition to using olive oil instead of butter, we're doing a healthy twist on a soufflé by using coconut milk instead of cream and just a touch of brown sugar. The coffee accentuates the flavor of the chocolate.

The recipe can easily be halved or doubled. I usually throw the cakes into the oven just as we sit down to dinner, and they tend to be done right on time for dessert. The seductive aroma of chocolate wafting from the kitchen will let you know when they're almost ready.

Special Equipment: 8 (5-ounce) ramekins

¼ cup extra-virgin olive oil,
plus more for greasing and garnish

7 ounces dark chocolate, chopped

2 Tablespoons natural cacao powder

2½ Tablespoons brown sugar

4 eggs

½ cup hot strong coffee or weak espresso

1 (14-ounce) can unsweetened coconut milk

Ice cream, optional

1. Preheat the oven to 350°F and "grease" each ramekin with the olive oil.

2. Pour a few inches of water into a small saucepan. Fit a heatproof bowl over the saucepan making sure it doesn't touch the water. Heat the water to a simmer. Add the chocolate to the bowl and stir gently to melt.

3. Use a silicone spatula to pour the melted chocolate into a blender. Add the cacao powder, sugar, eggs, coffee, and coconut milk. Blend on high until everything is well mixed. The longer you blend, the more your cakes will rise.

4. Pour the mixture evenly into the prepared ramekins.

5. Bake until a toothpick inserted in the center comes out clean or until you can clearly see that there is no more liquid on top, 30 to 35 minutes.

6. To garnish: this is your chance to let the olive oil stand out and make this dessert unique. I recommend anywhere from ½ teaspoon to 1 tablespoon extra-virgin olive drizzled on each cake, depending on your personal palate. I love olive oil—as by now you know! If you are serving with ice cream, pour the oil on top of the ice cream for a wow effect. Make sure to bring the bottle to the table.

Greek Yogurt Panna Cotta

WITH CHIANTISHIRE BLACKBERRIES

Think only Tuscans live in Tuscany? Think again. The Brits fell in love with Tuscany years ago, and with the strong British pound, they started gobbling up the best real estate in the region. Who could blame them? Given the dreary weather and pale cuisine of England, it's no wonder they bought an outpost in Tuscany, affectionately nicknamed "Chiantishire." I hope to do it myself one day. Plus, it's through movies and books by British authors like E.M. Forster and W. Somerset Maugham that we have our romantic image of this beautiful countryside.

Well, this recipe has nothing to do with the British-Tuscan implants themselves. I just love the name Chiantishire and think it goes perfectly with these blackberries cooked in Chianti.

These blackberries are great with panna cotta, which literally means "cooked cream," just as *terra cotta* means cooked earth, i.e. ceramics. But most panna cotta recipes don't require cooking; gelatin thickens the cream. This one is made with Greek yogurt, lemon zest, and a touch of raw honey, for a bright, rich, fresh flavor.

Serves 6

Special equipment: 6 (5-ounce) ramekins

For the Panna Cotta:

1½ cups Greek yogurt

1¾ cups heavy whipping cream

Zest of ½ lemon

½ teaspoon lemon juice

¼ cup plus one Tablespoon raw honey

1 teaspoon vanilla extract, optional

1 packet of gelatin

For the Blackberry Topping:

1 cup red wine

¼ cup raw honey

2 bay leaves

3 whole cloves

18 ounces blackberries
(3 standard containers), divided

Zest of two lemons

Prepare the Panna Cotta:

1. Put the yogurt, cream, lemon zest, lemon juice, honey, and vanilla in a mixing bowl, and whisk until well combined.

2. Pour ¼ cup of water in a small saucepan. Sprinkle the gelatin evenly over the water, and let it sit for one minute to soften. Turn the heat to low, and whisk the water until the gelatin is well incorporated and just about to reach a simmer. You DON'T want to boil the water. Pour the gelatin into the yogurt mixture, and whisk gently to combine.

3. Pour the yogurt mixture into the prepared ramekins, cover with plastic wrap, and refrigerate. Let it rest until it's set, anywhere from 4 hours to overnight

Prepare the Blackberry Topping:

4. Place a heavy-bottomed pan over medium heat and let it get hot for a couple of minutes.

5. Add the wine, honey, bay leaves, and cloves. Mix until the honey is dissolved.

6. Let bubble, stirring occasionally until the wine becomes syrupy and you can see the bottom of pan when swiped with your wooden spoon, about 10 minutes.

7. Remove from the heat. Carefully remove the bay leaves and whole cloves.

8. Add two-thirds of the blackberries, and toss to coat.

9. Transfer the contents of the pan to a blender or food processor, and pulse until it becomes a chunky puree. Don't overdo it.

10. Pour the puree into a serving bowl, add the rest of the blackberries, and gently mix to combine. Place in the refrigerator to cool.

11. Top the *Greek Yogurt Panna Cotta* with the blackberry topping, and finish with the lemon zest.

SUMMER PEACH VARIATION

I call this topping *Rosemary Grove Peaches.* It is pure summertime yum and really merits a recipe all its own. The peaches macerate in lemon juice and take on a subtle flavor of rosemary that is unexpected and enlivening.

3 white peaches, cut into 1-inch cubes

3 Tablespoons lemon juice, from 1 juicy lemon

2 sprigs fresh rosemary, cut into 1-inch pieces

½ cup *Toasted Pine Nuts* (Page 64)

1. Place the peaches in a large ziplock bag. Add the lemon juice and rosemary.

2. Squeeze the air out of the bag and seal. (Alternatively use a bowl with an airtight lid.) Let the mixture sit for at least three hours at room temperature, after which you can transfer it to the refrigerator until ready to use.

3. Top the *Greek Yogurt Panna Cotta* with the peaches and garnish with the toasted pine nuts and a piece of rosemary.

4. Pour a cold glass of Moscato d'Asti. EAT!

Dairy-Free Variation: Substitute the Greek yogurt with quality unsweetened coconut yogurt and substitute the cream with canned coconut milk. Continue as directed.

Cloud Nine Custard

I had just arrived at Zepporah's house in Sonoma (see *Sonoma Squash Soup,* Page 168) when she ran inside with a huge jar of milk and a carton filled with small blue eggs. "Look what the neighbors just dropped off! Feel the milk. It's still warm from the cow. And these are from their hens. They brought me this as a thank-you for letting their goats graze on my property."

And with that she put the milk in the fridge and set the eggs down, preparing to jump in her car. She was leaving for a week in San Francisco, while I'd house-sit and work on this book.

"What are you doing with all that milk?" I asked. "It'll go bad before you're back."

"I know, but I have nothing to do with it. You drink it."

I don't drink milk. I've never been able to stand the taste. And though I was willing to make an exception for milk this fresh, there was no way I could get through the whole jar. It would kill me to waste it.

So I set out to make a custard. I slowly heated the milk, tossed in some cardamom pods and cinnamon, and let the flavors gently infuse. I picked a branch from a juniper bush, and threw it in. I raided Zepporah's liquor cabinet and added some rose-infused gin. I let the flavors sit all day. Then, as one makes custard, I added a touch of sweet raw honey and the blue eggs. Finally, I mixed it all together and baked it.

Assuming you don't have cows nearby, or blue eggs, or a juniper tree, or rose-infused gin, I recreated this recipe with adjustments. Get the freshest milk you can find—raw if you live in a state where it's legal—and allow for the flavors to infuse. Don't rush this recipe. Allow time to stop, as it does, on Cloud Nine.

Serves 6 to 8

Special equipment: 9-inch tart pan

2 cups whole milk

2 cups whipping cream

3 cardamom pods, cracked open a bit with the side of a knife

4 juniper berries, cracked open a bit with the side of a knife

1 stick cinnamon

3 Tablespoons gin

½ teaspoon rosewater, optional

¼ cup raw honey

2 whole eggs

2 egg whites

1. Pour the milk and cream into a small saucepan. Add the cardamom, juniper berries, cinnamon, gin, and rosewater, if using. Heat uncovered on medium low to medium for two hours, whisking intermittently to integrate the skin that forms on the top with the rest of the mixture. You want your milk to be at an active simmer, steaming but not at a rolling boil. It's okay if a little milk sticks to the bottom of the pan. Liquid should be reduced to just over 2½ cups.

2. Let it rest uncovered for another two hours off the heat. Take a nap.

3. Preheat the oven to 325°F.

4. Lift the cardamom, juniper berries, and cinnamon stick out of the saucepan with a slotted spoon. Whisk in the honey, eggs, and egg whites.

5. Place a tart pan in a larger pan so that it fits and can hold some water on the side. It gets a little tricky carrying uncooked custard to the oven, so this is what I find helpful: Pull out the center rack of the oven and place your two pans on it. Pour the custard into the tart pan, and carefully add water to the outside pan until reaches halfway up the tart pan. (This is called a bain marie, and it helps to cook the custard evenly. Look how fancy you are!) Very carefully, scooch the oven rack in, close the oven, and let it cook for 80 minutes.

6. Remove the tart pan from the oven, and let it rest for 30 minutes, if you can control yourself. Cut and serve. It's also delicious cold or at room temperature. The cooler or colder it is, the better chance you have of serving it in neat pieces like a cake.

Cantucci Toscani

WITH VIN SANTO, ANISE, AND ORANGE

In Italian, *biscotti* means cookies. Any type of cookies, not only the oblong, crunchy ones that we consider "biscotti" in America. If you walk into a supermarket or a bakery in Italy and ask for a *biscotti*, you'll be asking for "one cookies," since *biscotti* is the plural, and they'll show you everything from butter cookies to chocolate chip.

If you want the "biscotti"-type cookie that's for dipping into dessert wine or coffee and you're in Tuscany, ask for *cantucci*, or the sweet diminutive, *cantuccini*. If you're in Rome, ask for *tozzetti*.

That said, the literal translation of *"biscotto"* means twice-cooked. And no matter what you call them, these cookies are exactly that. You will bake them, slice them, then bake them again. This will give them the proper crunch.

Cantucci are traditionally dipped into vin santo, a Tuscan dessert wine. I highly recommend you get some, so you can have the true taste of Tuscany right at your fingertips. (And it's great with chicken liver, as in *Maria's Crostini.*)

1¾ cup raw almonds

3 cups all-purpose flour

½ cup almond flour or almond meal

1 cup sugar

2 teaspoons baking powder

1 teaspoon kosher salt

Zest of 1 orange

1 teaspoon vanilla extract

1 teaspoon anise seeds

3 eggs

3 egg yolks, divided

2 Tablespoons unsalted butter, melted

2 Tablespoons vin santo, rum, cognac, brandy, or whiskey

1. Preheat the oven to 350˚F.

2. Place the almonds in a dish towel or a Ziplock bag, and smash them with a meat mallet or a hammer until lightly crushed. Place them on a baking sheet, and bake for 8 minutes. Let cool and set aside.

3. Place the flour, almond flour, sugar, baking powder, salt, zest, vanilla extract, anise seeds, 3 eggs, 2 egg yolks, butter, and vin santo into a large mixing bowl. Use your hands to squish all the ingredients into a dough. It should be just wet enough to stick together in a ball. If not, add a touch more vin santo. Now fold in the almonds until they are well distributed.

4. Cover a baking sheet with parchment paper, and sprinkle some flour on it.

5. Break the dough into 3 pieces, and mold each one into a flattened log, which should measure about 2 ½-inches wide, ½-inch tall, and 1-foot long. You want the flattened logs to be uniform so that the *cantucci* will bake evenly.

6. Brush the remaining egg yolk on the top and sides. This will give the *cantucci* a nice golden color.

7. Bake for 25 minutes or until the logs are just firm on top. Remove from the oven.

8. Let cool for 5 minutes, and slice each log crosswise at a diagonal about ½ to ¾-inch wide. Continue to let cool for another 25 minutes.

9. Roll the *cantucci* on their sides and bake again for 25 minutes, flipping them over halfway through baking.

10. Let them cool completely, if you can control yourself from eating them. The cooling process will make them crunchy.

11. Serve with vin santo, a dessert wine of your choice, tea, or coffee. Store leftovers in the freezer.

Sfratti

ITALIAN-JEWISH COOKIES FROM "LITTLE JERUSALEM"

Sfratto, the singular of *sfratti*, has two meanings in Italian: "stick" and "eviction notice." It refers to the rods that landlords used in Renaissance Italy to beat delinquent tenants out of their homes. The same *sfratti* were used to kick Jews out of town and send them roaming for a safe haven. In 1555, that safe haven was Pitigliano.

A little background: Renaissance Rome was ruled by the Pope, absolute monarch of the Papal States that spanned Central Italy. Living in Rome meant following Papal Law, which, like Soviet Rule or Shariah Law, was basically fascist. Starting in 1555, for over three-hundred years all Jews in the Papal States were ordered to live in ghettos, adhere to curfews, give up their right to own land, and practice only certain professions. Jews were also required to attend Catholic Mass, where they would insert earplugs to stop the "light of Jesus" from entering their brains.

To escape this oppression, Jews traveled to Tuscany, outside of the Papal States, and many settled in Pitigliano, a hilltop town protected from malaria by its altitude and from raiding warlords by its sheer rock walls. Here, they thrived. There weren't that many of them—only 200—but life was good. Many were moneylenders, a profession that the Church forbade Christians to practice but encouraged for Jews. (Note to future Popes: if you want to oppress a group, don't force them into finance.) Others became radiologists or wrote sitcoms.

Their adopted city was nicknamed *La Piccola Gerusalemme* (Little Jerusalem) not only for its golden landscape, which recalls the Holy City, but also because this small town, ruled by the lenient Orsini family, boasted a synagogue, a mikvah (ceremonial bath), a kosher bakery for matzoh and challah, and a school. Even after the famous Medici family took over southern Tuscany and forced its Jews back into ghettos, the Pitigliano community was granted unspoken immunity from certain legal restrictions, because they were so integral to the survival of the city.

Centuries ago, the Jews of Pitigliano reclaimed the *sfratto* by making a dessert in its honor. Before they're cut up, these delicious, traditional nut-and-honey-filled Rosh Hashanah treats look a little like sticks. You can't beat anyone with them, but they will beat your tastebuds into happy submission.

Today, even though only a few Jews remain in Pitigliano, as modern jobs enticed them to larger cities, the synagogue remains, as do historic remnants of the mikvah and bakery. However, the true living legacy of the Jews of Pitigliano is the *sfratto*: made famous by Pitigliano's renowned Jewess cookbook author, Edda Servi Machlin, and sold to tourists by a non-Jewish bakery in the old ghetto. This recipe is a gluten-free, *much* less sugary version of Servi Machlin's recipe.

For the Pastry;

3⅓ cups all-purpose or gluten-free flour

⅓ cup extra-virgin olive oil

½ cup brown or white sugar

¾ cup white wine

¼ cup whisky, cognac, or vin santo

A pinch of salt

For the Filling:

¾ cup raw honey

3 cups of walnuts, chopped

Zest of 2 to 3 oranges

⅓ teaspoon cinnamon

⅓ teaspoon ground cloves

⅓ whole nutmeg, grated

20 grinds of the pepper mill

Extra-virgin olive oil

Make the Pastry:

1. Place the flour, olive oil, sugar, white wine, whisky, and salt in a food processor, and pulse until the ingredients just come together.

2. Remove the dough from the food processor, grease it with a little olive oil, and cover with plastic wrap. Put it in the refrigerator for a good hour or overnight.

Make the Filling:

3. Pour the honey in a small saucepan over medium heat and let it "melt" for 3 minutes.

4. Add the walnuts, zest, cinnamon, cloves, nutmeg, and pepper. Stir and cook for another 5 minutes.

5. Transfer the filling to a small mixing bowl, and let it cool.

Assemble and Bake:

6. Preheat the oven to 350°F and line a baking sheet with parchment paper.

7. Form the pastry dough into 4 equal-sized balls.

8. Using a rolling pin or a makeshift rolling pin (such as a tall, strong drinking glass), flatten each ball of dough one at a time to make an 11 x 4-inch rectangle. Use extra flour as needed to prevent sticking.

9. Roll the filling into 4 ropes, about 1-inch in diameter, and place in the center of each rectangle. Gather the sides of the dough and pinch together to form a smooth seam over the filling. Be sure to close up the ends of the log as well. Place on the prepared baking sheet. Don't worry if it looks ugly. It's rustic, and you're cutting them later!

10. Bake the *sfratti* on the prepared baking sheet in the center of the oven for 20 minutes. Let cool and cut into 1-inch "sticks."

11. Enjoy with good coffee, vin santo, or whiskey, and share the story of *sfratti* to anyone willing to listen. Store in the freezer.

Shift Into Dance

"Don't take this the wrong way," Deena, a regular cooking student of *Meal and a Spiel,* says to me in front of a kitchen full of people. Whenever someone begins a soliloquy with "Don't take this the wrong way," it's best to brace yourself.

"What I love most about your classes is that you always mess something up."

Here I am—the teacher, business owner, and self-proclaimed expert, hired to put my students' time and money to good use—and she's pointing out my errors. Is she telling everyone I'm not worthy? My gut reaction is defensive: prove her wrong.

But how can I? It's true.

I've allowed bread to burn. Lamb stew to char. Swordfish to overcook. In my first pasta class ever, I burnt the garlic three times in a row! I've forgotten to bring ginger to Thai class and smoothie ingredients to detox class. I've even shown up with salmon that had gone bad. And this—THIS!—is what she thinks makes me a great teacher?

Deena's not alone. Countless students tell me that my mistakes are what teach them the most. In those moments, we're all forced to shift, to creatively adjust to the situation. It's a recipe for life and cooking. If we panic and freeze, we don't eat. And that's not an option!

Cooking is like dancing. At dance parties, there are two types of people.

There are those of us who dance all night. When an unfamiliar song starts to play, we may be hit with a jarring wave of sound, but we don't freeze. Even when we go from feeling like the smoothest operator on the dance floor to having two left feet, we trust that, as the music continues, our internal rhythm will adjust until our bodies find their way back in sync with the beat.

Then, there are those who only get on the dancefloor for the songs they know. These people can't cook, because they're afraid to improvise.

If this describes you, pour yourself a glass of wine, get in the kitchen, close the curtains, and blast the music. Find any recipe in this book and boogie and twirl your way through it, making as many mistakes as possible. Yep, screw it up. Just have fun!

Cooking demands that we shift into dance. We must stay open to the whims of the moment. We must adapt to sudden changes, whether they're in our control or not. Scrape the blackened side off the bread and continue making crostini. Take the lamb out of the burned pot and continue cooking it in more wine. Use galangal instead of ginger. And on rare occasions, if something is truly unfixable, like the spoiled salmon, well, just say you're sorry, take note, and be done with it. Go to the fridge, shift into dance, and waltz up something else!

" *Being at ease with not knowing is crucial for answers to come to you.*

—Eckhart Tolle

Classroom Corners

Life Lessons Through Food

Recipes by Title

Recipes by Category

Ingredients

THANK YOU TO ALL OF MY RECIPE TESTERS!

With your help I discovered and corrected confusing instructions, poorly measured ingredients, incorrect cooking times, and all kinds of ways to make these recipes more approachable and successful for cooks of all levels!

Ada Horwich
Alexandra (Sandy) Gleysteen
Alexandra Smothers
Alice Palombo
Alison Mayersohn
Alissa Roston
Allison Reisner Kerman
Amanda Jakubowicz
Amy Knobler
Andrea Bricker
Angelique Famulak
Anne Ima
Cathy Unger
Charlie Zabriskie
Christina A. Bozarth
Christine Neuharth
Cristina Topham
Daisy (Harveen) Radia
Daisy Radia
Danielle Eber Bloch
Debbie Pringle
Debora Dale
Deborah Lintz Sank
Deena Eberly Fleiner
Deena Gussman
Deena Wachtel
Delilah Urman
Denise Mandel-Becker
Dina Litt
Donna Lyons
Drew Patterson
Elana Rosenbaum
Elika Kormeili

Elina Gitig
Elke Ereshefsky
Heather Pettis
Heather Stewart
Hedda Leonardi
Helene Swartz
James Cory
James Uruba
Janna Fisher
Jessica Dreyer
Jim Cory
Julia Nickerson
Julia Sternfeld
Kayo Goto
KJ Luker
Laine Fletcher
Lauren Ravitz
Leslie Aslanian Williams
Leslie Button
Lily Lok
Linda Boyd
Linda G. Mayman
Lisa Wolken
Lori Herrscher
Lori Tessel
Loris Lunsford
Lynn Tarnow
Maria Ricci
Marisa Pick Graines
Marlene Grossman
Marni Isaacs
Martha Ljung
Martha McKinley

Megan Weber
Melissa Eklof
Michelle Richman
Mimi Mather
Nicole Caplan
Orna Wolens
Pam Baer
Peterann Siehl
Rachel Davidson
Rachel Farahnik
Randi Caldwell
Renee Silvestre
Robin Stevens
Robyn L. Goldberg
Rochelle Ginsburg
Sally Kravich
Samantha Barnett
Sharon Ware
Shira Feinstein
Shirin Behnia
Stephanie Batchelor
Susan Haymer
Suzanne Williams
Suzy Kaufman
Tamar Kagan Sajadi
Tamara Nevens
Tara Church
Teri Wilks
Theresa Diulus
Tiffany Yu
Toni Corwin
Yoko Ano
Zach Martinucci

Acknowledgments

My first thank you is to my parents, who have generously opened their beautiful home and kitchen to hundreds, if not thousands, of cooking students throughout the years. You have trusted the goodness of others, and your generosity has been felt by all. *Meal and a Spiel*, the cooking school and the book, would never have been possible without you.

Thank you to my creative editor Seth Grossman for your genius sense of humor that helps my jokes radiate and for your razor sharp red pen that keeps my long-windedness at bay. Working with you has been one of the great creative experiences of my life. And that day when I was feeling quite down and you cooked plate after plate of delicious food from your garden to cheer me up and celebrate the completion of our editing process goes down in the books as one of the most heroic acts of friendship ever.

Thank you Rachel Davidson, for believing in me and this cookbook whole-heartedly, even in moments when I didn't know what direction to go in. Thank you for holding and tying all the pieces together. If it wasn't for you *Meal and a Spiel* would likely still be a bunch of disorganized files on my drive.

Thank you Jessie Glass for your gorgeous design work, for elevating my vision to new levels, and for your patience with my need to see things one way, then another way, then the original way.

Thank you John Schell for the sensitivity of your eye, for allowing the food to have its own voice through your lens, and taking photos for this book that are more beautiful than I could have imagined.

Thank you Sheera Faris Thomas for your fabulous style and brilliant eye. Girl, you did it again. I love the way you dressed me for the photo shoots and the way you styled the plates with such casual elegance. You add chic to my rustic, and you upleveled this project by 1000%.

Thank you to Kevyn Allard for the caring way you approached editing my recipes so that they can be followed with ease. I am most grateful for the way you work with your heart and brain all at once.

Thank you Alice McLean for your keen copy editing and working with us on a tight clock! Thank you Rona Rodrig for checking over the manuscript before printing. Love having a *Meal and a Spiel* community member on the book team.

Thank you Chris Hemesath for joining the team in the 11th hour and managing the production of this book to get us to print on time!

Thank you to Dianne Jacob for encouraging me to focus the theme of the book and for guiding me along the way.

Thank you Patti Henry and Catherine Corpeny for sitting with me at We Care and helping me craft *My Story*. Thank you Caitlin Durham for helping me craft my *fashla* speech, much of which has been added word for word in *My Story*. Thank you Nancy King for giving me the best branding homework questions ever when I first started out. Much of the way I described my purpose and backstory then are used word for word here. You all helped me articulate for myself how the swirling road of life can often be the most direct route.

Thank you Irene, Malcolm, and Jen Caplan for opening your gorgeous Italian home to me over the last two decades. My life would not be the same if not for my time at Geggianello. All of the *Life Lessons through Food* were written there. Thank you Maria Torrini for showing me that the art of fabulous food lies in the touch of love and choice of ingredients. Most American girls in Italy don't get the experience of a true *mamma italiana*...I feel blessed.

Thank you Zepporah Glass for letting me work on my book in your peaceful home amidst the redwoods. Most of the *Classroom Corners* were written in your sanctuary.

Thank you to all those who have inspired recipes in this book: Andrea Pallaoro, Edo Brizio and his mom, Jeff Thickman, Francesca Fanti, Angie George, Joyce Goldstein, Edda Servi Machlin, and Andrew Coleman.

ABOUT THE AUTHOR:

Born to parents who defrosted Lean Cuisine for dinner, Elana Horwich began cooking as a young child because the kitchen was the only place in the house her mother couldn't find her. In her 20's she had an epiphany which took her to Italy for 5 years. There, she worked in bars, fell in and out of love, ate her way through the peninsula, and garnered life experiences that she would one day write about. While devouring every aspect of the local culture, she learned to cook from an Italian *mamma* in a Tuscan villa.

In 2010, back in her hometown of Los Angeles, Elana founded the **Meal and a Spiel** cooking school out of her parents' kitchen, and now travels the country teaching people how to make phenomenal food, easily.

Elana holds a B.A. from Brown University and a Masters from Middlebury College in Florence, both in Jewish Italian Studies. She is a former high school history teacher who has also written and performed stand-up comedy and led experiential vacations throughout the boot of Italy.

Elana has appeared on *Good Day LA, KCAL, KNBC*, and *KTLA* as an expert on healthy holiday cooking. She is a regular contributing writer for the Jewish Journal and her recipes have appeared in the *Huffington Post, Tablet Magazine, The Daily Meal*, and in newspapers throughout the country. She is the consulting chef for the UCLA Women's Cardiovascular Center.

Her ultimate dream is to live in a world where everyone shares love with one another through cooking.

Clean, fair food is accessible only to the privileged in our our country. This disheartens me. Thus, a portion of all sales of this book will be donated to **Slow Food USA**, part of the global Slow Food Movement that is creating dramatic change throughout the world and in 150 chapters in the United States. Slow Food is the opposite of fast food. By purchasing this book, you're helping to transform the way we produce, consume, and enjoy food.

Thank you for contributing.

XO,
Elana